808 42                    174308
Kri        Krieger, Murray

           The new apolo-
           gists for poetry

*THE NEW APOLOGISTS FOR*
*POETRY*

# The New Apologists for Poetry

## *by* MURRAY KRIEGER

GREENWOOD PRESS, PUBLISHERS
WESTPORT, CONNECTICUT

Library of Congress Cataloging in Publication Data

Krieger, Murray, 1923-
   The new apologists for poetry.

   Reprint of the ed. published by University of Minnesota
Press, Minneapolis.
   Includes bibliographical references and index.
   1. Poetry.  2. Criticism.  I.  Title.
[PN1031.K7 1977]        801'.951        77-21933
ISBN 0-8371-9787-2

Originally published in 1956 by the University of Minnesota Press,
Minneapolis

Reprinted with the permission of University of Minnesota Press

Reprinted in 1977 by Greenwood Press, Inc.

Library of Congress Catalog Card Number 77-21933

ISBN 0-8371-9787-2

Printed in the United States of America

*To my Mother and Father*

# PREFACE

It is, I suppose, proper, now that a study has been completed, to mention when it began. I first thought of doing an extended essay on contemporary poetics in 1947 and started my labors late in 1948. My work on it has of course gone through many stages and has assumed several forms; one or two of them I had erroneously thought complete only to have changed my mind or to have had it changed for me. This history is significant only because, in indicating the years and the shifting views which the study has seen on its way to completion, it intimates that there may be embedded in the essay a variety of motives which I have had to try to reconcile. And I feel that perhaps I should give some forewarning of this variety so that if there seem to be alternations in attitude, the reader may at least understand their genesis.

My original aspirations for this essay represented my most immodest attitude toward what might be done and, even more, what I might do. For I entered upon this study with what now appears to me to have been a shocking confidence that I could eventually come by the solutions to the theoretical problems I intended to pose and would be able to announce them, if not in this book, then surely in a sequel. As my knowledge of the problems deepened, I increasingly sensed my own incapacities ever to subdue them utterly. But if I was more realistic about my own powers, I remained as confident about the revelatory powers of systematic aesthetics. There have been times, however, when I abandoned the expectation and even the hope that solutions to the problems were at all accessible to methods of philosophical inquiry. I must even confess to anti-philosophical moments of jubilation, when I enjoyed my belief that the problems were invulnerable to the probings of discursive intelligence. But here, as a literary man anxious to preserve his obscure and perhaps too precious sanctuary, I was not (as I thought) retreating to the farthermost bounds of modesty. Rather I had returned to another kind of pride: a pride in the ineffable simply succeeded to my original pride in the limitlessness of philosophical mastery.

I do not mean to imply that these attitudes were chronologically ordered, that one took over from the one preceding. While it is true that they have sought to dominate my essay in about the order mentioned, it is true also that the earlier ones have never been without some influence on me and that I never entertained even the last except with reservations which the others occasioned. Indeed I suspect, or at least like to think, that every theorist concerned about poetic experience or, to invert, every lover of poetry concerned about theory vacillates in much the same way. My hope, then, is not that I have resolved these differences of attitude but only that I have done fairly well at inhibiting them, so that they do not too openly jar the uniformity of tone and intention. For whatever the reader's attitude toward the possibilities for answers to the questions as I formulate them, I have one conviction which I would like him to come to share: that, answerable or unanswerable, the questions are worth asking and worth asking in this way.

This essay was conceived as a unit, and all of the chapters were written with the whole in mind. Some of the material, however, was incorporated into articles by being reshaped in order to fit the more immediate occasion for which the particular article was designed. Consequently portions of this book originally appeared, although in a somewhat different form, in the *Sewanee Review*, a *Journal of English Literary History*, and *Comparative Literature*. I should like to thank the editors of these journals for permitting me to make use of these materials here.

There are many who have helped in this study, and I must here claim the privilege of thanking them. Dean Theodore G. Blegen and The Graduate School of the University of Minnesota enabled me to complete the book by awarding me a faculty research appointment for the summer of 1954. Miss Ruth Altmann of the University of Minnesota Press provided editorial assistance which proved to be an invaluable aid through my final reworkings of the manuscript.

Much of this study reflects those who have lent their learning and experience to me along the way. Mr. J. D. Stine, perhaps without knowing it, was crucially present at the start of it all. Professor René Wellek of Yale University helped me through my early flounderings with the "new criticism" and its relations to the theory of Coleridge. Through the wisdom of Professor M. O. Percival of the Ohio State University I was taught the limits of aesthetic inquiry. Professor Robert B. Heilman of the University of Washington was for me the rarest of gifts to the scholarly writer—a publisher's reader who coupled his generous reception of my work with the scrupulosity of an exacting taskmaster, thus persuading me to finish again, from first to last, what I had confidently assured myself was already finished. Then there were my colleagues and friends at the University of Minnesota: Professors Allen Tate and William Van O'Connor who read the manuscript with a sympathy that gave me needed encouragement; Professors Jay Vogelbaum and Leonard Unger who, through the warmth of many long and leisurely conversations, allowed me to borrow from the rich liberality of their minds.

My wife, Joan, helped me to think these problems through. She never let me rest secure with half an insight, and her probing questions made me recognize where I could not muster more than evasions: where they could not prompt me to wisdom they prompted me to humility. Equally indispensable was her untiring drudgery through each of the several stages of the manuscript. Finally I must claim my inestimable indebtedness, far beyond what any footnotes or acknowledgment can indicate, to Professor Eliseo Vivas of Northwestern University. I can mention that he taught me those aesthetic concepts that have guided my work, as will be all too evident in the pages that follow. I can mention too that he taught me never to forget the crucial relevance and intimate relationship of aesthetics to all matters of literary theory. But all that he taught me I cannot even hint at satisfactorily. In our day it is rare for the apprentice to have had his master, for the student to be able to say, "I have had a teacher." In Professor Vivas for many years now I have indeed had a teacher—one who surely deserved a better student.

M. K.

December 1955
University of Minnesota

# CONTENTS

[ xi ]

*The New Apologists for Poetry*

Contents

*The New Apologists for Poetry*

and hedonism distinguished · The transformation found in Brooks ·
The emotive versus the contextual · A new cognitive function for
poetry · How it differs from the romantic view of imaginative truth ·
How it differs from the experiential view of Max Eastman · Experience and art, chaos and order · Poetry, prose, and the problems of
context · Eastman and D. G. James on these problems · The apologist's burden

*THE NEW APOLOGISTS FOR*
*POETRY*

# INTRODUCTORY

## EXTENT AND LIMITATIONS

COUNTLESS studies could be written on modern literary criticism. A student of the field must from the outset limit himself severely—and perhaps arbitrarily—if he hopes, within reasonable limits, to achieve an effective focus; to eschew an encyclopedic compilation of authors, titles, and summaries in favor of a systematic, if quite inexhaustive, essay.

Upon what basis may such limits be placed? If the student is concerned about that which is unique in modern criticism, then the so-called "new criticism" presents itself as an obvious candidate for investigation. But those literary critics whom we usually include in that amorphous group would seem, upon close examination, to have little enough in common—too little, perhaps, to justify making a school of them. Although there have been numerous attempts to point out a common direction in their work, these either have failed to include some critics commonly associated with the group or have made the direction so broad that it is not very meaningful to the student of critical theory. If we say that they are characterized by an exclusive concern with the close reading of literature as literature, we ignore a social psychologist like Burke. If we call them all conservatives or traditionalists, besides still being troubled with Burke and others, we are hardly establishing a differentia which is specifically applicable to the realm of literary criticism.

## The New Apologists for Poetry

Certain adventitious circumstances seem to be all that these critics have in common. There are certain personal friendships and hence, perhaps, a certain cliquishness among them. They publish in the same literary quarterlies and take part in the same summer-school activities. They share some basic antagonisms: a scorn for the self-indulgence of critical impressionism and a disdain for the academicism of university English departments—even as they have taken their places within them. But none of these facts constitutes the basis for a common critical attitude which could define the group.

Yet these critics are commonly referred to as if they constituted a single and defined entity. This is an especially convenient device for those who want to issue a blanket condemnation of them. In attacks like those by Douglas Bush, R. S. Crane, Robert Gorham Davis, Malcolm Cowley, and Robert Hillyer, however widely these may vary in justness and in accuracy, there is no central attempt to differentiate among the many practitioners of "the new criticism," or to provide a definition which would include all the critics who are in the barrage area. Of course, in all justice it must be admitted that the term "the new criticism," under which such diverse critics have been brought together, often to be jointly whipped, was itself originally used with reference to this group by one of its leading members, John Crowe Ransom, in his book of that title.* And although several of them, taking the cue, perhaps, from Allen Tate, have disclaimed the existence of any such school, others have continued to press forward its contributions as an organized and collective accomplishment. But these

* Of course Ransom is hardly the first theorist in the history of criticism to use this phrase as a sympathetic characterization of the movement with which he associates himself. For example, very different "new criticisms" indeed were being heralded by Ferdinand Brunetière in his *Honoré de Balzac* (trans. R. L. Sanderson, London, 1906, p. 20); by Ludwig Lewisohn in the introduction to his anthology, *A Modern Book of Criticism* (New York, 1919, p. iv); by J. E. Spingarn in his essay of 1910, "The New Criticism," later reprinted in the anthology of Edwin Berry Burgum which also bore this phrase as its title (New York, 1930). It may be that every critical school must begin with some pretension of being "new" in order to find the zeal to get its work done, even if this pretension indicates that perhaps zeal is being inflated to arrogance. We may, however, rightfully distrust a school that ends with this pretension.

defenders of "the new criticism" have no more succeeded in defining the term than have its attackers.

Is there no such thing, then, as "the new criticism"? Very likely there are no aesthetically meaningful defining qualities which allow us both to call a man a "new critic" and to include all those who have gone by that name. Now some "new critics" view their movement as one born of a need, both theoretical and historical, and, consequently, as one with an aesthetic and social mission to fulfill. In a science-centered age which was damaging its culture by reducing the profoundest utterances of man's spirit to technological disciplines, this criticism had to affirm the uniqueness and indispensability of art's role in society. It had to refuse, for the sake of our complete humanity, to countenance any positivistic reductions. This perhaps unfortunate need to justify poetry in a way in which it had never to be justified before was a blessing in disguise for literary theory. The older pronouncements about literature, which allowed it to be didactic on the one hand and decorative on the other, would no longer do. For if we wanted truth, we had methods to arrive at it which were far more rigorous than those of poetry; and if we wanted pleasure, we could hope to get it in ways far less burdened with invalid attempts to describe our world. Thus, while refusing to subjugate literature to science or to philosophy by giving it the function of illuminating general truths, these "new critics" had equally to eschew an "art for art's sake" position which would trivialize literature. They had somehow to assert at once the autonomy of art and its unique power to give meaning to our experience, a power allowed only by its autonomy. This is a highly significant, if difficult, assertion. It can be understood only if we first abandon the common misconception which, insisting that an autonomous art can only be one practiced for its own sake, identifies "the new criticism" precisely with this dilettantism of the aesthete.

Much of "the new criticism" has done its work in terms of this more complex program. But there have been defections in the ranks. Some nominal members of the group have never had these aims, and some of the most important and most representative members of the group have, often unconsciously, lost sight of them from time to time. The reason is not far to seek. No defined program has ever been formulated in theoretical terms by these critics. Indeed, not only are they lacking a foundation of aesthetic theory, but some of them even prefer to be so lacking, in order (as they think) to preserve their literary sensitivity in an uninhibited state. The latter may argue—and very likely with justice—that if they had stopped at the start to analyze their problems at the aesthetic level, they could not have accomplished what they have. Be that as it may, the capacity of these critics to accommodate concepts springing from conflicting assumptions has been amazingly unlimited. And this neglect of system has allowed many heterogeneous elements to claim "the new criticism" as their own without any possibility of dispute.

The student, it seems to me, has no choice but to accept the impossibility of generalizing about all the "new critics." Again, if he is primarily interested in finding a common direction, he is forced to choose among them—and to choose somewhat arbitrarily. But the choice is not dictated by mere whimsy; rather it is determined by a particular interest, a principle of selection, which must come from outside the critics themselves. Now I am especially concerned with those of the "new critics" who are trying to answer the need, forced on them by historical pressures, to justify poetry by securing for it a unique function for which modern scientism cannot find a surrogate. These critics, then, by theorizing about what seems to them to be the difference between the nature and function of poetry and the nature and function of science, are collectively engaged in formulating a new "apology for poetry."

But I have said that the "new critics," generally, suffer from a common theoretical deficiency which vitiates their attempts at system-making. Thus, if a consistent and systematic "apology" is to be made, it must be made for these critics in terms of the requirements set for a theory of literature by the discipline of aesthetics. My objective here, however, is a considerably more modest one, although I believe it must be attained preliminary to the final apology which eventually may be systematically drawn from, or perhaps read into, the insights of these critics. In these days when professional philosophers have so often become as confident of their answers as they are proud of their ability to make them with confidence—outlawing as unaskable any question that might shake their confidence and their pride—I prefer only and finally to narrow the range within which one may ask questions, so that these may come closer to being the right questions, even if I can proclaim nothing but my confusion about the answers to them.

My interest in the work of those "new critics" who are concerned with such an apology has had the benefit of the systematically controlled concepts which my studies in aesthetics have made available to me. My critique of modern theorists and the cluster of questions it has been designed to raise have resulted from these critical and aesthetic studies. What I wish to do is to examine several theories—each inadequate and most of them inconsistent—in light of each other; to view them in terms of the problems of aesthetics; and to use them, so viewed, in order to point to those crucial questions on the answers to which a systematic apology depends. The simultaneous purposes that govern this inquiry involve it in a dialectical arrangement; and what may appear to be its unorthodox organization or even at times its rambling movement is a necessary outgrowth of my attempt to juggle these several considerations at once. For by what method can these various tasks be served except by the dialectical—with its returning of the argument upon itself, with its voluntary retreats and half-hearted advances, with its eager acceptances here which turn to cautious rejections there?

In the pages that follow, the reader will find analyses of the positions of a handful of critics who may be seen to contribute, consciously or otherwise, to the apology our society demands that they make. But the other interests of this essay dictate that these critics must not be treated completely, one at a time. First, they must be viewed in terms of each other. And in order that such comparisons may be implemented, the critics must be ranged about a common aesthetic problem. Now, if we want to talk about the function of poetry—and it is on the basis of its function that we must apologize for it—we have to know first what kind of thing it is whose function we are trying to determine. Thus we are led back to a consideration of what poetry, as aesthetic object, actually is. But in defining it, we must know what we mean by calling an object "aesthetic"; in this connection, then, we must say also what it is we mean by an aesthetic experience. We may push back the sequence of the aesthetic process yet one step farther by asking what kind of activity is required of the poet to produce the object as we wish to define it.

My inquiry, then, falls into three major sections: the first concerns the psychology of poetic creativity; the second concerns the structure of the poem as aesthetic object, viewed in terms of a definition of the aesthetic experience; and the last concerns the unique function of poetry. The various critics—or those aspects of them that are relevant to the problem under investigation—enter the scene when the dialectic calls for them. I try so to manipulate their entrances and exits, as well as what we learn of them while they are on-stage, that they may help me, as they in fact have, to narrow the range of considerations within which each of the three problems may be most successfully explored. And since what is said about each of the problems prepares the way for what may be said about the next, the last act, to which the other two point, is meant to be a proper finale to the piece, even if the piece is but a modest prelude to the more significant and solvent one which perhaps ought to have been written. If this third section is much shorter than the others, it is only because so much of the ground has been cleared by the time we arrive at it.

There are, of course, many other methods of treating modern criticism as there are many other interests in terms of which it may be viewed. If I may cite the method and interest least like my own, Stanley Edgar Hyman, in *The Armed Vision* (New York, 1948) treats various critics, one at a time, and tries to treat each of them exhaustively. His scientistic aim, precisely the opposite of mine, is to show that modern criticism should be "the organized use of non-literary techniques and bodies of knowledge [by which he primarily means science] to obtain insights into literature." For what I hope is my less simple and more humanistic objective, I have had to forgo this more obvious, catalogue-like approach. While the method of the essay that follows may be less obvious and more dense, I have not meant to use it to camouflage my confusion. I hope rather that it is demanded by the complexity of the materials I deal with and that it serves to clarify, without thinning, my subject-matter; in short, that it exhibits a many-faceted grasp instead of betraying a pointless muddlement.

It is inevitable in a procedure like mine that there be many omissions, since only those few critics are treated, and only those few aspects of the critics, which the flow of discourse seems to demand. My neglect of the work of R. P. Blackmur is only one obvious, if especially glaring, omission. My excuse—that I am dealing exclusively with theoretical criticism while his work concentrates very largely on practical criticism—must serve for others as well as for him; it must serve too for the great bulk of work by many of those critics I have included which is not treated along with what for my purposes seemed to be their most crucial writings. Further, I am sorry that, because of the recentness of publication, I have been unable to consider such important works as Philip Wheelwright's *The Burning Fountain* (Bloomington, Indiana, 1954). It is inevitable too, while I deal with only a slim selection of critics, that I may, as a kind of shorthand, use terms like "the new critics" or "our critics" when in fact I mean only the limited group within my survey. For these and, I am sure, many other lapses I must ask the reader's indulgence.

But for one flaw more serious than the rest, if I am guilty of it, forgiveness may be sought but not so readily granted. For it arises out of arrogance, that cardinal sin of the student and scholar who violates rather than embraces his tradition as he ought. It may perhaps appear that many a critic entertained between these covers is most inhospitably received, condescendingly treated, and finally ejected rudely with the label of "inadequacy" or "inconsistency" ungraciously hung round his neck. If this is how it appears, then I have indeed failed; but it is, I should hope, an error of stylistic judgment rather than a breach of scholarly morality. It has rather been my intention to welcome those who have grappled with these problems and to congratulate them for the brilliance they have so frequently displayed. If I have used most of my labor to expose what seems to me to be the incompleteness of what they say, I beg the reader to remember that I hardly claim any more completeness for myself. Since, even coming along after them, I am no more able than they are to see through the many problems to an adequate and consistent theory, I can hardly guarantee even that the problems are soluble and such a theory attainable. Thus I am scarcely in a position to do anything but applaud those whose valiant efforts have forced the problems to yield at least partial answers. But it would not be a service to their achievements and to the further promise of these achievements for me to claim more for them than is warranted. Rather the painstaking, and often painful, critique must proceed in order to mark off what is yet to be done or what is to be done again, and done differently. Surely this is a respectful procedure. I hope that in my hands it seems so.

### TOWARD A SYMPATHETIC READING

Ours is a period whose dominating academic philosophy would not recognize and could never countenance the general intention and direction of this essay, to say nothing of its treatment of specific problems. In an intellectual climate so coldly inhospitable to the self-important fervor of poetic apologetics, the literary man who would accord to poetry the consideration due it, who would treat poetry seriously—as more than a plaything—must be aware of his heterodoxy toward the strenuous modern dogmas of the schools. This awareness should lead him to try to make his peace with his reader; it should lead him to see the need to urge anew some old insistences: insistences, as old as poetics, about the reality and the real difficulty of his theoretical problems. Since these problems persist even into these positivist-ridden days, it is his duty to his subject to see that insistence keeps up with persistence. Thus he must plead his insistences in hopes of persuading his reader away from the disdain of our currently fashionable philosopher.

Thus, however systematic my orientation in this essay, I maintain from the outset that I undertake it as a literary man. I maintain, on the other hand, that when a literary man begins to speculate in a systematic way about problems in poetics it does not necessarily mark his fall from the grace of sensibility, as many literary men—including some new critics—would have us believe. But he does find himself aware of certain obligations which the less encumbered theorist may not share. His fidelity to the obligations his literary sensibility requires may these days seem to be a quixotic fealty. But his devotion allows in his utterances a refreshing, if unrigorous, engagement to his subject that may be of value to the purer aesthetician.

If I would be true to my literary obligations, then, I must begin by discussing a specific poem. For, as I have been intimating, the dedicated literary man is cursed with a rather curious and, he may like to think, old-fashioned empiricism. It is one which is dull and dogged. It requires that theoretical statements about poetics, if he is to appreciate them as relevant to his interests, must have immediate reference to the facts of his experience with poetry. It may be expressive of an unscientific bias in him that he feels constitutionally obliged to ignore more general investigations into such realms as those of psychology and semantic analysis unless, as they rarely are, they are centered about what he feels to be the peculiar powers of poetry in his constant experiencing of it. This fact of his poetic experience is for him the inescapable starting point of all theorizing; he clings to it as surely and as relentlessly as does the scientist to his laboratory-controlled facts. This constitutes his act of faith; and although he may have no warrant for his insistence except what some may wish to call an emotive one, he will not believe anyone who tells him so. Nor, he is convinced, will anyone else who has allowed a poem to work its full effects upon him.

As the literary man chooses to face it, then, the theoretical problem requires him to search out a poetics which will account with consistency for what he finds the poem to be, what he finds it can do. His primary criterion for a proposed theory is the consolingly operational one: will it allow him to make sense of poetry's value to him? Or, to put it more crudely, will it allow him to go on reading poetry as he does? For he must not give up the experiential fact of poetry, at any theoretical cost. In dealing with any theoretical claim, he must on principle always return to the poetic experience with which, for him, the claim must come to terms. If anyone charges this principle with being personal, idiosyncratic, introspective, the literary man dares not dispute it. In reply he can only point hopefully to his fellows, who with him can share wide areas of agreement or at least wide and agreed-upon grounds for disagreement.

But now to the poem. One may properly object to my using John Donne's "The Canonization," which is in many ways so obvious a choice and which, therefore, has already suffered from being critically overlabored. I mean, however, not to demonstrate my critical acumen, but rather to indicate in an immediate way some of the complexities of poetic discourse for which the literary theorist must account. Accordingly, I have tried to select an extreme and yet clear case in which these complexities must be bared even for the most elementary understanding of the poem. Perhaps because of this characteristic, the poem has been so attractive to modern critics that many of them have already discussed it.[1] Nevertheless, the poem can be used for my purposes here since much of what is true of it may, with more subtlety, be true of much of our poetry.

> For Godsake hold your tongue, and let me love,
>     Or chide my palsie, or my gout,
> My five gray haires, or ruin'd fortune flout,
>     With wealth your state, your minde with Arts improve,
>         Take you a course, get you a place,
>         Observe his honour, or his grace,
> Or the Kings reall, or his stamped face
>     Contemplate, what you will, approve,
>     So you will let me love.

Alas, alas, who's injur'd by my love?
    What merchants ships have my sighs drown'd?
Who saies my teares have overflow'd his ground?
    When did my colds a forward spring remove?
      When did the heats which my veines fill
      Adde one more to the plaguie Bill?
Soldiers finde warres, and lawyers finde out still
    Litigious men, which quarrels move,
    Though she and I do love.

Call us what you will, wee are made such by love;
    Call her one, mee another flye,
We'are Tapers too, and at our owne cost die,
    And wee in us finde the'Eagle and the Dove,
      The Phoenix ridle hath more wit
      By us, we two being one, are it.
So to one neutrall thing both sexes fit,
    Wee dye and rise the same, and prove
    Mysterious by this love.

Wee can dye by it, if not live by love,
    And if unfit for tombes and hearse
Our legend bee, it will be fit for verse;
    And if no peece of Chronicle wee prove,
      We'll build in sonnets pretty roomes;
      As well a well wrought urne becomes
The greatest ashes, as halfe-acre tombes,
    And by these hymnes, all shall approve
    Us *Canoniz'd* for Love:

And thus invoke us; You whom reverend love
    Made one anothers hermitage;
You, to whom love was peace, that now is rage;
    Who did the whole worlds soule contract, and drove
      Into the glasses of your eyes
      (So made such mirrors, and such spies,
That they did all to you epitomize,)
    Countries, Townes, Courts: Beg from above
    A patterne of your love!

To begin with, "The Canonization" has a very marked progression, and yet, beneath its surface of not uncommon speech and a seeming reasonableness, we find that its development is not, as it may first seem, really logical at all but rather is poetic, indeed contains a parody of logic. What I mean is that the poem is not adequate argument at all; rather the speaker is led on to his conclusion almost unknowingly, carried there on the vehicle of his metaphor. The metaphor is really taken seriously (or should I say wittily?) and is allowed to lead to as lofty a conclusion as its vehicle can reach. The very reasonableness of the tone of the poem allows the reader, if he seizes the vehicle rather than the tenor of the metaphor, to make absurdity seem like logic. Only too late does he realize that he has been taken in and that the case is not proved at all, except that poetically—that is, in terms of the language-context of the poem—it has.

It should be clear on the first reading that the poem moves from one extreme to another: the first two stanzas present the speaker's first argument defending the love between his mistress and him, while the last three stanzas allow him to justify his love in a much more positive way with an argument that is precisely opposed to his initial one. Thus the poem has a dialectical movement. The poet advances the first argument only to reach the second, which is the reverse of the first and far more powerful.

Now to become more specific. In the first stanza the speaker tells his listener to say or do anything he likes so long as he allows the speaker to love. He may criticize anything else about the speaker, and he may do anything he pleases to improve his worldly situation in complete disregard of the speaker's love. In the second stanza the speaker indicates why his love can safely be allowed by the man of the world he is addressing. For his love is insignificant as far as the world is concerned. It cannot possibly affect any of the important activities of mankind. Contrary to the Petrarchan conceit, it does not sink ships, start floods, affect nature, start plagues, or put an end to warfare or lawsuits. What harm, then, can come from the love of the speaker and his mistress? Why should it not be allowed?

With this argument completed, in the third stanza the speaker asks, in effect, "What if you should chide us for loving in spite of my concessions?" Suppose his friend should disparagingly call the lovers two flies (that is, minute insects who are short-lived and who use up their brief span continually reproducing) or candles which burn themselves out of existence. The lovers rather find that they resemble the eagle (an idealized masculine symbol) and the dove (an idealized feminine symbol), and then, beyond these, they discover that they together make up the phoenix riddle (the legendary bird of neither sex and of both which consumes itself by fire every five hundred years and rises to new life out of its own ashes). But by becoming the phoenix riddle, the lovers are also being granted a resurrection which will allow the world to look upon them as saints.

The fourth stanza gives further evidence of their qualifications for sainthood as the life of religion and the life of love are identified in their contrast to worldly existence. Their life story will be celebrated in verse rather than in a more pompous memorial. (But we must note that even as the speaker draws this contrast between the lovers and those who succeed in the world, he uses the word "legend" to apply to the tale about the lovers. And this word can also mean the story of a saint's life.) The worldly "Chronicle" is similarly contrasted to "sonnets" (that is, love poems) which, in turn, are transformed into the "hymns" by which the world canonizes them.

The last stanza contains the prayer made to the canonized lovers by the rest of the world. And with it the first argument (that of the first two stanzas) is turned on its head. The world (which, the speaker originally claimed, was entirely unaffected by the insignificant love of the speaker and his mistress) now wants to be ruled entirely ("Countries, towns, courts") according to the pattern of that love. For the complete mutual absorption of speaker and mistress allows the entire world to be contracted into their eyes, since when one lover looks into the eyes of the other, those eyes, as mirrors, reflect what is the entire world for the lover who gazes into them. Thus metaphorically, love, which before stood apart from the world, now absorbs it all. And for the lovers there is "peace," while, as we saw in the second stanza, the rest of the world had nothing but "rage."

There are certain crucial passages which merit closer attention.

The first two stanzas do not require much further comment. They merely set up the initial and tentative argument for love that is later to be overturned. There is nothing implausible here, and few special devices are needed. But let us return to the all-important third stanza in which the turning point occurs. I pointed out that the lovers are described in four ways, two by the outside world and two by themselves. And I also examined the implications of each of these ways. Now, the world calls them flies and tapers to emphasize their sensuality and their self-destructive passion. The first description applied by the lovers to themselves, eagle and dove, elevates the flies into much more glorious winged creatures. But this is only a point of transition for the lovers' description of themselves. For once having elevated flies to eagle and dove, the speaker combines this with the tapers (which burn themselves out) and reaches the phoenix. For this is a winged creature (fly, eagle and dove) which consumes itself by fire (tapers). Thus we see that the speaker has not rejected the description of the outside world at all. Rather he has used it to define his love in more glorious terms than he could have without it. Again the dialectic—except that the logic of its outward form has only a metaphorical foundation. With the phoenix, however, a new element has been added. (Of course this is hardly the speaker's fault. He was led to the phoenix inevitably, and now that he is arrived at it, he must take the consequences of anything he may discover about it.) It arises to new life out of the ashes from the fire in which it has consumed itself, just as the phoenix comparison arises out of the ashes of the previous comparisons. But this is resurrection and makes the lovers "mysterious," that is, saintly, in terms of Christian mystery. This is where the flies and tapers have led us.

But even this is not all. This stanza is also heavy with sexual implications. I have discussed the use of flies and tapers in this connection. It should be noted that each of the lovers is one fly, they are two tapers rather than one, and they are the eagle and the dove. But when we reach the climax with the phoenix, "*both* sexes fit" "to *one* neutral thing." Obviously this phrase has reference to sexual intercourse, the single "beast with two backs" of which the cynical Iago spoke. It is, then, the sexual embrace which allows the resurrection. Thus, like the phoenix, "we die and rise the same." And "die" has the usual metaphysical ambiguity which allows it to mean both the end of life and the sexual climax. Thus in one sense we have really not left the flies and tapers at all. They are indulging in the sensuality of which the world has accused them. And yet their love is much more than this; it is in another sense saintly. Donne's proof? The entire stanza. It may be sacrilege, but it is great poetry which reveals the unique capacities of poetry.

The movement of "verse" (the generic term) to "sonnets" (love verse) and finally to "hymns" (religious verse) in the fourth stanza was discussed earlier and is of a similar nature. The speaker is carried to the act of canonization without seeming to exert any logical pressure of his own. His language achieves it for him. By the end of stanza four the canonization has been reached—or, in the spirit of the poem, should I say "consummated"? All that remains is for the speaker to invert the situation of the first two stanzas, on the basis of his position as a result of stanzas three and four. He must have the world plead with the lovers as originally they pleaded with the world. And the very quality which before made love insignificant—its complete isolation from the world—having sanctified it by identifying it with the unworldly saintly life, now gives it the power to save the world.

But although the reader has been fooled by the absurdities which have been concealed under the seeming rationality of the poem and has taken the vehicles of the metaphors seriously instead of remaining within the confines of the tenors, nevertheless the poem has forced him also to take rationality along with him as a beguiling, covert guide. After all, sexual intercourse is not quite the conversion to sainthood, and Donne continually emphasizes this with his repeated use of sexual ambiguities in the passages which are most needed to yield the religious meanings. Nor are love verses meant to be regarded only as hymns to saints. And the lovers do not in any obvious way affect the business of the world, which can never forsake its "rage." The ambiguities prove that the reader was not meant only or merely to be fooled all the way. On the other hand, neither is he to look upon the poem merely as faulty argument or as a joke. For in one sense—through the operation of its language—it has proved its case.

I believe no more precise statement can be made about what the poem is saying. All I can do is point to the complex of internal relations, some few of which I have discussed, and say that the meaning of the poem is somehow there. To say, as a recent critic has said, that the poem celebrates the glories of a love that has more to it than lust, is seriously to cheapen and misrepresent it. This claim omits, among other things, the realistic presentation of the sensual life as the enabling act of resurrection. Further, any attempt at a more lengthy and more heavily qualified paraphrase of the poem's meaning would, I fear, be no more adequate, indeed might very well take us even farther from the poem; for it would very likely make the poem seem like capricious, self-contradictory foolishness.

Nevertheless, despite, or rather because of, the mutually qualifying complexities of its context which prevent the reader from extracting any assertion from the poem, it does show him some interrelationships among the problems of love, of religion, and of the worldly life in the many views it has simultaneously brought before him. If it gives him no single answer, it shows him why no single answer will do. For the poem is argument only as it is perverted and even parodied argument; and, as argument, it is convincing, and seriously convincing, only as it is nonsensical.

Now this, highly abbreviated in view of my limitations of space and the limitations of my critical language, is my reading of the poem. I must apologize especially for neglecting prosodic matters which would further complicate my account. The poem, perceived through this imperfect * rationalization of my experience of it, constitutes the text of my discourse. The problem is to work toward a poetics which has at least a personal validity, one that

---

* Necessarily imperfect since, despite my precautions, any such rationalization involves some translation of the terms of the poem and thus does some violence to the integrity of the experience it has afforded me.

will permit and will theoretically account for readings of this kind. Thus my appeal is empirical in this sense: if we accept this reading or the experience for which it seeks to account as a fact, then what kind of poetics would be needed to make theoretical sense of this fact? I want merely to account for such data as I have presented— data that would seem to have a psychological admissibility, if no other. Whatever theoretical claims I shall make must be construed as purely hypothetical, as the clause in the sentence which follows an "if" clause: if our interest is to deal adequately with this sort of poetic experience, then, in terms of this interest, what kind of object can we postulate which can facilitate this experience? what kind of creative process would be required to yield this kind of object? in what ways, besides affording us our experience of it, can we expect this kind of object to function for us? *

I shall be dealing with these questions, one at a time, throughout this study, since complete answers to them would put us well on the way to a systematic poetics valid for this kind of poetic experience. I should like, however, to deal with them briefly and in a preliminary way here. If one should ask about the legitimacy of other poetics needed to justify other possible experiences of the poem, I can hardly outlaw them. I prefer, at least tactically, to take refuge in my private interest, content about the quality of those who would share it with me even as they share poetic experiences roughly like mine. And here, in order to be safe from the slings and arrows of outrageous schoolmen masquerading as fortune, we will raise no issues—epistemological, ontological, or cosmological—to be slain in infancy. Nor will we for a moment insist on the truth-value or even the meaningfulness of the assumptions we use. Instead we shall plead only that we need to make them and that they have an intra-systematic, if not a referential, meaning; that their coherence, if not their correspondence to reality, makes them worth bothering about. We admit the circularity of our procedure; but ours, we like to think, is a friendly circle.

* These three questions are dealt with, respectively, in Sections II, I, and III of this study.

No one, then, must for a moment suspect that I shall be making a single objective claim. For I would not be so rash as to attempt a flight to what a contemporary analytic philosopher has scornfully termed the "onticsphere," [2] since I have alas no wings and literary men are notoriously poor mechanics. And such a flight would in any case be futile and reckless daring since these days we find ourselves confronted with some of the most proficient antiaircraft cannoneers western technological thought has pro-duced—and they are rarely less than fully armed.

In what direction, then, would my provisional definition of the aesthetic object tend to move? Obviously I would have to begin by making the recently common claim that there can be no separation between form and content, from which would have to follow the equally common claims about the organic unity and inviolable context of the poem which functions for us as aesthetic object. For to insist on these things in any less wholehearted a way would allow the poem to become fragmented into a para-phrase which would have a referential and propositional intention and a poetic overlay which, however attractive, could never trans-form the assertion into another kind of discourse. Any such divi-sion would be untrue to the integrity of my poetic experience and to the self-contained and self-sustaining world of linguistic inter-relationships which I have found, or rather in which I have lost myself, in the poem. I find that when I am reading well the poetic context controls my experience and the meanings I see in it. To allow the poem to function referentially is to break the context. It is to allow the poem to point outside itself and thus to lead me into the world of what meanings had been for me before I came to the poem; which is to say that I would be released from the control of the poetic context and, unhappy parolee, I would be returned to the uninspiring familiarities of the workaday world, having been denied the theoretical possibility of the unique view of the world which can come with the purely poetic experi-ence. I refuse to worry about this denial, however, since I have had this kind of poetic experience, and I prefer to reject the theory rather than the most valued and most intimate phases of my psychological history.

But this insistence upon the unqualified integrity of the poetic context, without which I cannot have the controlled poetic experiences I have had, raises many rather obvious theoretical difficulties. On the face of it, it seems rather absurd to try to maintain the self-containedness of the linguistic interrelations within a poem when clearly symbols cannot function unless they mean; and as soon as meaning enters the picture so does the outside world to which the words in the poem must have some reference. After all, I am trying to formulate a theory for poetry and not for nonsense.

There is yet another difficulty. As I shall try to indicate later, I do not mean to take refuge in an "art for art's sake" position. While I may be defending the autonomy of the poem, I will claim that the advantage of this position is not that it divorces poetry from life but rather that it enables poetry to reveal life to me in a unique and a fresh way, a revelation it could not manage were it not autonomous, were its relations to life as immediate as they are in more referential forms of discourse. Here again, then, I seem to be claiming that in some way poetry must be at once nonreferential (in terms of its inviolable context) and referential (in terms of the outside world from which in some sense it must spring and to which in some sense it must ultimately return).

Finally there is a difficulty in what may seem to be the unqualified organicism at the root of the position I have been advancing: How utterly self-contained can a poem be before its closed system would prove invulnerable to the reader's attempt to invade it? For the reader, never having encountered this system before, would not be able to probe for an opening in the poem's armor. But of course the reader does find a way in, and this clearly indicates that his terms cannot be so utterly unusable with respect to the contextually controlled terms within the poem. An equally forceful argument against an extreme organicism would point out, via the continuities we find in the history of literary tradition, that poems have common as well as unique properties.

These difficulties point up the apparent paradox which a poetics constructed in the way outlined here would have somehow to resolve. The poem must in one sense, as a special form of discourse, be nonreferential, even as it must be referential to be any form of discourse at all. It must, as organic, be autonomous, even as it illuminates human experience. If it is to be the ground of the integrated, disinterested, even selfless experience I would denominate as aesthetic, the poem must be distinguished by what have been termed "immanent meanings," [3] even though these cannot be discovered if I do not bring to the poem clearly specified meanings from the outside.

Of course the easy way out would be to refuse to admit this seeming paradox and to dismiss the organic and contextual characteristics in favor of the more obvious referential ones without which no discourse can function. And if this would deny to poetry the claim of being a special form of discourse and to the aesthetic the claim of being a special mode of experience, I suppose I would simply have to face up to the loss of my precious illusions in the greater name of simple common sense.

But the dedicated literary man dies harder than this. His experience with poetry forces him to maintain the contextual and autonomous claims for poetry even as he acknowledges its especially intimate relations to the outside world. And we have already seen what would be done to the status of poetry and to the very existence of the aesthetic mode of experience by depriving the poem of its self-containedness. In working toward a definition of the poem as aesthetic object, any aesthetic theory that would be responsible to the literary man's facts—the facts of his experience and the historical facts that indicate poetry's unique and indispensable role in society—would have to confront both sides of this paradox and be content with no answer that blinks either of them.

I should like now to reverse the chronology of the aesthetic process by moving from the poem as object, and my experiencing of it, to the creative act and the direction my theory of it would have to take. I am assuming, of course, that I must try to account with consistency for the way in which the aesthetic object I have just been discussing would be produced. I had to begin before by denying a form-content dichotomy to the poem and by asserting its contextual integrity. So here I must deny the common assumption that the successful poet—he who creates an object capable of forcing me into an aesthetic experience—begins with a preconceived idea of what he wants to say and then translates it into poetry in such a way that what emerges is pretty much the sort of thing he began with; that, with the execution fully under his control, his product is roughly similar to his intention. If the idea is prior to language and controls the language which is but its translation, then obviously we can hardly expect the poem which emerges to have the contextual characteristics I demanded earlier. It would seem quite inevitable that a theory which opposes form to content in the poem would oppose message to embellishment in the creative process. For the process itself would be thought of as mechanical if its product was.

Clearly, then, in terms of what has been said about the poem, language must be considered as a formative factor in the complex process of creation. I must say that the poet's original idea for his work, no matter how clearly thought out and complete he thinks it is, undergoes such radical transformations as language goes creatively to work upon it that the finished poem, in its full internal relations, is far removed from what the author thought he had when he began. I might be tempted to say that rather than the other way round, it is language that has created the poetic idea as this idea comes to be the complex of words that constitutes the completed poem. Since, according to what has been said about the poem itself, the context, being inviolable, is untranslatable, obviously this idea cannot have had any other locus than the poem itself.

But it must be admitted that to talk about language going creatively to work or about language creating the idea of the poem is only to talk metaphorically; and, even as metaphor, it is clearly an overstatement. For the poet is not here meant to be the mystic who, as divinely and passively possessed, transmits an inspiration whose creation has another source. Nor, of course, is language to be thought of as self-generating—whatever that would mean. It must be the poet—or, to use the traditional term, the poetic imagination—that goes creatively to work, that creates the possibilities which his language may exploit, and that rigorously controls the choice of language which informs, even as it expands, these possibilities.

But we must ask in terms of what principle or idea the poet does his controlling. If I say that he directs the process and its choices in terms of his original idea (the one he has before he begins submitting himself and it to his recalcitrant medium), then I am returned to the mechanical theory of the creative act, which sees the preconceived idea as all-governing and the working in language as mere translation. Yet in what other way could the work be directed, in terms of its own evolving *telos*, by a force outside itself? For, as I have said, language can hardly direct itself.

I am arrived, then, at what would seem to be another paradox in many ways analogous to the one I found in examining the poem as aesthetic object. And, also like the other, the two assertions that make it up seem equally partial and equally indispensable. In one sense the poet must be the creator of his work, directing its growth with his skills and in obedience to his intentions. Yet these intentions are continually modified and even transformed by the objective demands of an evolving context which seems to be creating its own intentions. Thus in another sense it is language— the developing language-context and the further possibilities afforded by the resources of language—which seems to be the master, forcing the submission of the poet and his intentions to the intention it seems somehow to be generating spontaneously. If one wished to construct a theory of the creative process that would meet the requirements set by my approach to the created object itself, then once more he would be obliged to conduct his search in recognition of the claims of both these formulations.

In turning to the third area of problems, I should like to touch briefly upon what I now can say about just one of the possible uses of the poem in addition to its allowing my immediate, felt experience of it: its capacity for telling me about the world. While I have said nothing about the nature of the aesthetic experience itself, it should be clear from my discussion of the poem as aesthetic object that I am assuming my aesthetic experience to be one of "intransitive attention." [4] It is this characteristic which allows me the claim of being contained and controlled by the poem, which allows me to insist on the integrity of the poem's context as it works upon me, and which allowed me to speak of my experience of the poem as "integrated, disinterested, even selfless." Needless to say, this is the kind of experience which I tried to communicate earlier.

It is difficult, in view of what I have said about the aesthetic experience and about the poem which is its ground, to see how anything can be said for the poem's effect on my view of the world. I anticipated in my discussion of the poem as aesthetic object that the difficulties encountered there would be reflected in my attempt to reconcile the autonomy of the poem with its revelatory powers. We would expect the claim that the poem is autonomous to lead me to deny any meaning to the poem. And in insisting that the poem's work would stop with the aesthetic experience, I might very well view the poem as purely emotive, perhaps even going so far as to join I. A. Richards in claiming that the poem intends to yield only "pseudo-statements." [5] Yet since I refused to shrink from the paradoxical and insisted at the same time that the poem had also to be in some sense referential, I might be expected to view the poem as making unverified and often unverifiable assertions, saying with Morris Weitz that the poem can make "truth claims." [6]

My discussion of "The Canonization" should be helpful here. While, in the way I viewed it, surely something was being said about divine and earthly love, it was difficult to conceive this *something* as an assertion, in view of the complexity of the poem's internal relations, the simultaneity of the several conflicting points of view, and the mixed use of logic and parody of logic as its principle of development. Thus I can hold neither with the emotive claims nor with the propositional ones. Between these positions there is one, differently enunciated by Max Eastman and John Hospers as well as by some of the so-called "new critics," [7] which would see poetry not as giving knowledge in the normally accepted sense but as giving us an experiential grasp of our world which eludes the systematized abstractions of the knowledge-giving disciplines. This is a tempting idea, one which on the face of it does not suffer from the inadequacies of the other two. In spite of what I must claim to be its partiality, I know of no other current formulation that seems in many ways to answer our needs so well.

But one final time I must broach the paradox. On the one side the poem is, to use Hospers' term, "true-to" the fullness of our worldly experience, thanks to its complexities of context and its more than referential interests; but on the other side—as I have indicated earlier—it is all control and discipline, characteristics which, by calling a halt to the complexities, order them and thus seal the poem off from the chaos of our pre-analytic experience. Thus even as, through complexity, it reveals experience, through control it disdains the messiness of experience. This control, in making the poem responsible to something besides our worldly experience, has a role perhaps analogous to the function of logic in philosophical discourse. It is this, finally, which makes the seeming self-containedness and intransitiveness of the poetic response possible. "The Canonization" ought again to be a case in point, although my analysis of it barely touched on so-called formal elements at all. What is said about the strange relations among religion, love, and the practical world is clearly delimited even as it seems so full. The line that separates artful complexity from natural chaos is finely drawn. And what the poem adds to our attitudes toward life would very likely be impoverished rather than enriched if it spilled over into experience from the austere plenitude of art. If at her highest, art deters us with what Clive Bell has called her "cold, white peaks," we must dare draw near to discover that, for those who abide with her the chill becomes a warmth that can sustain vigorous life—a warmth that never cloys.

But this is to restate the paradox and to do it metaphorically—which, I will be told, will never do. For this is to justify emotively what I have been unhappy with rationally; in effect, it is to convert paradox into miracle. And, however tempting and even satisfying this may be, I must for now resist it. Rather I have asked us not to rest in the paradox but to try to work our way through it without ignoring it or simply collapsing it. And it may very well be that this task will be the most difficult and yet the most crucial in the further exploration of that boggy and insidious area which encloses the problem of the meaning of poetry. Yet I have meant to show that it is a problem which is not likely to be solved in isolation from the other aesthetic problems I have discussed. Perhaps it is just this interrelatedness of the various problems and the need for consistency among the answers proposed for each which make it profitable for us to keep aesthetics—despite the frightening and often unmanageable heterogeneity of the fields within it—a single, if highly federated, domain.

I do not mean to be wayward, perverse, or self-consciously obscure in my persistence about the paradoxical. It is simply the best I can do to account for the difficulties I meet as I try to theorize about my experiences with poetry. It may very well be, as some will say, that all these difficulties I have dreamed up are really semantic confusions which would fade with a proper clarification of the terms I use. Unequipped as a literary man must be for this rigorous sort of task, I welcome those who would furnish the kind of linguistic analysis which would rid me of these thorny problems by showing me they never existed. But as I think of my perplexities and of the likely charge that they are imaginary, I may be permitted to wonder whose the illusion is: mine for seeing visionary difficulties or theirs for seeing analysis of language as the universal solvent. If it should be mine, all I can do is point to the limitations of the literary man and lament that one does only what he can, and with what he has.

I mean to raise questions rather than to settle them. But I must admit too that I mean to insist persuasively that they are questions still, at least to some readers of poetry. And thus it may be better that I raise rather than settle them. For, as with dust, perhaps by raising questions I can keep them about us in the air—in which case I am content that I never shall see them settled. And if we are blinded by them from some pressing matters, perhaps we can use this kind of blinding to rediscover our powers of vision—and that is what the aesthetic life is for.

# THE CREATIVE PROCESS:
# SCIENCE, POETRY, AND THE IMAGINATION

# Chapter 1

# T. E. Hulme: CLASSICISM AND THE IMAGINATION

ALTHOUGH modern criticism has done its most valuable work on the literary text, much of its emphasis and terminology has been greatly influenced by the psychological considerations about the creative imagination which have distinguished aesthetic thinking for the past century and a half. But it is not the "imagination" defined by traditional British philosophy which has held this key position. As the word was used from Hobbes to Locke and as it was used when Addison borrowed it from the latter for his *Spectator* papers on "The Pleasures of the Imagination," it had little which could inspire a literary criticism. Those twentieth-century theorists for whom the word has indicated a new direction have rather followed the example of Coleridge, who, seeing the inadequacy of a concept of imagination inhibited by a mechanical psychology of association, turned to the organicism of German transcendental philosophy. As a result, what served as imagination for Addison was from this time forward relegated to "fancy." Seen through the interests of twentieth-century critics, the meaning Coleridge attached to these two terms may be briefly summarized. "Imagination" is that spontaneous power of mind which allows it to express itself in a literally creative way; through imagination the mind infuses organic life into the lifeless mental impressions it has gathered from a lifeless world. "Fancy" is the faculty which, while it also chooses among the many impressions stored by the mind, remains essentially passive; bound by the law of association, it can only bind together additively the selections it has made from the mind's associative memories. For these critics, the imagination, thus derived from Coleridge, is the empowering faculty for our best poetry.[1]

The work of Coleridge was the culmination of the investigations of German aestheticians from Kant to Schelling, and it marked a new emphasis in thinking about art which would never allow the followers of Coleridge to return to the easy assurance of British empiricism. Its dominantly psychological interest may be seen in Coleridge's insistence that the question "What is poetry?" is almost the same as "What is a poet?" Of course these formulations left much to be done by any followers of Coleridge. For, as we shall see, all the questions about poetry that must be answered cannot be collapsed into the narrow dimensions of the poet's psychology. And in the criticism of a poem we must do more than attribute various of its parts to one or another faculty in a transcendental psychology.[2] Yet this is, for the most part, what Coleridge has left to us in his practical criticism. Later, when we come to consider what modern criticism has had to say about the aesthetic object, we shall be concerned with the ways devised by modern critics to judge literary texts objectively, without recourse to psychological speculations. Yet there too we shall see that the influence of Coleridge has been considerable, that often objective criteria have somehow been established through extensions of Coleridge's psychologizing. But here I shall restrict my concern to Coleridge's own field of special interest, to the question of the activity of the poet.

In contrast to these claims about the influence of Coleridge on twentieth-century theorists, it may justly be argued that in their battle against romanticism some of the most influential of modern critics have set themselves against the completely romantic Coleridgean imagination. It would be strange if they did not, in view of the avowed anti-romanticism of modern poetic theory. Indeed it is strange that Coleridge's theory is not more widely condemned by modern critics than it is. This condemnation is especially apparent in the theoretical tradition begun by T. E.

Hulme. But even Hulme, who, as an anti-romantic, explicitly leads away from the Coleridgean imagination, must, as I shall show, end by returning to a markedly similar theory of poetic creativity.

Hulme feels that the essence of romanticism is located in its idolatry of the individual who, for the romantics, should have unlimited aspirations since he has unlimited powers.[3] The transcendental faculties given the individual by German Idealism and by Coleridge embody these unlimited powers and therefore must be denied by the classicist for whose advent Hulme prays. For the classicist, according to Hulme, sees man as an extremely limited being who needs all kinds of severely imposed disciplines if he is to function as he should in his proper sphere. Thus Hulme, defending the view of the classicist, rejects a concept of imagination which would substitute a monism for Christian dualism and would make of man a god. For the attribution to man of the power to create absolutely, *ex nihilo*, could mean little less. Thus Hulme explicitly calls for a poetry of fancy rather than the poetry of unbounded imagination which he feels contaminated English verse in the nineteenth and early twentieth centuries. He calls for a poetry that is formally precise and whose pretensions are limited to simple and vivid description. One might say he calls for a return to a theory of imitation and opposes the reigning theory of expression, the introduction of which was so largely Coleridge's responsibility.

But there is also a quite different side of Hulme. In his essay on Bergson, in which he expounds sympathetically the aesthetic of his master in philosophy, there is a description of the poet's activity that seems nearly as transcendental as Coleridge's.[4] Here Hulme distinguishes between intuition and stock perception and characterizes artistic creativity as the former. It is only the artist, he claims, who can break through the mere static recognition of the world about us which practical life demands; he alone can see through to the dynamic flux which characterizes essential reality. And as artist he makes this vision available to others who, without the artist, could never see beyond the stereotyped world of practicality.

This conception gives the poet a far higher and more romantic function than Hulme has assigned him in his severe "Romanticism and Classicism," which repeats, in more narrowly literary terms, the general argument of his more ambitious "Humanism and the Religious Attitude." For while Hulme, as influenced by Bergson, still wants the poet to be descriptive, he adds a metaphysical dimension to this objective. He would have the poet describe the world about him not merely as it seems to be but rather as it really is behind the veil that hides it from most of us. The poet must not give us as the world "the film of familiarity and selfish solicitude" [5] (note how apt this Coleridgean phrase is here) which our senses normally allow to us; rather he must give us the rare world beyond, which he somehow intuits. Now this is a handsome objective; and the intuitive faculty which is to fulfill it for Hulme seems not far removed from the imagination invoked by Coleridge.* Surely we may doubt the power of fancy to operate at these profound levels. Hence, we cannot accept Hulme's plea for a poetry of fancy and his condemnation of a poetry of imagination as his final or his only word. Similarly we may be disposed to categorize Hulme as a severe classicist who wants to return poetic theory to the well-ordered stalls of classical imitation from its chaotic refuge of romantic expressionism; but again Hulme's essay on Bergson should give us pause. For while the poet, as envisaged by Hulme in this essay, may in some metaphysical sense

* It is important, however, to note a significant difference involved in the relation of these faculties to the particular and the universal. In true German style, Coleridge often seems, like Schelling, to conceive of the universal as lying immanently within the particular. The poet's imagination, in dealing with the particular, can, through its creativity and its organic powers of unification, harmonize the concrete and the finite with the universal, the infinite, the real. But for Hulme, following Bergson, universals are not reality but are arid superimpositions upon reality which are demanded by our practical propensities. It is the uniquely particular—the dynamic, ever changing instantaneous—that is the real, veiled from an action-ridden mankind. Thus the essential reality to which the Coleridgean imagination is to pierce is far removed from the fluid reality to which the Bergsonian intuition is to pierce. The similarity between the two faculties here being marked is one of function: each, as revelatory of the real, is our most significantly cognitive power. We may also see in the differing concept of the real given us by Bergson through Hulme a principal reason for the special concern of modern poetic criticism for freshness, precision, and concreteness.

be said to imitate reality, only if we stretch the traditional meaning of the concept of imitation in an extraordinary way—one which would make it broad enough to accommodate anti-classicists as extreme as Schelling—can we make it apply here.

Of course, we can dismiss the entire problem by calling Hulme's two positions the damning inconsistency of a muddled mind. But even if this were true, as it very well may be, the problem simply takes another form, since we are still left with the need to account for this inconsistency if we are to see its significance for modern poetic theory. And Hulme's enormous influence on the direction this criticism has taken, an influence that stems from both aspects of his speculations, cannot be gainsaid. For, if we follow down the line that starts with Hulme, we find the same seemingly contradictory duality in most of its major exponents: an uncompromising prejudice against romanticism coupled with an invocation of romantic and Coleridgean concepts, even when Coleridge has been slandered by name. For example, the attraction of these critics to romantic theory is betrayed by their constant use of the now common "organic" concept in discussions of either creative activity or poetry itself, as they either use Coleridge's psychologizing or seek to transform it into objective criticism.

Thus, having forced a disjunction between romanticism and classicism, recent theorists, in the footsteps of Hulme, desire to justify classicism with the theoretical tools of romanticism, yet without permitting a reconciliation between the two. Perhaps their reasoning may become clearer if we examine, from another perspective, their general attitude toward this concept of imagination which some, like Hulme, explicitly reject even as they smuggle it into their theory. Of course, it must be admitted that other critics—I. A. Richards, Cleanth Brooks, and Robert Penn Warren particularly—hold Coleridge and his concept of imagination in high regard. And yet their theories are not necessarily much more similar to each other than they are to those of their critical brethren—like Hulme, Eliot, and Ransom—who have less esteem for the theory of Coleridge. In fact, although the former group of critics shares with Kenneth Burke, for example, its admiration for Coleridge, any one of this group is, in terms of poetic theory, perhaps more closely allied to any one of the latter group than he is to Burke.

To the overtly anti-Coleridgean critics, Coleridge's concept of imagination came swathed in the added meanings it had picked up during its use later in the nineteenth century. Writers like Ruskin had thought of themselves as Coleridgeans and had re-defined imagination and fancy for their own uses. For Ruskin, the difference between the two consists mainly in the playfulness of fancy as against the dead earnestness of imagination, the finite as against the infinite.[6] No one who reads Coleridge closely, espe-cially his practical criticism, can deny that this serious-playful dichotomy is involved in his own distinction between the two terms: witness his implied condemnation of the metaphysical poets as being fanciful rather than imaginative.[7] But if Coleridge's practical application of his theory displays this tendency to equate the imaginative with the serious, there is nothing in his theoretical statement of the distinction between imagination and fancy which demands this kind of application. The self-conscious, humorless seriousness which characterizes the so-called romantic disposition is what bothers the modern critic most, since because of it the romantic becomes vulnerable to irony by not being able to supply his own. And the kind of poetry the romantic would try to justify with his theory would be of the unsmiling variety.

But the value of Coleridge's theory lies in its usefulness to those outside his period and beyond its attitudes; its value lies, as with every philosophical contribution, in whatever claim it can make about leading us toward solving the problems our experience sets for us. And the substance of his distinction does not concern seriousness and playfulness. His definition of imagination does not necessarily dictate against the poems of Donne, although it cer-tainly may dictate, and rightfully so, against some of them. But what a Ruskin or a Carlyle did was to take the accidental aspects of Coleridge's definition—those whose applicability was completely controlled by the prejudices of Coleridge's own era—and to use them for the substantial aspects of his own definition, which he then assumed to be Coleridgean. And thus the serious and the witty came to characterize the imagination and the fancy, respectively.

This brief historical sketch is no mere digression. It partly reveals the reason that Hulme could throw out Coleridge and his imagination on one page and advocate similar aesthetic concepts on the next. Hulme was, in a way, repeating the error of Ruskin. Since he wanted above all a tough poetry—a poetry of wit, as his followers would say—obviously the imagination, with its meaning restricted to unleavened seriousness, would not do for him or his followers. If fancy allowed Hulme and his followers their conceits, then by all means they would take fancy. But when they examine the art of making witty verse, not only do they attribute to the poet the qualities Coleridge included in his concept of imagination, but they insist that only this kind of verse reveals these qualities; that, with few exceptions, the serious verse of the nineteenth-century variety, called imaginative by earlier Coleridgeans, reveals only those qualities that Coleridge relegated to fancy. Now this confusion does not necessarily imply that the distinction is a useless one. Rather two conclusions can be drawn from it: the obvious one is that judgments are so conditioned by epoch that it may seem at times almost futile even to strive for objectivity; a more important one is that neither imagination nor fancy has as its essential attribute the one bestowed on it by its most important post-Coleridgean definers—seriousness or playfulness, respectively—and, as a corollary, that only some quality which transcends these is basic to the meaning of imagination as this word has influenced our post-Coleridgean critical tradition.

Of course, this historical extenuation of Hulme's seeming inconsistencies does not reconcile them. Nor is it meant to. It cannot explain how Hulme, in his "Romanticism and Classicism," can deny to the poet the possibility of moving beyond the world about him and yet, in his "Bergson's Theory of Art," can import the term "intuition" to allow precisely for this possibility. Those who would defend Hulme's consistency may point out that, after all, his discussion in the closing pages of "Romanticism and Classicism" is carried on completely in the Bergsonian terms that characterize his other key essay. But this would hardly alter the charge. It would simply make the inconsistency more unforgivable, since now it would be seen to exist within the limits of a single brief essay.*

Other readers of Hulme may insist that I should not even have extenuated the charge to the extent I have done. In "Romanticism and Classicism," they can claim, Hulme clearly realizes that Coleridge's definitions of imagination and fancy are not Ruskin's. In fact Hulme, in quoting Ruskin's definitions of imagination, prefaces the quotations by conceding that Ruskin may be using the word in a highly distorted sense. He is quoting Ruskin, he tells us, to show us the romantic attitude, not to indicate anything about the concept of imagination. Thus might one not say that the concept of imagination that is under attack by Hulme is far less parochial than Ruskin's, so that any subsequent invocation of this faculty constitutes far more serious an inconsistency than was suggested earlier? Before I can answer, however, several other considerations must enter which should clarify the precise nature of Hulme's inconsistency.

To begin with, although it is true that Hulme does not accept Ruskin's concept of imagination as necessarily identical with that of Coleridge (and it is the latter against which he intends to argue), he still carries along many of Ruskin's connotations in his own uses of the word. For example, late in the essay, when

* In this entire discussion it may be well to recall Sir Herbert Read's claim in his introduction to *Speculations* (p. xv) that Hulme "was not, by design, a systematic thinker. He was, in one sense at least, a poet: he preferred to see things in the emotional light of a metaphor rather than to reach reality through scientific analysis." Even if this be the case, it nevertheless must be my task to examine his statements rigorously, however carelessly they may have been related to each other. It is the characteristic of many of the critics to be examined here that they are unsystematic by design. That is much of the reason that this study was deemed necessary. For whatever his design, a theoretical writer can be talked about only if we are aware of the justice he does to those obligations to logic which he incurs, willingly or not, when he begins to record his speculations. In the case of Hulme, however, it is true that his ambivalence is so baffling that I must move cautiously, making qualification upon qualification, if I am to avoid premature judgments and thus do him justice on the theoretical level.

Hulme is discussing fancy, he says, "where . . . your only objection to this kind of fancy is that it is not serious in the effect it produces, then I think the objection to be entirely invalid." But an objection of this kind could come only from a defender of a concept of imagination that is close to Ruskin's. Elsewhere in this essay Hulme disparagingly characterizes all theories that derive from German romantic aesthetics as conceiving that the artist partakes in a vague infinite. Similarly, he says, although in another connection, ". . . there you seem to me to have the highest kind of verse, even though the subject be trivial and the emotions of the infinite far away." He distinguishes in yet another way between imagination and fancy: ". . . where you get this quality [of concrete and fresh imagery] exhibited in the realm of the emotions you get imagination, and . . . where you get this quality exhibited in the contemplation of finite things you get fancy." It is evident in these passages that Hulme considers the imagination to be distinguished from fancy because it is serious rather than witty, because it reveals the infinite rather than the limited, and because it deals with vague emotions rather than with concrete things. Now the former characteristics of these pairs follow from Ruskin's concept of imagination—and, to some extent, perhaps, from the imagination we could derive from Coleridge's practical criticism. But none of them appears as the defining quality of the imagination delineated in Coleridge's theory.

Yet at the end of the essay, when Hulme speaks of Coleridge's distinction between vital or organic complexity and mechanical complexity—which has seemed to be the essential feature of Coleridge's distinction between imagination and fancy—he treats this distinction sympathetically, strangely enough, and proceeds, on the basis of a careful analysis of this distinction, to outlaw romanticism and the poetry of the imagination. In other words, he seems to be defending organicism even as he attacks the romantic theory of imagination. Obviously Hulme does not intend to judge against this concept of imagination by using a law furnished him by this very concept. It should be clear, then, that Hulme is not defining imagination, as Coleridge originally did,

in terms of the organic concept; that instead he is still characterizing the imagination largely by the traits attributed to it by
Ruskin. In this way Hulme can both favor organicism and oppose
the imagination, despite the fact that Coleridge's importance to
us lies in the fact that he firmly identified the two. Further, in
this last discussion, Hulme, as a faithful Bergsonian, uses "vital"
complexity to characterize *all* art, in contrast to the mechanical
complexity by which he characterizes the operations of the intellect. For he is as anxious to avoid "the old classical view," which
defines beauty "as lying in conformity to certain standard fixed
forms" (any such fixity would be abhorrent to Bergson), as he
is to avoid "the romantic view which drags in the infinite." In a
similar vein, Hulme earlier says of fancy that it "is not mere
decoration added on to plain speech. Plain speech is essentially
inaccurate. It is only by new metaphors, that is, by fancy, that
it can be made precise." Then he goes on to describe a form of
fancy that is inferior to imagination. So here he is defining fancy
(as "not mere decoration") in the very way that Richards and
Brooks, for example, taking their lead from Coleridge, define
imagination. For it is the concept of the functional, rather than
the merely decorative, metaphor which characterizes that modern
criticism which is admittedly Coleridgean.

It follows from these various passages, first, that the imagination excluded by Hulme is not excluded by reason of the definition
Coleridge gave to it. On the contrary, the differentia established
by Coleridge for the imagination is the very one Hulme uses to
define all art—and here Hulme properly sees Coleridge and Bergson as agreeing. Secondly, Hulme's idea of fancy appears to be
essentially no different from Coleridge's imagination, unless we
import Ruskin's claims about the kinds of attitudes and subjects
appropriate to each. In manner of operation, or in the kind of
mental faculty involved, there is no important difference. To put
it another way, if we look at the problem from the point of view
of the Coleridgean imagination, Hulme is not actually calling for
a different faculty; he is calling for a different use of the same

faculty. He wants it to be addressed to different subject matter, to be at the service of different attitudes.

Hulme is reacting against a "Weltanschauung" [8] and a metaphysic more than against a literary theory. And this realization leads to another source of his confusion. In many of his essays Hulme uses the term "romanticism" to cover a multitude of sins. He collapses within this single term two quite antithetical movements, which would involve two quite different metaphysics and aesthetics. He often sees romanticism as best typified by the ideas behind the French Revolution—by what might be termed rationalistic progressivism. "Here is the root of all romanticism: that man, the individual, is an infinite reservoir of possibilities; and if you can so rearrange society by the destruction of oppressive order then these possibilities will have a chance and you will get Progress." He opposes to this political romanticism the belief in order and tradition, just as he opposes to the self-indulgent seriousness of literary romanticism the toughness of his proposed classical poetry.

But having established his definition of romanticism on the ideas, let us say, of a Thomas Paine, he proceeds to use the derogatory term to put what I shall term Germanic romanticism in its place.* But this is not entirely just. It perhaps springs from a confusion which commonly lumps all English and German romanticism together without first making the necessary distinctions. For example, Edmund Burke, who is indeed one of the earlier Germanic romantics, opposed to the rationalistic defenses of the French Revolution the very virtues—order and tradition—which Hulme claims to be the antidotes to romanticism. And the German romantics are equally conservative and equally traditional. Indeed, the number of converts they gave to Catholicism should certainly have pleased Hulme. With Burke they stood for the organic concept, which resists the mechanism of the rationalistic progressive. If segments of British romanticism were Godwinian,

* I call it here "Germanic" rather than "German" romanticism because some non-Germans shared in the movement although the ideas were most fully explored by Germans.

this is hardly reason to damn as a Godwinian anyone who has ever been called a romantic. Hulme has earned the right to condemn romanticism only by his arguments against the antitraditional progressives; he proceeds to prosecute the Germanic romantics (including, of course, Coleridge) on the wrong grounds, therefore. He would need a new series of objections to press the case. Similarly, when he disparages literary romanticism by citing its unleavened seriousness, we must conclude that he is unmindful of the sometimes tough-minded self-criticism of romantic irony (not entirely unlike the "irony" of modern criticism), which is displayed in some German romantic literature and proclaimed in much of its literary theory. Again he seems not to have realized sufficiently that much of English and Germanic romanticism has little in common beside the not very judiciously applied name.* In failing to classify the enemy more carefully, he fails also to note the points on which there may be some agreement between them and him. In his anxiety to make the romantic-classical cleavage too clean, he ignores certain all-important overlappings—all-important because so many of his followers are heavily dependent upon the romantic (Germanic romantic) concepts they have adapted to their own uses.

This is not to say that Hulme, had he seen the necessary distinctions among romantics, would have felt very much kinship with the Germanic variety. There still would remain the problem of metaphysics; and certainly few thinkers in the history of philosophy are more open to Hulme's charge that they "drag in the infinite" than these romantics are. Their frequent recourse to metaphysical monism, which would detract from God's transcendence in order to exalt His immanence, must have seemed sufficient reason for Hulme to give them the label of romanticism. And certainly they deserved it, at least on these grounds. But aesthetically, and often politically too, he would, and unconsciously did, find many of their ideas congenial to his own. And in his

* While it may seem difficult to account for these oversights of Hulme in view of the fact that he spent time in Germany studying continually and profoundly, I do not believe his failure to make certain crucial distinctions among those whom he calls romantics can permit an alternative explanation.

literary theory, like Bergson before him, he put their dynamic organicism to good use. Whether this organicism can flow consistently from Hulme's rigidly dualistic metaphysics is a question which need not concern us here.

While I may seem to have strayed a good distance from poetic creativity, I do not believe that I have. Surely the term "imagination," as conceived by Coleridge, is central to modern theoretical discussions of this problem. Now I have shown at the outset that Hulme, one of the pioneers of the movement under study, argued against this conception of imagination. And since critics in the wake of Hulme have, like him, been battling romanticism with the tools furnished them by romanticism, it seemed crucial to clarify the precise intellectual relationships between these critics and their romantic ancestor-enemies.

Several of the chapters which follow will be dedicated to proving that the duality I have been tracing in Hulme is hardly confined to him. We shall see many of his followers paralleling his attempt to make the best of two conflicting theoretical traditions. And they often do considerably less well with them than Hulme has done. For example, we shall shortly be concerned with the serious theoretical difficulties in the work of T. S. Eliot, in whom a classical interest, which demands an impersonal poetry that is "an escape from emotion . . . an escape from personality," is constantly accompanied by a romantically expressionistic interest, which calls for the famous objective correlative. If we assume for the moment what will be amply shown later—that similar and similarly serious difficulties exist in the work of Eliot and others— then it would seem clearly important to return to what has been said about Hulme to learn the precise direction his apparent inconsistencies have given to the more extensive and detailed poetic theories that followed.

Clearly it would seem that Hulme is trying to maintain a position which at once includes classical imitation and romantic expressionism, obedience to mechanical rules and individual creativity.[9] His distaste for nineteenth-century poetry, as well as for nineteenth-century criticism and philosophy, forces him to think of himself as a defender of another neoclassicism. But at the same time his devotion to Bergson forces him to adopt the principle of an organicism or vitalism that must resist all fixity. To say merely that Hulme tries to stand between these extremes and to utilize the best that each has to offer would be radically incomplete; it would make of him no more than a reckless eclectic who would have little to contribute. Instead he made his way to a completely independent position which, to use his words again, avoids the "standard fixed forms" of "the old classical view" as well as "the romantic view which drags in the infinite." To clarify this position and the direction it has given, it is necessary to add yet another element to those shown to be at work so far.

As imagist, Hulme is especially concerned with language. We have seen that for Hulme, the disciple of Bergson, the poet must break through the stock recognitions which plague practical life and thus must make it possible for us to see things in their uniqueness. But Hulme does not allow these intuitions to take place in a vacuum; he is anti-romanticist enough not to believe in the self-sufficiency of the mind. Not only do intuitions take linguistic form, he claims, but they are dependent upon language. For just as most of us look at the world through stereotypes, so do we speak of the world through the equally fixed forms of language. Since thinking can take place only in a medium, it may very well be that we cannot have a fresh perception of the world unless we have first dislocated language in order to force fresh ways of expression from it. Thus, to the problem with which Hulme was seen to be concerned earlier—the artist's need to see the world in a new way—another must now be added which is perhaps prior to, or at least inseparable from, the first: the artist's need to use his language in a new way.

Here, in Hulme's insistence on the primary place of language in the poet's vision, is the clue to the most important difference between Coleridge's theory of imagination and Hulme's theory of intuition. I must postpone treating the total impact of this difference, however, until certain other views of creativity have been presented. But it is, as will appear later, a difference which has been of paramount significance in establishing a criticism that could, for the sake of insight-via-language, endorse poetic experiment even as, in the name of classical restraint, it forbade idiosyncratic recklessness.

# Chapter 2

# T. S. Eliot: EXPRESSION AND IMPERSONALITY

It was T. S. Eliot who, in terms of his own genius, elaborated Hulme's scattered insights and transmitted them in the form which became one of the two major streams of influence that culminated in much of what goes by the name of the "new criticism." His attitude toward romanticism in general and Coleridge in particular resembles Hulme's. Eliot is perhaps as self-consciously classical as any other modern critic, with the possible exception of Yvor Winters. But, as with Hulme, there is in Eliot's discussions of poetic creation a strange duality which suggests contradiction.

Eliot's early theoretical treatments of poetic creativity divide into two main groups: those controlled by the concept of the unity of sensibility and those controlled by the concept of the objective correlative. Eliot's poet of unified sensibility "is constantly amalgamating disparate experience." [1] He can make no distinction between the intellectual and the emotional: all is utterly fused. And when this magnificently integrated mind sets to work in language, great poetry results. Thus we may explain the greatness of the successful metaphysical poems in which, to use Johnson's less well-meant characterization, "the most heterogeneous ideas are yoked by violence together." In fact Eliot indicates that he would accept this definition as an approving one if "yoked" were replaced with "united." [2]

But it has been precisely on the ground of the unification of the

disparate that the modern defenders of Coleridge, like Richards
and Brooks, have proclaimed the usefulness of their master's concept of imagination.[3] And Brooks' *Modern Poetry and the Tradition* (1939) performs the marriage between Eliot's unity of sensibility and Coleridge's imagination, modified by Richards' broad
interpretation, since Brooks discovers that both require the same
kind of poetry, and, more important for my immediate interests
here, the same kind of poetic activity. For we can compare with
Eliot's unity of sensibility the passage from Coleridge from which
Brooks likes to claim support for his concept of irony:

. . . [the imagination] reveals itself in the balance or reconciliation
of opposite or discordant qualities: of sameness, with difference;
of the general, with the concrete; the idea, with the image; the
individual, with the representative; the sense of novelty and freshness, with old and familiar objects; a more than usual state of
emotion, with more than usual order . . .[4]

Brooks might as effectively have quoted Coleridge's praise of the
fusion of elements he finds in the couplet from *Venus and Adonis*,

> Look! how a bright star shooteth from the sky;
> So glides he in the night from Venus' eye,

which Coleridge cites as an example of imagination and which
I. A. Richards discusses to show the usefulness to practical criticism of this concept of imagination:

How many images and feelings are here brought together without effort and without discord, in the beauty of Adonis, the
rapidity of his flight, the yearning, yet hopelessness, of the enam-
oured gazer, while a shadowy ideal character is thrown over the
whole.[5]

And just before quoting the couplet, Coleridge says, in a passage
not quoted by Richards,

In its [the imagination's] tranquil and purely pleasurable operation,
it acts chiefly by creating out of many things, as they would have
appeared in the description of an ordinary mind, detailed in unimpassioned succession, a oneness, even as nature, the greatest of
poets, acts upon us, when we open our eyes upon an extended
prospect.

To this couplet Coleridge, and later Richards, oppose a passage produced by fancy:

> Full gently now she takes him by the hand,
> A lily prisoned in a jail of snow,
> Or ivory in an alabaster band:
> So white a friend ingirts so white a foe! [6]

Coleridge claims this second, the merely fanciful, passage is characterized by "the faculty of bringing together images dissimilar in the main by some one point or more of likeness . . ." [7] Richards adds to this Coleridge's later claim that in fancy the images brought together "have no connection natural or moral, but are yoked together by the poet by means of some accidental coincidence." [8] At this point we should recall that it was just this word yoked which Eliot objected to in Johnson's definition and which he would replace with united in order to do justice to the operation of sensibility in the metaphysical poets. Like Eliot, Coleridge uses this very word to distinguish the arbitrary connections of fancy from the inevitable fusions of imagination. Certainly it must be admitted, then, that the kinds of psychology called for by Eliot and Coleridge are quite similar, although Eliot's concept seems to be historically rather than philosophically derived. Thus Eliot, like Hulme, betrays himself as a defender of the organic theory of imagination which he has elsewhere disparaged.[9]

But after we have seen Eliot's definition of unity of sensibility, which seems to control his discussion in "The Metaphysical Poets," we may be quite surprised, later in the same essay, to discover his statement that these poets "were, at best, engaged in the task of trying to find verbal equivalents for states of mind and feeling." [10] For here, suddenly, we are to understand that poetic activity is merely the effort to translate the pre-existing mental and emotional state of the poet. And this is a form of expressionist theory which is too romantic even for the formulations of Coleridge. Clearly this is not the same kind of creative activity as that utterly fused intellectual-emotional grasp which characterizes the poet of unified sensibility. Nothing more is said in this essay about the "objective correlative," but it is taken up in some detail elsewhere.[11] But the more Eliot talks about it the more inconsistent it seems with his ideas about the unity of sensibility.

Even within his discussions of the objective correlative, however, there seem to be several ideas which cannot be reconciled with each other. Eliot seems frequently to be proposing a theory of the expression of the poet's emotion that seems highly romantic and highly inadequate.[12] This rather naive notion finds the poet looking for "a set of objects, a situation, a chain of events which shall be the formula of that *particular* emotion" which he is seeking to express.[13] While no emotion *as such* appears in the work, the poem as a whole is the translation into objective action of the original emotions which inspired it. And it is to evoke those same emotions in the audience. Thus the poem is to be the emotionless bridge between the similar emotions of the poet and his audience. The poet gets rid of his emotions by sublimating them in his poem's objectivity and, by means of this device, he shifts his emotional burden from his own shoulders to those of his audience. One can well say with Eliseo Vivas that "Eliot grafts a somewhat revamped doctrine of catharsis on to the popular theory of expression, and uses the product to justify poetry therapeutically. Poetry is on this theory a psychic antitoxin and makes action possible."

It must be granted that Eliot's theory—and in particular his questionable judgment about *Hamlet* (that in being an insufficient objective correlative it is motivated by emotions which are "in excess of the facts as they appear" in the action [14])—provided a general principle which prompted younger critics like Cleanth Brooks to many perhaps sounder critical pronouncements about the ungrounded emotionalism they call sentimentality. But regardless of the aid this furnished for practical criticism, it should be seen that it involves a very mechanical conception of the creative act, one that would hardly seem consistent with the organic implications found in the concept of the unity of sensibility. The poet must have a store of disembodied abstract items called emotions,\* which he apparently must pretty clearly under-

\* We may well wonder just what sort of thing a disembodied emotion

stand before they come to be expressed if he is to know where to search for their objective equivalents. When he discovers the things or actions which can successfully contain an emotion, he transfers the subjective emotion to its secret enclosure within the objective things or actions. There it lurks in waiting for the spectator who, baited by the objective properties of the poem, has the emotion spring fully upon him from its hiding place. And thus the original emotions of the poet, the emotions expressed by the poem, and the emotions aroused in the spectator—three quite different affairs, it would seem [15]—are here carelessly equated.

Eliot cleverly retains his "impersonal" and would-be classical theory of art by keeping the poem from exhibiting any emotion as such, although as in very romantic theory, it expresses the poet's emotions and relays them on to the reader. And yet the reader's emotions, we are told, are to be purely aesthetic emotions. Not only might a psychologist have difficulty in conceiving of emotions that differ in kind from each other,* but he would surely wonder how the emotions aroused by the poem could be any more aesthetic when they reached the reader than they had been when they existed untouched, before the writing of the poem, in the poet's mind.

The mechanical nature of this description of the poet's psychology should now be apparent. If the situation discovered by the poet to embody the emotion is adequate to that emotion, then just as the emotion is not to be "in excess of the facts as they appear," so neither should the reverse be true: the facts should not be in excess of the motivating emotion. There should be no surplusage in either direction. But this predicates a highly static

would be, since an existent emotion sufficiently specific to guide the poet's choice would seem to be defined by its object rather than to await in a generic state a specific object which will allow it to manifest itself.

* If we assume that emotions are defined by their objects, it would seem that all one can mean by an aesthetic emotion, as distinguished from a non-aesthetic emotion, is that the former happens to be aroused by a work of art while the latter happens to be aroused by something else. And this merely returns us to the problem instead of solving it. For we must ask what distinguishes the work of art from non-art. And what I shall say here will make it less and less likely that the emotion expressed in the total poem is necessarily very close to the original emotions of the poet or to those aroused in the reader.

situation. The poet must completely understand his emotion prior to its realization or else he could not tell so precisely how the objective facts measure up to it. What, then, has he gained from his work besides his unburdening of himself? (Eliot would hardly allow this to stand as the sole justification of the poet's activity, even though he does speak of poetry as "an escape from emotion . . . an escape from personality." [16]) The objectification of the emotion cannot have added at all to the poet's understanding of it since it was in terms of this clearly comprehended emotion that the objective situation was selected. Objectification is then no more than mechanical transference.

It is especially odd to see these implicit claims by Eliot who, as a faithful follower of Hulme, often shows his utter devotion to the medium of poetry, its language. For where he concerns himself with the objective correlative, there is no evidence of the poet's need for language in order to bring his emotion to his full understanding. The emotion exists prior to language, and acts, in this prelinguistic state, as the judgmental factor in the entire creative act. What need, then, for the use of language, which Eliot continually assures us is necessary for the growth of sensibility? Yet like Hulme, who views language as requisite to insight, Eliot sees poetry as having the social function of vitalizing the language of its audience in order to vitalize their perceptions of the world. And this—the refreshing of a nation's sensibility through the refreshing of its language—we find Eliot enunciating as late as 1945, which indicates how much he is still influenced by Hulme.[17]

It is difficult to trace Eliot to this Bergsonian position from a theory which seems hardly to recognize the indispensability of language. And yet even in this essay, "The Social Function of Poetry," significant remnants of the objective correlative still lurk. Wherever Hulme would use the word *intuition*, Eliot uses *feelings* or *emotions*. The poet, we are told, gives "people words for their feelings" and gives them too knowledge of feelings which they have never experienced. But these feelings do not have the cognitive power of Bergson's intuitions. As a matter of fact, we are told plainly that the poet's function is not in any way a cog-

*174308*

nitive one. Eliot says here, as he has frequently said elsewhere, that the poet has nothing to do with thinking. Whatever ideas there are in the poem are ideas the poet has borrowed. The poem is designed "to convey an emotional equivalent for the ideas."

While this concept may seem to be more relevant to the relation of poetry to knowledge, one of my later considerations, than it is to the question of creativity, it is important now to note where Eliot's concern with the objective correlative leads him when he tries to carry it with him along the path set for him by Hulme. Just as he talks about the need for language—language which his objective correlative has made a subservient instrument—so too he talks about the insights given us by poetry, except that he must restrict these insights to emotional ones. As a result, where Hulme sees the poet laying bare the structure of reality, Eliot sees him as working with shopworn ideas. Hulme's poet infuses life into the world by showing it to us as we can never see it without his aid; Eliot's infuses new life into old ideas—ideas that are easily accessible to us without his aid. Thus there are two epistemologies lying behind these conceptions of poetic creativity, and Hulme's allows his poet to be immeasurably more creative than Eliot's can be.* Hulme here has the consistency to remain close to Coleridge in that he allows to the poet the function of showing us that in the world which no one else can show us. Eliot retreats from these extensions of the organic aspect of his theory, which stresses the great poet's unity of sensibility. He seems rather to draw a limit to the poet's function so that the poet can give us nothing that was not in our world before his entrance upon it. He can merely reshuffle it for us.

But this entire discussion, a defender of Eliot may claim, looks only at one half of Eliot's statements about the objective correlative. Although it is true that a substantial portion of these essays is concerned with the expression of the poet's emotion, is it not unjust to emphasize only this concept without taking equal notice

---

* This despite Hulme's insistence that "art merely reveals, it never creates" ("Bergson's Theory of Art," *Speculations*, p. 151). For Hulme treats artistic revelation as a sacred and irreplaceable function.

of Eliot's insistence on the impersonal quality of art, on the separation in good art between "the man who suffers and the mind which creates"? In reply I might say that there is nothing in these statements for which I have not already accounted. While I have looked at Eliot's objective correlative mainly as an expression theory, I have also shown that there is to be no emotion as such in the poetry. And the objections introduced at this point, in light of Eliot's impersonal theory, merely stress the *objective* side of the objective correlative just as I have stressed the expressive or *correlative* side. If the work contains objective situations and the emotions themselves are kept out of it, then the poem is impersonal even as it expresses those emotions; the artist works in terms of the objective action he has selected as the equivalent of his emotions rather than in terms of the emotions themselves. Thus "the mind which creates" is shown to be separate from "the man who suffers" without my being forced to modify my exposition of the objective correlative. Indeed, it becomes clear how Vivas can justly say that Eliot is "chasing with the hounds of modernism while running with the hares of classicism."

This attempt by Eliot to make a complete breach between the work and the emotions which it serves to objectify, however attractive it may seem, can hardly be reconciled with the mechanical conception of the creative act which I examined earlier. I showed then that all too little consideration was given to the literary medium, that the emotion must have existed in a fully coherent, albeit disembodied, state prior to its objectification; that while language was needed to pass it on to other people, the poet himself did not need language to clarify it for himself. The one-to-one relation between the poet's emotional intentions and those of the work is sufficiently precise even to suggest "the intentional fallacy" which so many followers of Eliot repudiate.[18] This mechanical concept makes it difficult for us, much as we would like to, to accept, in the context of his discussion, Eliot's statement that "the difference between art and the event is always absolute." [19] And, if we did not know his ideas so well, we might be surprised, in view of Eliot's primary theoretical concern with

[ 53 ]

emotions and situations rather than with language, to find him saying "that the poet has, not a 'personality' to express, but a particular medium, which is only a medium and not a personality." [20] There are more explicit statements of the same kind, statements even more at odds with his objective correlative, in *The Use of Poetry and the Use of Criticism*:

We have to communicate—if it is communication, for the word may beg the question—an experience which is not an experience in the ordinary sense, for it may only exist, formed out of many personal experiences ordered in some way which may be very different from the way of valuation of practical life, in the expression of it. If poetry is a form of "communication," yet that which is to be communicated is the poem itself, and only incidentally the experience and the thought which have gone into it. The poem's existence is somewhere between the writer and the reader; it has a reality which is not simply the reality of what the writer is trying to "express," or of his experience of writing it, or of the experience of the reader or of the writer as reader. Consequently the problem of what a poem "means" is a good deal more difficult than it at first appears . . . But a poem is not just either what the poet "planned" or what the reader conceives, nor is its "use" restricted wholly to what the author intended or to what it actually does for readers.[21]

Here, as in parts of "The Social Function of Poetry," Eliot returns to Hulme's sound aesthetic concern with language and gives one of the clearest statements we have of the aesthetic which seems implicitly to underlie much of modern criticism. It is this concern with the poet as technician—one who deals with words in order to deal with emotions or with their objective equivalents—that features Eliot's most valuable criticism.

Interestingly enough, this concern is dominant in a crucial passage in Eliot's most recent theoretical work, in which he approaches poetic creation almost exactly as I shall shortly be trying to do, and with his customary brilliance of style. It must be admitted that Eliot, here paraphrasing Gottfried Benn, is speaking of only one of several kinds of verse (the "meditative"), so that this is for him only one of several varieties of the creative process and the only one which satisfies the requirements I seem to be setting up. But its more consistent adherence to an organic theory than many of his earlier utterances and its implicit denial of the objective correlative make the passage worth quoting in full here:

What, asks Herr Benn in this lecture, does the writer of such a poem, "addressed to no one", start with? There is first, he says, an inert embryo or "creative germ" (*ein dumpfer schöpferischer Keim*) and, on the other hand, the Language, the resources of the words at the poet's command. He has something germinating in him for which he must find words; but he cannot know what words he wants until he has found the words; he cannot identify this embryo until it has been transformed into an arrangement of the right words in the right order. When you have found the words for it, the "thing" for which the words had to be found has disappeared, replaced by a poem. What you start from is nothing so definite as an emotion, in any ordinary sense; it is still more certainly not an idea; it is—to adapt two lines of Beddoes to a different meaning—a

> bodiless childful of life in the gloom
> Crying with frog voice, "what shall I be?"

I agree with Gottfried Benn, and I would go a little further. In a poem which is neither didactic nor narrative, and not animated by any other social purpose, the poet may be concerned solely with expressing in verse—using all his resources of words, with their history, their connotations, their music—this obscure impulse. He does not know what he has to say until he has said it; and in the effort to say it he is not concerned with making other people understand anything. He is not concerned, at this stage, with other people at all: only with finding the right words or, anyhow, the least wrong words. He is not concerned whether anybody else will ever listen to them or not, or whether anybody else will ever understand them if he does. He is oppressed by a burden which he must bring to birth in order to obtain relief. Or, to change the figure of speech, he is haunted by a demon, a demon against which he feels powerless, because in its first manifestation it has no face, no name, nothing; and the words, the poem he makes, are a kind of form of exorcism of this demon.[22]

But it is hard to follow the steps by which Eliot can move from a theory of self-expression to one which focuses on the manipulation of a communicable medium, to one, that is, which sees the object as an independent entity, a world of values whose separate status is "absolute." The poem which is the objective translation of an already fully articulate emotion, or which deals with emotional equivalents of already formulated nonaesthetic ideas, can hardly have such an absolute status. His concern with language here would follow from his admiration for the unity of sensibility. His most influential invention, however, the objective correlative, poses a view of the creative act which can hardly justify the poet's being primarily concerned with his technical problems as a poet rather than with his emotional problems as a man.

# Chapter 3

# I. A. Richards: NEUROLOGICAL AND
# POETIC ORGANIZATION

I. A. RICHARDS has joined with Eliot to exercise perhaps the greatest influence on the new critics. We might say that it is through the fusion of the theories of Richards and Eliot that much of what passes for the new criticism has taken form. But it may seem odd to discover that Eliot, in his most detailed discussion of poetic activity, should at many points seem strikingly similar to the thinker who, perhaps as influential, starts from diametrically opposed assumptions. Of course, one great difference between those of their statements about the creative act which are similar is that with Eliot we can point to other discussions which partially nullify, even if they contradict, what is objectionable in his theory of the objective correlative; I. A. Richards, on the other hand, really means what he says. His greater consistency arises from his eagerness to accept the logical consequences of his position, while Eliot, at times perhaps fortunately, seems not to be totally aware of what those consequences are.

The early Richards, as a materialist and would-be neurologist, must view poetic creativity in consistently quantitative and mechanistic terms to keep this activity the same in kind as nonartistic activity. He sees the mind as no more than a bundle of impulses, each of which seeks satisfaction at the expense of the others.[1] Thus human action is reducible to the satisfaction of man's most insistent impulses—those impulses upon whose satisfaction the fulfillment of the greatest number of other impulses depends. The end of any individual's existence must be to keep himself as slightly frustrated as he can, so to organize his life that as many impulses as possible can be fulfilled as often as possible. The person in the healthiest mental state is the one who has brought most of himself into play.[2] While in ordinary life, with its demand for action, we can satisfy only one or very few of these impulses at a time, and satisfy them only at the cost of frustrating innumerable others, poetry allows us to organize for satisfaction many impulses at once, since we are not involved in action.[3] And since the more impulses, and the more opposed impulses, we satisfy the better, the poem that allows the fullest organization of impulses is best. But experience of any kind allows these organizations, so that no place can be provided for an exclusively aesthetic experience. Of course, since aesthetic experience, being unconcerned with practical or cognitive problems, can concentrate more completely on the complex organization of impulses than can the other varieties of experience—the latter all being more or less world-weighted—art is a handy thing to have around. But, Richards must insist in a way far less sophisticated than Dewey's, art is experience, so that there is no such disposition as an *aesthetic* state within an observer and no such quality as an *aesthetic* value in an object.[4]

I am here interested, however, in the activity of the poet, although I approach him by way of the function of his art. If the end of life is the attainment of an ever richer organization of impulses, then the function of art must be to communicate to a more poorly organized public the highly elaborate experience of an individual, the poet. Needless to say, this individual can have this experience, beyond the reach of most of us, because of his fine neurological organization, his extreme mental health, at least as far as his reaction to this experience is concerned. Through the medium of art, we are to come as close to duplicating his experience as we can, thus enriching our own organization.[5] This identification of the artist's experience with the reader's—an ideal, if not an actual, identification, as will appear when I examine Richards later in another connection—forces Richards into a description of the creative act which is at least as mechanical as Eliot's was sometimes found to be. The poetic process is described with almost no reference to the medium; and this neglect is once more surprising, emerging as it does from a theorist whose interest in literary problems seems largely motivated by his semanticist's interest in language.

The characteristic which sets off the artist for Richards, it must be noted, is not at all the artist's craft in working in a given material; it is his healthy organization of impulses which allows him to undergo such rich experiences. It is this undifferentiated concept of experience and his theoretical neglect of the medium which allow Richards to make such broad analogies among the various arts.[6] Thus there is no explanation in such a theory for the fact that the artist chooses the particular art that he does or, to narrow the field to literature, the particular genre that he does. In fact, we can see no reason for him to bother to communicate his experience at all, except out of a sheerly altruistic regard for the less highly organized people about him. For, not unlike Eliot's artist, he apparently does not need the expressive act to create or, indeed, even to organize his experience. The experience exists, in its complete form, prior to the act of communication.

This belief in an experience which is fully formed and apparently fully comprehended prior to the act of expression is the source of much of the trouble into which his theory leads Richards. It leads not merely to a distinction between, but to a separation of, content and form that is as primitive as any in the recent history of literary theory. This despite Richards' explicit contempt for any such dichotomy.[7] Richards is thus led to distinguish in the act of judgment a "critical part" and a "technical part." [8] The former determines the value of the experience, the latter the effectiveness of the object as communication. Since value can be predicated only of experiences and not of objects, only the critical estimate, Richards warns, is a judgment of value: the critic must beware of mistaking any technical deficiencies for detractions from the value of the experience. Thus he is led to the distinction between a "bad poem" and a "defective" one. In the first, the experience itself is worthless (that is, it does not offer an organization of impulses that is rich enough), while in the second the work fails as communication.[9] He does admit that a poem may be both bad and defective. But to call a poem defective is not to offer an evaluation, since value can exist only in the original experience. And this experience somehow exists and is accessible to us outside the words which embody it in the poem.

This dichotomy seems completely worthless. We are shown two poems, one bad and one merely defective. Somehow the defective one, which fails as communication because it does not control our experience so as to make it approximate the poet's, is still somehow to indicate to us that the original experience was probably worth while. In other words, the poet probably had a sufficiently broad organization of impulses. That this was not sufficiently communicated cannot be attributed to the poet's experience. In dealing with a bad poem, exemplified by a sonnet by Ella Wheeler Wilcox, Richards condemns the experience as without value, because the stock responses it arouses hardly constitute a complex organization of impulses; but he insists that it has succeeded as communication.

I have carried Richards' argument this far, even though it extends beyond the creative process, in order to show with what consistency and tenacity he holds to his concept of the creative act and to what lengths it takes him in other areas of his theory. His similarity to Eliot should be clear. Richards' poet does not need the poem in order to realize his experience—the organization of his impulses—any more than Eliot's poet, as defined in "Hamlet and His Problems," needs it in order to realize his emotions. The experience of the one and the emotions of the other are completely formed and understood before they are embodied. The poets achieve their status primarily by their respective abilities to experience deeply or to feel deeply rather than to write well. And it must be repeated that these conclusions are all the more astounding in view of the fact that few critics have more constantly immersed themselves in problems of language.

What must be repeated too is that, while Richards cannot point to other aspects of his theory which, though contradictory, might lend depth and complexity to his idea of the poet, Eliot can always remind us of his claims about impersonality as well as his insistence on the unity of sensibility. And if these, when contrasted with his mechanical concepts, make Eliot less of a systematic theorist, as compensation they make him a more faithful reporter of the complex struggle undergone by the artist in his throes of creativity. For my examination thus far should have revealed that we need a concept of the creative act that will permit us, when we come to judge the poem, to see it as a work of art; not to see through it to a disembodied idea or emotion or experience which somehow is said to exist outside and prior to it. We cannot judge any such unavailable entity—unavailable precisely because it is not realized, does not come ultimately to its fully defined existence until it speaks, not *in* the work, but *as* the work. What existence can we attribute to the unformed mass which is the poet's emotion and his experience before he has provided them with the objective forms which alone can define them? With what experience of the poet *as* poet can we be conversant except the experience which is expressed as his poem? And it is the artist rather than the man who leads us to his work. Or are we to return to the grandiose, if aesthetically rather empty, suggestions which led Legouis to conceive of Spenser as a potential Titian? [10]

Richards, as a mechanist, is again more consistent, if less adequate, in his discussion of imagination than is Eliot in his analogous discussion of the unity of sensibility. Richards warns us from the first, in his *Coleridge on Imagination*, that he will convert the transcendental theories of Coleridge into materialistic terms.[11] Coleridge's contributions, Richards insists, come from his interests in psychology and language, which have no necessary connection with his philosophy. But, though Richards fails to grant this, Coleridge's hierarchical faculty psychology, so different from Richards' descriptive impulse psychology, is actually an expression of that philosophy, an analytical extension of transcendental epistemology. There is no possibility of separation.

It follows that Richards is unable to appreciate the full meaning of Coleridge's distinction between imagination and fancy simply because he cannot comprehend the full extent of creativity that is given the imagination in German transcendentalism. There is no way for traditional British empiricism to cope with these concepts, and Richards—the self-styled Benthamite [12]—is unable to step outside his narrow philosophic tradition even for purposes of faithful exposition. The creative power of the imagination is for him merely the expression and result of past experiences. While this is partially the case for Coleridge, it is not the whole story. Richards cannot see that in this fusing power there is also for Coleridge an originally (because Divine) creative element which makes the product completely new. The combination has something in it, something added, that is not in any of its elements. And no naturalistic theory can with consistency allow for it. Richards rather says, "prior experiencing *determines* how it [the self] will experience in the future." [13] Similarly he indulges in considerable dialectic to place Coleridge's concept of free will within the framework of determinism, but he is not very convincing in showing that the view he is presenting is Coleridge's.

Indeed Richards' epistemological presentation of the imagination is probably not far from what Coleridge meant by fancy.* What, then, does Richards do with fancy? It would seem that the distinction Richards draws between imagination and fancy is really that which, in another connection, he draws between contextual association and the linear stream of association.[14] Thus we have Richards' favored kind of association, needed for his entire critical theory, related to the imagination, while the old

* It must be granted that in his extension of these terms to practical criticism Richards seems far more faithful to what Coleridge meant by them; and this extension has certainly been extremely useful. Coleridge's distinction between imagination and fancy becomes for Richards an analysis of tenor-vehicle relationships in the metaphor. The imagination is displayed in an image which is internal and functional, the organizing principle of the passage; a passage is produced only by fancy if its image is merely external, accidental, decorative. In fancy the tenor and vehicle are always distinct; in imagination the tenor is fused into its vehicle. Thus the imaginative metaphor is untranslatable; the fanciful one is merely a transparent analogy. See *Coleridge on Imagination,* pp. 75–84.

associationist view, like Hartley's, is related to fancy. Richards does not sufficiently see the fancy as also a unifying agent, since unification for him is the differentia for the imagination; unity distinguishes contextual from linear association. Passages of fancy may then contain irrelevancies. Actually, for Coleridge the fancy unifies as well as the imagination except that the former operates on a much lower level, since there is nothing originally creative about it. In effect, Richards seems to have transformed Coleridge's all-important metaphysical distinction between the organic and creative on the one hand and the mechanistic and passive on the other into a descriptive distinction between two naturalistic psychologies: the Gestalt as opposed to the more naively empirical theories of association.* And although Richards joins the modern critics in their celebration of organic unity, it is clear that in his discussion of the poet's mental capacities he precludes the creativity which alone can allow him to speak of the poem as organic. For if the work only transcribes combinations of the poet's past experiences, then there is no way for it to assume that life of its own—a life answerable only to its own laws—which a thoroughgoing organic theory must grant to it.

* In this connection it is important to note that Richards objects to the fact that Coleridge places fancy and imagination within a hierarchy of value. As a psychologist Richards must restrict himself to descriptive observations, avoiding the normative. (See *Coleridge on Imagination*, pp. 91–97.) Of course, Coleridge's attribution of far greater value to imagination is justified by the fact that his psychology is a branch of his transcendental philosophy and thus need not, like Richards', be value-free.

# The Requirements of an Organic Theory of Poetic Creation

IT IS now possible to tie some of the strands of this discussion together. The three writers I have examined have talked about two closely related problems involved in the study of poetic creation. They each have had something to say about a theory of mind, about the mental powers which engage in the making of poetry; and they each have been concerned with the ways in which these powers are related to the poetry they produce. These would seem to be the two primary considerations in any adequate treatment of the creative act: first, what mental equipment must the poet possess and, secondly, how does this equipment work upon language to convert it into poetry? Or, put yet another way, what is the relation of the poet's mind to the material given it by his experience in the world, and what is the relation of the poet's mind to the objective medium with which it works to produce poetry? [1]

Hulme deals with the former of these problems in his ambivalent discussions of fancy, imagination, and intuition; Eliot deals with it mainly in his use of the unity of sensibility; and Richards deals with it in his interpretation of Coleridge's distinction between fancy and imagination. Hulme sees the artist sometimes as possessing faculties which allow him to go beyond what most of us find around us, sometimes as limited to simple descriptions of what has been afforded by the external world. Eliot sees the poet of unified sensibility as impressing the stamp of his unique psychological integration on everything around him, thereby giving it the newness of life. But there is another Eliot who sees the poet as the mere translator of already existing entities into the language of objectified emotion. Finally, Richards sees the poet as controlled by the law of association—though it is contextual rather than linear association—so that he can put nothing in the work except that which the world has provided him. He may make different combinations, but there is nothing in Richards' system to allow his poet the uniqueness and novelty that a truly organic concept could provide. These discussions of the problem, then, seek to answer this question: to what extent is the poet literally creative—that is, to what extent does he add to the materials provided him by the world—and to what extent is he passive, an amasser and combiner of the experience he has discovered in the world?

It should be clear that, since these critics take an organic or, in Hulme's sense, a vitalistic approach to poetry when they are discussing it as aesthetic object, they can with consistency conceive of the relation of the poet's mind to his previous experience only in terms of the more organic parts of the theories of creativity of Hulme and Eliot. This need for an Idealistic theory of mind would preclude the possibility of using Richards' modified version of Lockean empiricism. If a theorist is to deny any dichotomy between form and content when he discusses the aesthetic object, he must begin to allow for this unity in his discussion of the creative act. And, from the standpoint of consistency, it is the creativity provided by Coleridge's imagination that would seem best to characterize the relation of the poet's mind to the data furnished him by his world. True, a very large part of the work he creates may be traced to his experience; but what makes the work stand up aesthetically as an individual entity would have to be the organic life that has been infused into it by the purely creative act of a mind that somehow sends forth more than it has taken in. How else is the consistent organicist to account for the utter newness of the true work of art? How else for the all-important additions which Eliot persuades us the first-rate artist can make to the tradition which has spawned him? [2] A theory that would limit the poet to mechanical reshuffling, no matter how thorough that reshuffling may be, cannot satisfy the organic theorist. For the differences among the various combinations can be only differences of degree, while a difference in kind seems to be called for if he is to do justice to the quiet but nevertheless profound revolution that each great poem works upon the tradition.

But this is only half the story, and unless the organic theorist supplements it by considering the second problem—that of the objective medium, language—it perhaps is not even adequate as far as it goes. For thus far, following Coleridge in using a transcendental psychology which holds for all men, he would be claiming powers for the poet which may seem to exist independently of his power to make poetry. It may seem that he would be giving these powers to him as a mind, apart from his skill in language. If he should be claiming that the work of the creative imagination were complete prior to, or independently of, its embodiment in its medium (and this, if we substitute *intuition* for *creative imagination*, is essentially the contention of Croce and Collingwood), then my complaints against Eliot and Richards for proposing, respectively, a disembodied emotion and a disembodied experience, would have to be turned against him as well. He too would be able to talk of Spenser as a potential Titian. The role of the poet's medium must enter at this point to qualify his treatment of the activity of the imagination. This, then, is the second major consideration outlined above: how the poet's imaginative faculty converts language into poetry. But like Croce, Coleridge, as an Idealist, cannot lead into the realm of the medium and make the latter a sufficiently formative factor in the poetic process. This is true despite Richards' claims to the contrary; in fact, as has been pointed out, Richards himself is most inadequate on this point. Coleridge can only posit the imagination as a mental faculty, an independent power which somehow seems able to exercise itself without a medium. To see the imagination as a power which needs a medium in order to function, it is necessary to supplement Coleridge's Idealism and subjectivity with more Realistic and objective modern theories which, beginning as Coleridge does with a creative mental power, limit the possibilities of this power's activity to the recalcitrant medium which can bring the power to life.

It is on this question of the role of the medium in the creative act that I have shown Richards and the Eliot of the objective correlative to be thoroughly inadequate. For to the extent that Richards' "experience" or Eliot's "emotion" is realized prior to its embodiment, the medium does not enter the creative process as an essential, formative factor. Of course, those portions of Eliot's work in which he is close to Hulme—the portions in which he talks of the poet's task as a struggle with language and sees the poem as an independent and objective entity—do bring him to treat this second major problem.

But it is in Hulme himself that this problem has been fully discussed. We have seen that for Hulme the poet cannot hope to have fresh insights into experience unless he has the ability to bend to the service of these insights the medium by means of which they are to take shape. If most people see the world in a stereotyped manner, it is because they are limited by their stereotyped use of language: fixed patterns of language dictate fixed patterns of thought. Thus for Hulme there can be no pre-existing fresh idea for which the poet then seeks fresh embodiment. The idea becomes fresh as it is worked by him across the grain of language habits. It emerges unique as his individual, and thus unique, purposes triumphantly elude the persuasive grooves of common passage. Thus the idea does not merely take place in language; the language *is* the idea—an objectified and communicable phenomenon, not merely a mental and purely private one. This concept is one which will justify me, when I come to speak of the object, in insisting on the unity of form and content. For there will never have been a separation, from the genesis of the poem to the time it reaches and affects the reader.

The advance Hulme worked upon poetic theory should, then, be clear. His anti-romanticism was not a full-cycle return to classicism. Rather, within the framework of a romantic aesthetic which still allowed the poet to be creative, Hulme returned linguistic responsibility to the poet: once again the poet was bound to matter.* Without forsaking the creativity of the poet, Hulme was anxious to curb the extravagances which the unbridled Coleridgean imagination seemed to him to sanction in nineteenth-century poetry. Thus he returned the poet from dreams of a vague, formless self-indulgence to a disciplined love for the endless capacities of his objective and traditionally developed medium. The poet could be unique, but he had to earn this right in his self-conscious struggles with the fixed and yet pliable demands of language. The poet could appeal to the romantic imagination provided it was now defined by the language which creates its vision. Thus not only was the poet to continue to supply us with insights, but he was to supply us also with the freshened language which creates the possibility for insight. That the critical theorists who followed Hulme did not, in their discussions of poetic creation, adhere consistently to his newer view does not lessen the importance of his contribution.

Agreement with Hulme's central idea is to be found in many influential modern aestheticians and, less explicitly, in the introspective writings of such self-conscious authors as Henry James. It has been worked out in an especially lucid fashion by Samuel Alexander,[3] and by John Dewey, who may have borrowed liberally

* It may seem difficult to maintain that language, the medium of poetry, is "matter" in the sense that, for example, the media of the plastic arts are. Recent symbolic philosophers of language, like Cassirer, have been able, within the framework of Idealism, to treat language as a mental construct and to show how creative and formative a factor this symbolic structure is in all human activity. They of course can insist that, while they deny that language is "matter," they nevertheless do not neglect the function of language in poetic creation as I have been arguing that Coleridge, as an Idealist, does neglect it. Without entering into any essential philosophical differences, I can say that at this point I would have little disagreement with them. Their Idealism is not Coleridge's and seems to have been modified in the direction indicated by Hulme (or should I say his master, Bergson?). I should like also to point out, however, that as language exists for the poet coming upon it at a point in the history of an already well-developed culture—as a racial repository of existent and possible meanings and of conventional grammatical and poetic forms—it may indeed seem to be an objective and material thing capable of the kind of manipulation we associate with physical mediums.

from Alexander in his least instrumentalist work, *Art as Experience*. In view of the correctives that Hulme and these others have furnished, in view of the difficulties so many modern theorists reveal in their discussions of poetic creation, and in view of their agreement about the organic nature of the created poem, it would seem that the process would have to be described in something like the following manner. The poet begins with a vague impulse, a vague something-he-wants-to-say; but this something need have little relation to what his work finally will say. It seems to be something new to him, something unique and important. He cannot say precisely what it is, or else his poem would already be written. He may think he can tell us what it is he has to say; he may write prose notes in his journal or in a letter to a friend. But, to the extent that it is a good poem he is writing, this preliminary statement will seem utterly incomplete, if not misleading, next to it: otherwise why bother to write the poem? *

The poet then submits this vague idea to his ability to work in language. He is controlled here by certain fixities, and yet he has certain freedoms within these fixities. First, he must be limited to some extent by the everyday uses of language, by the elementary laws which cannot be ignored if his work is to have any meaning at all for other users of his language: he must to some extent respect the meanings of words and the conventions

---

* In studies like Phyllis Bartlett's *Poems in Process* (New York, 1951), we find that, in actual practice, poets follow an infinity of methods in working through to the completed poems (see especially pp. 3–15, 78–154). Not only does the method of poetic creation vary from poet to poet, but it also varies from work to work of a single poet. And not infrequently our best poets do indeed begin with prose notes, and they may indeed believe that the poem is but a translation of these notes (see pp. 112–20). But it must nevertheless be insisted here that this indisputable variety among the ways in which poets create does not preclude the validity of the single method being described here. For, viewed in terms of the organically unified entity which is the completed poem, the poetic process must be seen as one that does not permit of a pre-existing prose equivalent which is then merely translated into poetry. In order to maintain an organic and contextual theory of the poem as aesthetic object, we must insist that, to the extent that the poem is good, any prior conception of it must be completely made over in terms of the demands of the medium. And even the fullest prose notes which precede the act of poetic composition must be seen as utterly inchoate, as little more than a vague impulse to create, next to the fully formed product.

of syntax. Secondly, he must be limited to some extent by the artistic traditions which have grown about the art form he has chosen, by the conventions with which he cannot break too sharply if his work is to have any aesthetic meaning for the members of his culture. But both these limiting factors—the conventions of language and those of artistic tradition—are what Bergson or Hulme would call fixed forms. Merely to submit the initial impulse to the demands of everyday semantics and syntax and to the demands of artistic traditions would ensure the poet's coming up with an utter stereotype; he could hardly *create*, could hardly bring something uniquely new into the world if he merely glided down these parallel sets of grooves. His result would have to be as unoriginal as the roads which led to it: the work would be mechanical rather than organic. The initial impulse would be adapted to the fixed forms, and as much of it would be admitted as the forms could comfortably accommodate. Thus the finished work would have to be less than the initial impulse, or at best certainly no more than it.

Here the poet's freedom must enter the picture as a counterbalance to these tendencies toward the stereotype. His unique, felt purpose, though still vague, yet in some mysterious manner also controls the poet to the extent that he is a creative artist. It must struggle with the fixed forms of both language as language and language as poetic convention. Yet it must continually respect the virtues of its antagonists, since to do otherwise would lead to a complete anarchy in which the poet would do no more than talk to himself. And why should he bother to work in a medium, the essence of which is its communicability, if he wishes only to indulge himself recklessly? By foregoing the struggle with the two fixed demands which are made upon him, he makes communication impossible with man as man as well as with man as cultivated reader of poetry. Thus, neither yielding to the demands nor ignoring them, he welcomes them and yet meets them head-on. On his artistic temperament depends his ability to "feel" what is right or wrong for his amorphous and as yet inexpressible impulse to create this poem.* He must often bend dangerously, indeed at times to the breaking point, the rigidities of everyday language and poetic tradition. But, while yielding thus far to the distortions and dislocations demanded by the uniqueness of his motivating drive, he must always stop short of the actual destruction of the forms he needs for communication. And yet, as far as the total meaning of the work is concerned, even this restraint must be felt not as a niggardly and rankling concession but as a further triumph.

But there is still another step to be taken. The restraint, the modification of certain demands of the initial impulse, might seem very well to be a concession if the only value of the two fixed demands—the only reason for the poet's needing them—was the one broached here: the opening up of communication. If this were the whole story, then every compromise might seem to be a setback to the poet's initial drive. He would have to be content to win a little and lose a little in the cause of communicating with his fellow-man. But he might dream blissfully of the unsounded depths he could reach if he were not thus inhibited. Then my discussion thus far still does not answer completely the recklessly romantic attitude. I have observed that the poet who ignored the legalistic demands of semantics, syntax, and tradition would be talking only to himself, that he need not have bothered to work in a medium that enables him to share his vision. But he may very well answer that if the fixed demands upon his spontaneity—which he would insist were costly to the integrity of his intentions—were valuable only because they allowed others to share his now debilitated insights, then he would prefer to remain speechlessly and uncompromisingly profound.

To do justice to the process of symbolization, I must rather maintain that this poet, should he ignore the demands of language and tradition, can succeed in talking to himself no more than he

* I say "feel" because any more consciously intellectual a judgment could be made only in terms of a more precise initial idea than I am allowing. It should be said once more that some poets may think they are making their choices rationally, in accordance with their preconceived idea, but to the extent that their works are aesthetically successful it is in terms of the poem's still incompletely realized *telos* that they are instinctively choosing.

succeeds in making his poem a possible instrument of communication to others. If his lawlessness has made his poem meaningless to others, it is essentially meaningless to himself as well. Not only are the objective demands necessary for communication, but they bring about the very possibility of expression.[4] For it must be remembered that the initial ideas about the poem were necessarily vague; they needed the making of the poem to clarify themselves. The clarification, we saw, results from the use of language. And language is a system which, like any system, depends on certain laws—laws of semantics and syntax—in order to work. The submission of the amorphous motivating ideas to these laws, then, is essential to the clarification of what these ideas precisely are. The ideas of the anarchically inclined poet must then remain as undefined after he uses language—if he ignores its principles of procedure—as they were originally. And if he prefers not to use language at all in order not to defile his original impulse, then he is no worse off. But in neither case has he achieved the clarification he thinks he has had all the while. He still has nothing to say to anyone, including himself. For the act of expression *is* the precise idea. He cannot have the idea-as-meaningful without it.

Similarly, traditional artistic forms are necessary norms which, by allowing deviations, help lead the poet to the complete realization of the unique thing he must express. It is these conventions, these disciplines, which from the first, though in a superficial way, set off the work of the poet from other forms of discourse. These conventions are literally of art, artificial. They frame the poem, temporarily cut it off from life to give the poet a chance to create for it a life of its own. While some adherence to the rules of language discussed earlier is demanded of all discourse, it is the additional if partial adherence to the rules of poetic tradition that gets poetry under way; it is the latter adherence that transforms the former one so that poetry is enabled, in the hands of a good poet, to become much more than mere language conventionally methodized.* Thus the poet's original roughhewn idea, insofar as

* In this essay I mean to use poetry in its broadest or Aristotelian sense as including all imaginative literature, fiction as well as verse. Yet in this and later

it is a poetic rather than a philosophic or scientific idea, must also undergo the refinements of formal demands in order to realize itself. An organic theory, then, seems destined to claim that the poet's initial intellectual-emotional impulse—which here for lack of a better term, I have mainly been calling his vague or rough idea—if it is to be developed at all, must develop finally and fully by emerging successfully from the conflict between objective demands and the unique purposes of the poet as seer.

To return now to pick up the step-by-step study of the creative act, we left the poet submitting his vague impulsion to create to the objective demands of language and of art, demands which he both respects and resists for the reasons already examined at some length. His initial motivation drives him to strain the recalcitrant fixities of these demands, but he stops short of openly destroying them. And the result of what might seem to be a partially lost battle is to be an aid, rather than a hindrance, to the realization of his artistic intention. Now, in terms of a theory of creativity consonant with an organic and contextual theory of the poem, this give-and-take struggle must be seen to be involved throughout the entire composition of the poem, from the first line to the last of the first draft to the last. As the struggle develops, the initial rough idea grows in precision and depth—in other words, gradually comes to contextual meaning. It is a far cry from what it was before the poem was undertaken. As the poet creates, he discovers

discussions it may seem at times that I am using the term to mean verse as distinguished from all prose writings, fiction as well as nonfiction. The reason for this seeming ambiguity is that I am discussing poetry on the levels of language and of conventional literary forms, and it is quite difficult to distinguish on these levels between fictional and nonfictional prose. Somehow the language of prose fiction must also be shown to develop the contextual characteristics necessary to form an autonomous world if contemporary organic theory is to discover a way to treat prose fiction as a form of poetic discourse. I do not believe, as later in this study the neo-Aristotelians will be seen to believe, that the treatment of poetry primarily in terms of language prevents the inclusion of prose fiction as a form of poetry. I would rather argue that if we refrained from treating poetry in terms of language, as the neo-Aristotelians would, then it would become impossible to distinguish at all between verse and prose fiction or to justify the conventional forms of verse. Nevertheless the crucial task of showing how, theoretically, the prose-poetry distinction here developed allows prose fiction to be considered as poetry remains a difficult one—just one of the many thorny problems I am bequeathing to future theorists in this tradition.

what it is he is creating. At each step he meets his problem, creates anew, in light of what he has discovered about his creation thus far. And it is not until he has completed the work that, in the spirit of the spectator or critic, he can learn what his idea, his artistic intention, really has been. But he may prefer to believe that the poem is merely an embodiment of what seems to him to have been a thoroughly lucid original idea. To the extent that he is an artist he will be—happily—mistaken; and if he persists in this belief, it will remain for the critic to show him what he has really done.

What further can be said about the organic nature of the process? We have seen that the two kinds of objective demands placed on the poet have been fixed and therefore mechanical ones. The rules of language and of artistic conventions are to a large degree rigid: they can be flexed only so far. How, then, does the interaction of these mechanical demands with the poet's individuality issue in an organic product? The answer to a further question would seem to point out the direction in which an answer to this one would lie: Is the form of a given poem merely the formal elements of the tradition, the objective demands in terms of which it has been built? It should be clear by now that the answer cannot be an unqualified affirmative. It has been shown that the formal demands must be distorted in keeping with the unique purpose of the poet. If they are not so distorted, then the result cannot be individual but can only be typical. And since the distortions forced by the poet's individuality characterize the poem even more than do the norms in terms of which the distortions have taken place, the final forms of no two poems can be alike. The violations of the mechanical formal demands are wrought while at the same time the poet respects these demands, since to ignore them would preclude the possibility of his producing art. Thus the poet disrupts mechanical form in order to emerge with a unique organic form. He rebels against the common elements of form in order to discover and create the absolute form which this particular poem must take: he does violence to form in order to celebrate form. Or, if we may invert the formula, by achieving the endless dimensions, the richness, of his unique form, the poet demonstrates the poverty of generic form. In much the same way we may conclude from his distortions of the procedures of language—even while he remains limited by them—that the poet does violence to the principles of discourse in order to achieve in his poem a unique and closed system of discourse which can break through the inherent incapacities of all nonpoetic uses of language: he damages language to show how much it can do. Thus, as with form, the poet does violence to language in order to celebrate language. And, again to invert, by achieving the endless dimensions of his closed system of language—one which cannot be used except in this poem—the poet demonstrates the comparative poverty of more general systems of language.

While the general direction of this sketch has been pointed out for me by those modern aestheticians who have tried to account for artistic creation in a way consistent with what they wish to say about the organic character of the aesthetic object, I must assume responsibility for the detailed extensions of their accounts. But, as it is presented here, this sketch does not pretend to be a scientific description of what actually goes on during the making of a poem. It is rather meant to be a necessary description deduced from what those critics who concern me seem to feel about the created poem. Thus the only evidence to be appealed to would be the evidence of the poem itself and what it indicates about the way it had to have been produced. Nor is this sketch mistakenly intended as an answer to those crucial questions it raises. It rather is to show which answers will not do and what considerations cannot be ignored by any answer that will do.

We may reject as conducive to the irresponsible in literature the notion that the poet is a translator of a private, pre-existing idea by which the developing poetic context is controlled, indeed to which the developing poetic context is restricted and the traditional demands of the medium are sacrificed. And we may reject as conducive to the dully mechanical in literature the notion that the poet abandons to the unyielding legalism of linguistic and poetic convention as much of the uniqueness of his idea as the seemingly inflexible medium demands. Now I have spoken of the transformation of mechanical form into organic form through the interaction of the poet's unique but unformed intention with a medium which is flexible even as it is fixed; but this is a formulation which beggingly betrays the lack of an explanation more than it furnishes one. Those who would pursue this direction in poetics would have to describe precisely what sort of thing this transformation is. They would have also to explain what is meant by what I have been calling the poet's original, vague, unformed idea. It cannot be any more than this or else it becomes so defined that it precludes any possibility of transformation at the hands of the medium. Yet how can it be any kind of idea at all if it is thus undefined? And somehow it must be sufficiently precise to allow the poet to do his share in the interaction with the medium. To what extent, then, can the poet control what finally emerges when his initial idea—the main controlling agent at his disposal—must be so amorphous? After all, to the extent that he consciously controls what the final product shall be, this product will not vary from his initial idea; and the creative process will not have done its work. Yet his medium can hardly do its work without his collaboration. How, then, can he collaborate without depriving the medium of its formative role in the emergent product? These and other considerations must be accounted for by any theory of creativity which seeks to account for the production of poetic objects which are distinguished by the contextual characteristics claimed for poetry by much of modern criticism.

# Chapter 5

# The Organic Theory: SUPPORT
## AND DEFECTION

THE phenomenology of the creative act I have suggested is the only one which can with consistency carry out the tendencies toward organicism in the claims about poetic creativity made by the members of the critical movement under study—an organicism upon which we shall see many of them insisting in their treatment of the aesthetic object and of the function of art. As I have pointed out in Eliot, and as I shall shortly remark in others, the critics in question often have too little a sense of the need for this view of the creative act and too little an awareness of the inconsistencies into which some others of their ideas about creativity may throw them.* Nor does their theoretical inadequacy bother many of them who, if in nothing else, are at least consistent in their disdain for philosophy and its disciplines.[1] Despite their attitude, or perhaps because of it, the task of seeing whether a systematic aesthetic can be worked out from the inklings of insights they have given us becomes all-important. And a consistently organic theorist will have to include in his conception of the creative act much of the above description and, of course, much more, since he will have also to supply answers to the questions my skeletal description has raised. Of course, he will have to fuse with this

* While this is not quite the case with the early Richards, who marches with his assumptions boldly and unswervingly into the narrow cage of reductionism, it must be realized that, despite his influence on modern criticism, Richards' neurologizing has hardly been in tone with the work of those who have found him most useful.

fuller description the Coleridgean conception of a truly creative imagination. But he can no longer view this imagination, in the way Coleridge viewed it, as a self-reliant spontaneous power of mind. Rather he must view it as a power which not only reveals itself but actually discovers itself in its workings with an objective medium.[2]

To return for a moment to the difficulties surrounding Hulme's rejection of Coleridge and German Idealism even as he used the organicism of their concept of imagination, we should be in a better position to account for his ambivalent attitude. His principal objection should now be seen as an objection to their Idealistic theory of mind, one which, as he claims, "drags in the infinite." He perceives that the activity of Coleridge's imagination is completely mental so that this conception must fail to do justice to language as a medium, an aspect which, to Hulme as poet-theorist, is all-important. Thus Hulme must, as philosopher, counter this Idealism with his greater Realism as, in the role of poet, he must counter the romantic emphasis on subjectivity and self-expression with an emphasis on the objective and controlling disciplines of a necessarily imposed medium. Hulme's poet, then, is less of a god than is Coleridge's in that he finds himself continually restricted by the laws of the finite material world; but he can still be a human (that is, a lesser) creator by triumphing over these laws even as he obeys them. In this way Hulme, while denying the romantic theory of self-expression, still avoids being reduced to the other extreme, the theory that poetry is mere communication.

There are among modern critics other sanctions too for the theory of the creative act called for here, except that in most cases the critics do not envision it as lucidly as do Hulme and aestheticians like Alexander and Dewey. For example, Eliot, in that important and many-sided essay, "Tradition and the Individual Talent" (which has earlier been shown to contain a formulation of the objective correlative), establishes in a very general way the poet's need to use, and yet in using to surpass and to transform, the artistic tradition he inherits. Clearly this indicates an acceptance by Eliot of the notion of creativity being advanced in this essay: it is precisely this struggle between the uniqueness of the poet's purpose and the generality and fixity of traditional forms which has been traced above. But, of course, Eliot fails consistently to develop this crucial idea in other parts of his theorizing.[3]

Similarly Yvor Winters, who surely would not be gratified at being coupled with Eliot, sees the poet as ever refining the possibilities for originality in even the least flexible of conventions. Thus, in his brilliant discussion of the heroic couplet, he goes so far as to claim that the less flexible the convention, the more meaningful are the individual variations the poet can work within it.[4] While there would obviously be disputes between Winters and Eliot as to what constitutes a living tradition and what a merely superficial convention, while the two would argue about such questions of valuation as the degree of conformity and the degree of innovation to be allowed, nevertheless it is important to recognize their fundamental agreement about the nature of the struggle between the poet and his tradition in the creative process.

It must be added that, again like Eliot, Winters has other areas of his theory which do not carry this insight forward consistently in the direction I tried to indicate in the preceding chapter. The main body of his critical theory proceeds from his distinction between reason and emotion, which, since his discussion is limited to the linguistic level, he equates with what he thinks of as denotation and connotation, respectively.[5] Thus through their denotative or conceptual power the words of a poem should make "a defensible rational statement about human experience" and provide, through their connotations, the emotions which this experience ought to motivate.[6] The poet uses his poem to render his moral judgment of experience, accompanying this judgment with the emotions proper to the experience; and the critic is morally to judge the poet's judgment.

Now Winters tries in two ways to circumvent the likely danger he foresees that his theory will be viewed as one that is incurably didactic, as one that splits the act of poetic creation into two separate kinds of activity and sees the poet as mechanically adding emotive connotations onto a previously fully formed prose argument. First, he seems to be maintaining the notion of the contextual uniqueness of the poem by insisting throughout that the poem cannot be exhausted by its prose paraphrase, that the nonrational elements somehow contribute to its total meaning. Indeed, taking off from Mallarmé, he goes so far as to say that the perfect poem should be "a new word," its contextual unity apparently providing its own definition.[7] Secondly, he continually tries to demonstrate that such formal elements as meter have "moral significance." These are elements of discipline and control; as such they help to define judgment.[8] Apparently the poet's unique judgment is rendered neither by the rational statement yielded by the denotations of his words nor by the emotional connotations initially motivated by the conceptual content. It is rendered rather by the relationship between these as this relationship is adjusted by the formal controls which furnish the limiting frame for the denotative and connotative activities of language. Thus it is the obedience to form that proves the poet's mastery of—his ability to judge—the experience he is presenting both rationally and emotionally. In the truly classical spirit which relates restraint to morality, Winters sees formal control as reflecting the poet's spiritual control in the face of his disturbing experience. The poet's unhappy alternative is to surrender limply to what Winters calls the fallacy of imitative or expressive form. That is, the poet in such a surrender allows his subject matter—the experience he is attempting to communicate and to judge—to dictate to an unresisting form. And, abandoning the one element which can permit him to assert his mastery over the experience, the poet, while he may communicate something of the subjective chaos of the experience, is no longer able to judge it and thus to become its lord.[9] Thus Winters tries to weld the rational and emotional dimensions of the language of poetry into a single, unified mode of discourse—the new word of which he spoke—made one by the controlling and judgmental element of poetic form.

But these attempts to make the poem as aesthetic object an

organic whole whose elements are inseparable seem doomed to failure. For there seems to be no way in Winters' system to allow these apparent efforts at organicism to flow consistently from his initial intransigent dichotomy. Indeed he explicitly and somewhat scornfully rejects what he calls "the earlier romantic doctrine of organic form sponsored by Coleridge," [10] so that it becomes difficult to see how he can consistently manage the unification of rational and emotional elements which he needs in order to assert that the poem and the judgment rendered by it are more than its paraphrase, that the poem is a new word. His original insistence on the poet's rational argument would seem to imply a clarity of experience and of judgment that exists prior to the writing of the poem, so that, like other such theories of creativity which I have examined, this one vitiates from the start any complete unity of form and content. And if this unity is later insisted on, then we can see it only as an *ad hoc* postulation which has not been prepared for in the foundation of the theory. Similarly, Winters' refusal to permit poetic form to be organic or, as he often prefers to call it, "expressive," prevents him from maintaining consistently that there is any significant interaction between the poet's experience and his chosen form. The relationship between them seems dictatorial and the dictation seems to flow in only one direction. Winters would thus be hard put to explain the justifiable reasons for any dislocations or variations within an otherwise mechanical and purely arbitrary form.*

It would seem, then, that tempting as some of Winters' very rewarding formulations may be, as much as they may seem to lead toward a conception of the poem as a unified and therefore independent entity, they have not been logically earned; they have already had the ground cut away from under them. For Winters' continual emphasis on the poet's task of moral judgment and the critic's task of moral judgment once removed, coupled with his

* In fairness to Winters it must be noted that he tries at one point to circumvent this very difficulty by showing how a poetic form may somehow be expressive while eluding the trap of expressive or imitative form. But this attempt to play both sides of the street succeeds only in confusing at least one reader. (See *In Defense of Reason*, pp. 545–50.)

failure adequately to relate moral and aesthetic judgment, forces him to violate from the start the self-containedness of the values of the poem. As a result we must wonder how formative a function he can justly assign to the give-and-take struggle between the individual and his tradition.

John Crowe Ransom is even more concerned with this relationship than are the others I have examined. Perhaps more than any other modern critic, he has set out in the direction I have indicated for a specific, step-by-step description of poetic creation.[11] And this is what might be expected from a critic who is calling for an "ontological" criticism, by which he means a criticism that treats the poem as having a completely independent and self-contained "mode of existence," if I may borrow a phrase from René Wellek.[12]

Ransom details for us the struggle between the poet and his linguistic medium. The poet, we are told, begins with a "determinate meaning," the prose statement he wishes to make. He chooses to present this meaning in one of the possible formal patterns which have been impressed on his medium by his tradition. Thus, along with his "determinate meaning" he begins with a "determinate sound." Now inasmuch as Ransom calls these factors "determinate," he clearly regards both of them as fixed and unyielding. But when the poet tries to unite these two independently chosen patterns in his poem, obviously one or the other or both of them will have to give. For the poet has thought through his bare determinate meaning without worrying about whether or not it was compatible with any particular pattern of meter and rhyme; and the converse is equally true. The conflict between the two determinate patterns forces certain compromises in the favor of one or the other. These compromises emerge in the form of either "indeterminate meaning" (when the thought is somehow altered so that the formal pattern may be maintained) or "indeterminate sound" (when the sense of the prose paraphrase is maintained at the expense of the strict formal pattern). Thus, so far as meaning is concerned, Ransom is led to his distinction between "structure" and "texture." For him structure is what he calls the strict "logical" paraphrase,* the determinate meaning with which the poet began. The indeterminacies of meaning, into which the poet is forced by his devotion to the determinate sound, constitute the poem's texture. Texture, then, consists of "logical" irrelevancies.†

Now to define texture in this way is to make a grave charge, although Ransom hardly means it disparagingly. It is one that has opened Ransom to much criticism, including the obvious one that he is operating in terms of a form-content or message-embellishment dichotomy not unlike the "decoration theories" of the eighteenth century, and that as a result he blocks himself from his objective of achieving an ontological criticism of the poem as an organic entity.‡ Indeed, at the superficial level at least, it may seem that he is echoing the "sound" and "sense" prescriptions of Pope. For the texture seems to have no inevitable function within the poem's integrity, but seems to subsist on its own to furnish us a wayward pleasure. In terms of my description of the creative act it becomes clear that Ransom, like Eliot, Richards, and Winters, is attributing to the poet, by having him begin

* Like other of our critics Ransom uses the term "logic," or "logical" in a way strange to the philosopher. A detailed discussion of this problem occurs on pp. 146–48, below. For our immediate purposes I believe we can safely translate Ransom's "logic" as "prose argument" or "prose paraphrase."

† It is important, in view of the direction this discussion is later to take, to note that Cleanth Brooks, who has a view of the creative act closer to the one suggested in this study (see note 2 to this chapter), takes a more positive view toward the "meanderings" of a poem and a more negative one toward its "logic." See The Well Wrought Urn, pp. 185–96.

‡ Ransom is also open to the charge, which finds support in Phyllis Bartlett's Poems in Process, that he is tracing only one of many possible ways of writing poems (see note on p. 69, above). I have acknowledged that this charge could also be levelled at the approach I have suggested. I have claimed also, however, that, for purposes of an organic theory of the aesthetic object, my approach might still be taken as a tentative description of what really is happening in poetic creation. But Ransom's theory would be more hard put to deny that it describes only a single, idiosyncratic method of writing poetry, since it is not a theory which allows his "ontological" conception of poetry to follow from it. His seems concerned more with revealing how one poet writes a poem than with analyzing what would be required of the creative process to allow what we find in poetry to follow systematically from it. Thus, even if it should be granted that the description of poetic creativity advanced by me has no more empirical justification than Ransom's has, at least one could argue that it has a theoretical justification which his cannot claim.

with a *determinate* meaning, a far too coherent and complete idea of what he intends to say in the poem before he becomes involved with language. And on the other hand, by tying the poet from the outset to a determinate sound, Ransom forces him to be too conscious of mechanical form at the expense of organic form. Would not the determination of these two elements, meaning and sound, seem, for the organic theorist, to be achieved by the writing of the poem, and not before?

Similarly, by continually stressing the "logical" irrelevance of texture—though this may be a not completely erroneous concept—is not Ransom misplacing his emphasis? For necessarily the argument of all discourse is nonpoetic: in a metaphor the vehicle certainly exceeds the prosaic demands of its tenor. But what is at issue here is whether or not the paraphrase *as such* exists as a prior element which is then violated, whether it exists as a standard in terms of which the complete meaning of the vehicle may be measured. And we are returned to Ransom's insistence that the poet, before he writes a line of his poem, has a thorough and well-ordered argument to make in it. We cannot escape the impression that Ransom conceives of the poet as first writing out a prose account of what he means to say and then converting his statement into poetry to increase its attractiveness at the cost of some of its argumentative precision. Here we are reminded of Ransom's claim elsewhere that the biological sanction for poetry is found in man's need for love: poems are to deal with "precious objects," objects which we love for their own sake although this love is in excess of, or irrelevant to, their utility value.[18] It would seem that just as our feeling for the precious object exceeds by the extra dimension of love its mere usefulness to us, so in the poem the texture represents our affection, which exceeds the object's function in the prose argument. But what still must be seen as missing is the theoretical means to return this extra and even excessive dimension to the poem as part of its organic unity.

The key to Ransom's doctrine may be found in the vigorous anti-Platonism which pervades his writings. For him Platonism is characterized by its octopus-like power of absorption, by its power to convert all things, however seemingly autonomous, into servants functioning in the interests of a unified end. It is to this universally synthetic power that, according to Ransom, all totalitarian—and therefore all nonpoetic—discourse is dedicated. No portion of this discourse can claim any right to exist apart from its relevance to the relentlessly pursued, common prosaic objective. And poetry written to promulgate a thesis, being a renegade in the service of the loveless tyrant, is properly castigated by the denomination of "Platonic." [14] Thus it is poetry properly pursued that stands up against the eviscerated world of ruthless efficiency which is the domain of nonpoetic discourse. In defiance of Platonism, poetry asserts its love for the individual object; a love that is revealed by its willingness to dwell on the object for its own sake even at the cost of introducing matter that is irrelevant to logic, the unyielding overlord of other forms of discourse. In the more relaxed atmosphere of poetry there is time for play, time to pause musingly over the autonomous units which the democratic state of poetry allows. It is as if Ransom is freely extending Coleridge's claim that in poetry, as distinguished from prose, "the reader should be carried forward, not merely or chiefly by the mechanical impulse of curiosity, or by a restless desire to arrive at the final solution; but by the pleasurable activity of mind excited by the attractions of the journey itself." [15]

If we stopped here, however, short of returning the texture to the flow of poetic discourse, we would not be doing full justice to Ransom's theory.* For after stressing so dangerously the neces-

* The following discussion is based only on *The New Criticism*, pp. 314–16. This is the one place I have found in his writings where he does try to restore textural irrelevancies to the unified body of the poem, although to my knowledge none of his commentators credits him even with this attempt. (See, for example, Wimsatt, "The Concrete Universal," *The Verbal Icon*, p. 76.) I grant of course that elsewhere he gaily courts irrelevancy, insisting upon it as the antidote for Platonism. For example, in "Criticism as Pure Speculation," published at much the same time as *The New Criticism*, Ransom presents in brief form much the same position that he does in the book, except that here structure and texture are kept irrevocably separate in the interests of anti-Platonism (here thought of as anti-Hegelianism). But in the passage from *The New Criticism* here being discussed and quoted in part, Ransom is closer to Brooks (see second note on p. 83 above) except that the latter would abandon Ransom's prescription of "logic."

sity of indeterminacy and irrelevance as the unavoidable compromise between argument and poetry as well as the poet's declaration of independence against a single-minded purposefulness, he suddenly introduces an unexpected distinction, one between "positive" indeterminacy and "negative and corrupt" indeterminacy. So indeterminacy is not to be indiscriminately desirable. Here he seems to be saying that, led into the wayward paths of irrelevance, the poet somehow, in his enjoyment of these bypaths, can hack his way back to the main prosaic road by clearing the area between the structure and the texture so that the paths and the road are joined into a broad highway, newly conceived, in which the irrelevancies are made relevant. The metaphor is mine, but I feel it is necessitated by Ransom's failure to provide earlier in his system for this possibility and, therefore, his failure to make it literally meaningful. It merely illuminates the area of problems to be solved; it doesn't begin to solve them any more than I pretended to in my preceding chapter. But Ransom does, in this one place in his writings, stick by his claim that while "bad" indeterminacy remains completely irrelevant, this "valuable" indeterminacy transforms poetry into a new kind of discourse, which has dimensions far beyond those of mere logic. And as a result the good poet is not merely led into this kind of indeterminacy but rather, knowing that he is a poet rather than a rhetorician, "he begins to indulge it voluntarily."

And this is the principle: the importations which the imagination introduces into discourse have the value of developing the "particularity" which lurks in the "body," and under the surface, of apparently determinate situations. When Marvell is persuaded by the rhyme-consideration to invest the Humber with a tide, or to furnish his abstract calendar with specifications about the Flood, and the conversion of the Jews, he does not make these additions reluctantly. On the contrary, he knows that the brilliance of the poetry depends on the shock, accompanied at once by the realism or the naturalness, of its powerful particularity. But the mere syllabic measure, and not only the rhyme, can induce this effect. When the poet investigates the suitability of a rhyme-word for his discourse, he tries the imaginative context in which it could figure;

but the process is the same when he tries many new phrases, proposed in the interest of the rhythm, for their suitability, though his imagination has to do without the sharp stimuli of the rhymewords. And by suitability I mean the propriety which consists in their denoting the particularity which really belongs to the logical object. In this way what is irrelevant for one kind of discourse becomes the content for another kind, and presently the new kind stands up firmly if we have the courage to stand by it. . . . As for Marvell, we are unwilling to praise or to condemn the peccadilloes of his logic, and here is a case where we take no account of the indeterminacy of the bad sort that results from the metering process, and that distresses so many hard-headed readers. This is all overshadowed, and we are absorbed by the power of his positive particulars, so unprepared for by his commonplace argument.[16]

Ransom's statements here are clearly analogous to the description of the creative act, given above, which saw the poet transforming would-be compromises into triumphs, dislocating mechanical form into organic form. It is this positive indeterminacy which, for Ransom, gives poetry its unique ontological status, which "induces the provision of icons among the symbols," which, in short, "launches poetry upon its career." [17] As will appear in a later connection, it can allow poetry a unique function that can make possible the pursuit of a modern apology for its existence.

It may be difficult to understand how Ransom can avoid seeing himself as a Platonist—in his meaning of the term—if he finds a place for seeming irrelevance in the higher, the more than "logical" or other than "logical," unity of the poem. Perhaps this is an inconsistency which cannot be resolved. It must be remembered, however, that the indeterminacy, no matter how "positive" it may finally prove to be, does remain free from the acquisitive society of resolutely marshalled words. That it may, in its freedom, merge into a new and more tolerant community of discourse is perhaps a tribute to poetry's "miraculism"—that attractive and evasive word Ransom has used in another connection.[18] In this way it may be that Ransom can avoid for poetry the Platonism he attributes to nonpoetic discourse, and, in its spite, can achieve a conception of the poem as a unified entity.

## The Creative Process

Allen Tate, in his well-known essay, "Tension in Poetry," [19] uses terms very analogous to those we have been considering in Winters and Ransom, although he is speaking explicitly of the poem itself rather than of the creative process. By "tension," in which, we are told, the meaning of the poem is to be found, Tate means "the full organized body of all the extension and intension that we can find in it." It is clear that, in his use of the logical term "extension," he means pretty much what Ransom means by "logic" and what Winters means by "motive" or "denotation." Similarly, his concept of "intension" is akin to Ransom's texture and Winters' emotion or connotation. Tate gives us examples of poems that fail to achieve tension either because the fuzzy aura of intension is not firmly rooted to the sound denotation of palpable objects or because the literal level of extension is firmly maintained only by ignoring the other, the richer intensive, levels of language into which it ought to open. While the latter of these failures simply reveals the lack of a poetic imagination sufficient to make the language of poetry more than that of prose, the former, which ought immediately to remind us of what Winters calls "pseudo-reference," [20] is the failure commonly attributed by these critics to the romantic poets.

But, again like Winters and Ransom, Tate tries to amend the dichotomy which initiates his theory: "tension" is not merely an anagrammatic device to combine "extension" and "intension"; it is a transformation of the immediate meanings of words and of their accretions into a new and self-contained mode of discourse.

The remotest figurative significance that we can derive does not invalidate the extensions of the literal statement. Or we may begin with the literal statement and by stages develop the complications of metaphor: at every stage we may pause to state the meaning so far apprehended, and at every stage the meaning will be coherent.[21]

Now this is a most rewarding formula for poetic analysis; but, as with Winters and Ransom, we may wonder to what extent the opposed components (here extension and intension) are separable entities in the poem or—more to the purpose here—in the creative process, and how they manage—if they do—to lose their identities in their resultant (tension). And, as we must ask of Winters' "motive" or Ransom's "logic," we must ask of Tate's "extension" whether it desists from its prosaic function of denoting objects, under pressure from "tension" to create a unique and self-contained mode of discourse. Since, in view of my quotations from Tate, above, it would seem that it does not so desist, how can the poem of "tension" be more than a well-embellished literal statement? How can the poem have, as we shall see it must have for these critics, a contextually autonomous status when one of the two components which make up its tension cannot relinquish its denotative precision—that is to say, its immediate, point-by-point dependence on the outside world to which it must then seek to lead us?

We have now observed several theorists who share a common systematic difficulty: their initial assumptions about the creative act, implicit or explicit, prevent them from asserting with complete consistency the organic unity of poetry. So promising are some passages in Ransom's discussion that it is especially unfortunate with him that the basis of his theory, with the excessive rigidity of its dichotomy, provides an insufficient framework to contain his most fruitful insights. Yvor Winters may be correct when he claims that Ransom is only attempting scientifically to describe what occurs in the making of poetry, that he has no way of measuring how much indeterminacy may be allowed since this is a question of value beyond the limits of mere description.[22] Much the same charge may be leveled against the description of the creative act toward which I have tried to point. What Winters does not seem to realize is that the discussion of poetic creativity must be primarily descriptive, that value questions must await discussion of other factors in the aesthetic process. But it has been the task of this section thus far to suggest the kind of descriptive theory of creativity which is consonant with the tone of modern criticism and which will allow the basic position of our critics with respect to the aesthetic object and the effects of poetry to emerge with theoretical consistency.

# Chapter 6

# The Uniqueness of the Poetic Imagination

### THE UNCONSCIOUS AND THE IMAGINATION

THERE is yet one final problem which I must focus upon before leaving the creative act, although it has been discussed implicitly by the theorists I have examined. I must set forth in what sense, if any, the poetic imagination may be said to be different from the operations of man's mind when it is engaged in other modes of activity. Hulme, we should remember, in drawing a distinction between the aesthetic intuition and the stereotyped recognition of objects, was opposing the faculties used in artistic creativity to those used in the life of practicality or in that of rational cognition. Even Richards, whose theory of continuity predisposes him against all distinctions in kind, distinguishes the poetic from the moral and the cognitive act. For the poet's organization of impulses, which enables him to create effectively, at the same time blocks any practical activity since the carrying out of any one impulse into the action toward which it directs itself would mean the stifling of the opposed impulses and hence the disintegration of the organized complex of impulses; thus only by not acting can he create. Similarly, as will emerge more clearly when we look at what Richards has to say about the effects of art, it is only by virtue of being nonreferential, and hence noncognitive and purely emotive, that the poem can function aesthetically. Like the Kant whom he scorns, Richards limits the areas upon which certain modes of activity are to operate, in order to increase the effectiveness of these modes within these bounds. Eliot's impersonal theory and his ideas about poetry and beliefs also set off man as poet from man as knower or man as doer. And to the extent that Winters and Ransom insist that the complete poem is more than its logical paraphrase, they are making of poetry a unique activity. We could go on with other critics in this group, showing how each of them comes to his theory by opposing the act of poetic creation to the act of cognition and of practical choice. The Kantian triad of faculties, transformed by Coleridge, via his concept of imagination, into the distinction between the poem and the work of science, is evidently at the root of all these theories.*

It is largely for this reason that I have done so little with Freud and with the obviously key role of the unconscious in the creative act. For in Freud's discussions of art, as well as in the work of many of his followers among critics, the poet, even in his activity as poet, is seen to be not essentially different from the normal man.[1] The problems of the poet with which Freudian analysis enables us to deal are the problems of the everyday neurotic; nor can we, using these tools of diagnosis, distinguish between the symbolism of the fully fashioned and communicable poem and the symbolism of the amorphous and purely private dream. But we have seen that what the critics I have been discussing are interested in with respect to the creative act is that which distinguishes the poet from the rest of us and the poet's work from the less controlled forms of expression to which the rest of us are restricted.[2] In light of the critical objectives of these writers, we may say that the poem arises out of a manipulation of a recalcitrant and traditionally developed medium; a manipulation that sees the poet con-

* Most of our critics collapse the cognitive and the practical simply into the nonpoetic, as Coleridge did in order to create his opposition between poetry and science, the opposition repeatedly used in organizing this essay. Despite the philosophical carelessness which allows one to see science or philosophy at times as practical and at times as cognitive in its objective (and the reader is referred, for a more analytical corrective, to C. W. Morris in the essays mentioned in note 16 to Chapter 5), this has been a workable dichotomy in recent poetic theory. Thus what ought to be the cautious distinctions between the cognitive and the practical on the one hand and the poetic on the other will be more recklessly treated as the distinction between poetry and science or between poetry and prose (with fiction excepted—see note on p. 72, above).

trolled by his medium and by the context emerging from it even as he (as an individual with an unconscious life which seeks expression) controls it. Thus in the making of the poem there is an activity and self-consciousness—in short, a responsibility—that is lacking in the dream. This is but another way of saying that there is in the making of the poem the formative catalytic agency of the medium that is lacking in the dream. Consequently there arises in the poem a formal context which resists the violence done to its integrity by those who would extrapolate individual symbols for non-contextual interpretation. The medium and the artistic intention it allows distort endlessly; they exist as obstacles to protect symbols in the poem from being recklessly referred to events in the poet's life, conscious or unconscious. And thus the wide gulf, which Eliot has pointed out to his grateful followers, between "the man who suffers" and the mind we see through the created poem.

Finally, for all the critics I have thus far discussed, successful poetry is not the unmodified expression of a neurotic's frustrations; it is, in its conquest of the medium by reconciliation with it, rather a victory over frustration. It is a mark of health, not a sublimation of disease. Like other theories that treat art only as an expression of one force or another (whether it be a personal or a social-historical force), the Freudian theory blinks the crucial transformation which the poet works upon whatever is being expressed in the act of expressing it poetically. And as *form* is the root of *transformation*, so this transformation is the root of poetry.

It should be added, however, that within the general direction I have indicated for a description of creativity there is much room for investigation of the workings of the unconscious during the throes of poetic production. For I had to insist that the poet, propelled into creativity by the vaguest of impulses, was somehow able, thanks to his imagination, to feel his way through the possibilities offered him by language. And I rejected in part the theories of Ransom and Winters, for example, because the poet was seen by them to begin with too definite and too coherent an idea of his intention—an idea that would inhibit his free working with language. We might say that the objection to Ransom and Winters was based on the fact that their conception would make the creative act too completely conscious. If their poet knew so precisely what it was he wanted to say, then his completed poem, which they insist is different from and more than the initial logical paraphrase, would be hard-put to locate itself around a new gravitational center. The alternative theory for which I have tried to provide would leave far more place to unconsciously "felt" choices. But if psychology is to clarify for us just what operations lie behind these choices, it will have to do so—if it is to remain consistent with modern critical theories—by following a direction it has shown no disposition to follow: that is, by examining the workings of the creative imagination as a faculty different in kind from those which govern our everyday practical and cognitive activities, and by examining it only in terms of its constant interrelations with language.

### THE NEO-ARISTOTELIANS: PLOT VERSUS IMAGINATION

It is at this point, however, that an important attack on the new criticism has been made by the neo-Aristotelians of the University of Chicago.[3] My discussion of the creative act thus far has posited a unique and creative power which achieves its ends by working in a resistant medium. This all-unifying imagination, derived from Coleridge, is being used here to differentiate poetry from science and morality. It must be admitted, however, that, as R. S. Crane, the leading spokesman of the Aristotelians, insists, modern critics have not generally seen the important distinction Coleridge draws between "poem" and "poetry" and the effect this distinction might have on the function they attribute to the imagination.[4] "Poetry," Coleridge tells us, is the direct reflection of the imagination. It occurs only in inspired passages and thus may appear in works of prose as well as in "poems." In fact, no "poem" can be all "poetry." What for Coleridge distinguishes the "poem," in which faculties other than the imagination may also be mirrored, is, first, its immediate end of pleasure, as opposed to the end of science, which is truth, and, secondly, its organic unity which allows a pleasure from its parts commensurate with the pleasure from the whole. Thus

Crane shows that the opposition of poetic to scientific discourse appears only in Coleridge's definition of the "poem" (and it is a difference based largely on the final cause rather than on language, which is for the Aristotelian the less significant material cause), while the imagination appears only in the definition of "poetry." And since "poetry" does not differentiate the "poem" from other modes of discourse, the Coleridgean imagination cannot be used to oppose poetic to scientific discourse. Thus, even if the Aristotelians were to grant the reduction of the imagination to linguistics (a reduction commonly practiced by modern critics ever since Richards transformed the distinction between fancy and imagination to one between ornamental simile and functional metaphor,[5]) they would observe that the differentiae of poetry cannot be so reduced. This argument, they claim, tears modern critical theory apart at its foundations. In all fairness to our critics, however, it should be noted that Coleridge seems to mean the imagination to have also the function of fusing the many nonpoetic elements (those which are direct reflections of faculties other than the imagination) of the "poem" with the "poetry" (the direct reflection of the imagination). And since the peculiar organic ordering of the parts is also a differentiating feature of poetic discourse, the imagination, working in this particular way, may legitimately be considered also as distinctly the property of the "poem."

But after all, faithfulness to Coleridge is not the criterion of critical theory. The underlying objection of the Aristotelians is their opposition to the reduction of criticism to mere commentary on language, to what they think of as grammatical apparatus. And it is true that from their science-poetry distinction onward, our critics have tried to show, even in their most esoteric interpretations of complexities, that the language of poetry is the key to everything else. Despite the inconsistencies in their theories of creativity, as practical critics they see language as prior to any of the many symbolic dimensions of poetry. Perhaps, since so many of them are practicing poets, their concern with technique has intruded into their theory. And, of course, there is the matter too of Hulme's influence. In opposition to these critics the Aristotelians consistently assert the primacy of plot-architecture, or principle of progression, in imaginative literature.[6] They thus explain Aristotle's insistence that the action is the "soul of tragedy." Elder Olson emphatically expresses this antilinguistic concept:

Nowadays when the nature of poetry has become so uncertain that everyone is trying to define it, definitions usually begin: "Poetry is words which, or language which, or discourse which," and so forth. As a matter of fact, it is nothing of the kind. Just as we should not define a chair as wood which has such and such characteristics—for a chair is not a kind of wood but a kind of furniture—so we ought not to define poetry as a kind of language. The chair is not wood but wooden; poetry is not words but verbal. In one sense, of course, the words are of the utmost importance; if we do not grasp them, we do not grasp the poem. In another sense, they are the least important element in the poem, for they do not determine the character of anything else in the poem; on the contrary, they are determined by everything else. They are the only things we see or hear; yet they are governed by imperceptible things which are inferred from them. And when we are moved by poetry, we are not moved by the words, except in so far as sound and rhythm move us; we are moved by the things that the words stand for.[7]

Now this is certainly the other extreme from that of the new critics. While the latter may seem, in their practical criticism, to reduce all to words, Olson, with a blind faith in the unfailing and unclouded referentiality of the language of poetry, seems almost to exclude verbal considerations from the poetic process. If nothing else, it should be obvious by now that, in terms of the theory consistent with the tone of the new criticism, the art product, unpredictable until it has been created, emerges from the struggle of the artist with his medium. It is in no sense preformed without reference to the objective means in which it is to be embodied; rather it is only in the medium that the creative experience can be expressed, or for that matter, can exist. Now this conception of the creative act, which, it has been claimed, can alone lead to a poem that has organic unity, can hardly be held by the Aristotelians, who indeed claim to be interested only in the object itself so that they need not theorize about the poet's act of creation. But they can hardly claim such immunity if, as they do, they hold to a poetics which insists on organic unity * but which involves by implication a theory of creativity that would preclude such organicism. For if the structure of action is the primary element, if it is the soul which exists before and beyond the words, its mere outer covering, then the poet uses his medium only to embellish what is already completely formed.

If, however, the Aristotelians overemphasize the pre-existing synopsis—that is, if they see the crucial work of the poet as preceding his involvement with the medium—our critics, at the other extreme, seem at times not to recognize that any non-linguistic factor can enter into the synthesis which is the act of expression.† Thus Cleanth Brooks, for example, can at times speak as if words by themselves, as it were, had the power of spontaneous generation:

Such an emphasis naturally stresses a close reading of the text, and, since poems are written in words, careful attention to language. But, though the text must provide the ultimate sanction for the meaning of the work, that does not mean that close textual reading is to be conceived of as a sort of verbal piddling. Words open out into the larger symbolizations on all levels—for example, into archetypal symbol, ritual, and myth. The critic's concern for "language" need not be conceived narrowly, even if his concern leads to an intensive examination: it can be extended to the largest symbolizations possible. A renewed respect for words and a sense of their complexities are matters for congratulation.[8]

* This organicism is implied by their insistence on interrelations among the parts of a structure of a kind that yield for each work a unique plot-form (see "The Plot of *Tom Jones*"). This claim for uniqueness is as incompatible with their consciousness of classes as it seems to be (see my further dicussion of them in Chapter 9).

† It must again be emphasized that I am speaking of the implicit theory that seems to emerge from their criticism of actual works. It should by this time be obvious that in their explicit claims about the creative act the function of language is often neglected rather than overemphasized. One of my main objectives thus far has been to point out the self-defeating tendency of their occasional claim that the poem is only a translation or an embodiment of some pre-existing entity. That their practical criticism is so largely centered on the creative powers of a language that seems to discover its content is evidence of my claim that the aesthetic demanded by their critical attitude is one with which their statements about poetic creation are not always consistent.

Elsewhere he tells us in a similar vein,

T. S. Eliot has commented upon "that perpetual slight alteration of language, words perpetually juxtaposed in new and sudden combinations," which occurs in poetry. It *is* perpetual; it cannot be kept out of the poem; it can only be directed and controlled.[9]

In a like spirit Wellek and Warren, who try to solidify the gains made by the new critics by establishing a theoretical framework for them, suggest that the three main levels of the poem, each expanding naturally into the succeeding one, are, first, the "sound-stratum," secondly, the units of meaning—words and the syntactic structures composed of words—and thirdly, the poet's world.[10] This linguistic reduction, common to these critics, may finally be seen to be as fundamental to the methodology of the moralistic Winters as it is to that of the positivistic Richards.

But we shall see in the next section that, in transforming the poetry-science dichotomy of the romantics, the new critics were anxious to grant that the language of the two is essentially the same. There are no peculiarly poetic words as there are no peculiarly poetic objects. The difference between science and poetry was rather established in terms of the complexities of the poetic context. But the efficient cause of poetry's contextual character has to be more than linguistic, since the words themselves are not special. It may be said that in poetry the arrangements and combinations of words are peculiar, even if the words themselves are not; but in this case the cause for this arrangement, since the latter cannot be controlled by the individual words themselves, which are neutral, must be supralinguistic. Consistent theorists in this aesthetic tradition would locate this cause in the symbolizing power of the imagination (as distinguished from the signifying power of the intellect). But the imagination cannot be reduced to mere diction. It has its motivating force, its structural and conceptual aspects, which at times may even be as clearly distinguished in the poem as are its verbal techniques, from which, however, the others are never separated.

Here we are returned to those unanswered questions raised earlier; and on the answers depends the possibility of a fully satisfactory description of the poetic process. How can we settle the respective claims of language and of the poet? Of course it would be nonsense to assert that language goes it alone in the making of a poem. But the poet can control the emerging product only in accordance with some idea he has of what it is to be. And to the extent that his prediction is accurate, the poem's organic and contextual autonomy is threatened. For what the emerging context and the language medium do or do not allow also casts its shadow upon the work still to be done; and the good poet has to relax his scheme accordingly. Thus he has to yield up his own precious intentions in the face of emerging intentions which, even as they are forced on him, he has somehow himself fostered.

Short of solving these riddles, the theorist who is aware of them and of their implications may say on trust that while the poetic imagination works in words and can reveal itself only in words, yet it cannot be utterly reduced to them. While the idea finally exists as the poem or as language, it so exists only because the imagination, by struggling with the medium and manipulating it successfully, has in some yet unexplained way allowed it to exist. But even such a cautious statement goes far beyond the Aristotelians in paying homage to the creative and even telic potentialities of a language set in motion but never put entirely on its own.

### D. G. JAMES: THE UBIQUITY OF IMAGINATION

This reintroduction of the imagination returns us to Crane's claim that this faculty cannot, in Coleridgean terms, differentiate poetry from science. The assertion that the imagination is not peculiar to art was made at some length earlier by D. G. James in his *Scepticism and Poetry*. His thesis, based partly on his interpretation of Coleridge, may seem to strike at the very root of modern criticism as well as to render futile the corrective I have just suggested. Although this book takes me afield into epistemology, I should like to consider it in some detail here. For this is a highly significant and widely influential work [11] both for my dealings with the creative act and for my later discussion of the function of poetry. It represents one of the few attempts made by recent critics to look at poetic theory anew in the light of the analysis of the "given" made by some contemporary philosophers of science.[12] James' theory involves a completely neutral universe without substance; there can be as many "imaginative" constructions of what this universe supposedly is as there are viewers with differing purposes. Given this view of a noncommittal physical reality, foisted onto the theories of Coleridge and Kant, in what sense can we say that the imagination has a unique task to perform, when it seems to be involved in all our knowing?

James begins by asserting the presence of the imagination in all human perception.[13] Its activity in poetry is different from that in ordinary perception only in degree but not in kind. The primary imagination is the everyday use of the faculty, while the secondary imagination is either its poetic or its scientific use. The primary is constructive of experience and is an automatic part of our every perception; the secondary, set into action by conscious artistic or scientific purpose, dissolves the ordinary world furnished by the primary in order to recreate it poetically or to recreate it in terms of the objectives of science. But the similarity of the various imaginations is founded on the belief that each is constructive of a world, whether it be the ordinary world of the primary, the individual artistic world of the poetic, or the mechanical world of the scientific. On this basis, James continually emphasizes the similarities rather than the differences in the operations of the imagination in poetry, in everyday life, and in science.

But what is the nature of human perception, in which the imagination has its role? James here explicitly derives his epistemology from Coleridge who, he claims, was in turn indebted to Kant. He ignores the extent of Schelling's influence on Coleridge. Actually he cannot afford to recognize this influence, since he wants to maintain that the imagination is skeptical, that it does not reveal knowledge since it can only construct upon reality a mythic hypothesis which is beyond the realm of the knowable. While Kant, who limits the cognitive power of a faculty in order to increase its practical function, may permit of such a development, Schelling extends actual cognition to the intuitive level of the imagination. In fact it is the imagination which for Schelling yields the highest kind of knowledge. And Coleridge's definition of the imagination has long been acknowledged (even by Coleridge himself, in fact [14]) to be very close to Schelling's. But James prefers to stick with Kant and, despite certain scholarly objections, we can hardly dismiss his theory because of this distortion of Coleridge. His interpretation of Kant, as will appear later, is also not beyond question, and, in trying to show a consistent view of the imagination on the part of Kant, he presents a theory of perception for which one may prefer his taking credit himself.

For James the function of the imagination is determined by that which is given to man's senses. What is the nature of the physical universe which is outside man and independent of his perception? James will not budge from a complete agnosticism, waiving as meaningless the problem of the world's reality—that is, whether it is three-dimensional objects or only sense data that are actually outside us. Although he seems throughout to oppose the materialist, and indeed concludes with a plea for dogmatic religion, in advancing his argument he seems often to accept without question a completely physicalist doctrine of the "given." Sense data for him are "patches of color and sounds, etc."—we are given, that is to say, only a two-dimensional, relatively undifferentiated continuum.[15] He does not attempt to say whether or not the real world consists of anything more. Rather he claims support from Kant in insisting that we cannot know whether or not it does. However, because he assumes without argument that this too was Kant's conception of the "given" as well as the extent of Kant's Realism, he will have to give to Kant's imagination a very puny function.

It is up to the imagination, says James, to construct the world in which we live from the chaos which we sense: ". . . we must view the mind as 'interpreting' or 'constructing,' into a three-dimensional order, elements which as such could never afford such apprehension." [16] We now can see the place he gives to the imagination in his interpretation of Kant. He claims that there are three faculties at work for Kant in perception: sensibility, which apprehends the "given"; understanding, through whose a priori principles the given sense data are ordered through general laws; and the imagination, which, also working from sense data, constructs from them the individual three-dimensional object. The understanding and imagination both work from the raw materials furnished by sensibility, but while the understanding generalizes, it is only the imagination that can see the object as a particular. The understanding may be the key to all our science, but it is the imagination that gives us a world in which we can live. This, then, is his total conception of the primary imagination, as he insists it was Kant's and Coleridge's. But Kant's imagination, which may also be interpreted as constructive, confers upon the natural object a telic significance, so that it sees the object as having a "finality" which contributes to an aesthetic value.[17] It certainly does more than merely recognize the object as thing. And Coleridge's imagination, thanks to Schelling, is, as we have seen, even more transcendental.

In a theory of the "given" in which the three-dimensionality of objects was available to the senses, James' imagination (but neither Kant's nor Coleridge's) would apparently disappear, since it has no more exalted a function than to construct the three-dimensional object out of the clues afforded by the given sense data. To imagine something is no more than, in everyday language, to see it. He can use the word *imagine* because of his skeptical terminology in which the things of ordinary sight are converted into myths. If we see anything beyond what James tells us we are given, then we are imagining we see it. Anxious to be a non-naturalist by faith only, he tries to remain at the ontological level an agnostic. Thus he will not say with the complete physicalist that nothing but his vague "given" is outside man's perception any more than he will say with the Realist that the whole object is there. The complete physicalist, asserting the limited nature of the external universe, can see man's mind as constructive of his everyday world and can insist upon the mythic character of that construction. On the other hand, the complete Realist, whose everyday world is not constructed but is discovered, can reserve higher powers for the imagination since it is not needed for normal sensation. But if the world that James has the imagination construct really should exist independently as three-dimensional (and he never denies this possibility any more than he does the opposing one), then surely it is available to the senses, and the imagination, in terms of the function he gives it, is superfluous. How can we be the imaginative creators of a commonplace world which may actually exist outside us? How, in other words, can James accept the physicalist's "given" as a basis for his argument when only a physicalist's ontology can support such a "given"?

Now we can better understand the interpretation James gives to the Coleridgean imagination. He asserts that the primary imagination is equally present in all our activities, aesthetic or nonaesthetic, using as support Coleridge's assumption that this faculty is "the living power and prime agent of all human perception." [18] He then uses a quotation from Coleridge, taken from another context, which describes Wordsworth's attempt to make wonderful the commonplace world, normally veiled by "the film of familiarity and selfish solicitude." [19] Coleridge saw Wordsworth's task, James claims, as the general task of the secondary imagination. It is to break down the practical everyday world and to create a new aesthetic one. The important point to be considered here is that James is identifying in kind one faculty which gives us only the practical world of stock recognitions and another which seems truly and metaphysically creative. As stated earlier, he can also call the primary imagination creative inasmuch as his concept of the "given" forces every view of any object in the world, no matter how stale, to be inferential and therefore creative. That is, we see more than is given us to see, so that the difference between the "given" and the seen must be attributed to the powers of our projection or creation. Thus he argues again and again that "the world of familiarity and selfish solicitude is the world of the primary imagination."

The most basic objections to this epistemology have already been discussed. What must be emphasized is that, regardless of the epistemological problems, even granting his theory of the "given," we cannot but see that the function he attributes to the primary imagination has little or nothing in common with the one he attributes to the secondary. If the primary is only the power which infers the third dimension, and thus thinghood, from our sense data, then its real activity would be restricted to our infancy, after which time mere conditioning and habit would do the job of creating the world for our everyday needs. Our simply taking stock of objects, as we use them or ignore them, is certainly not an imaginative act.* This, however, is not to deny that the imagination plays a role in our everyday lives. But it does so when we, asserting our humanity, break through stock recognitions, as Hulme puts it, in order to see the object for a moment as an end in itself. What is needed here is an assertion of the difference between stock recognition and real perception, a distinction which is surely common currency in contemporary aesthetics. This distinction marks off the activity of the primary imagination and separates the human from the animal. On the other hand, James would be forced to attribute his primary imagination to some higher animals as well, if we were to establish that without it they could no more live successfully in the sense data which are his "given" than we can.

On this basis the similarities James finds among the poetic, scientific, and everyday uses of the imagination are insignificant, so that the opposition between science and poetry imposed by modern criticism is not seriously threatened. The different imaginations he suggests have a single common function: each merely constructs a hypothetical world. Now the various worlds the different imaginations postulate can be mutually incompatible without our worrying about them, since they are equally unprovable.

* It is instructive to note how James here is at the opposite pole from the Bergsonian Hulme. Both begin with sensations; but while for James imagination in the first instance shows itself by converting sensations into the things of practical life, for Hulme the stereotypes of thinghood veil the dynamics of the reality we ought to sense, so that it is the function of intuition to restore us, through however great an effort, to sensuous immediacy. Thus for James it is the conversion from sensation to thing which requires imaginative effort, while the converse is true for Hulme. Our adult experience would, I am sure, make Hulme's seem to be the far more accurate description.

The everyday imagination infers a commonplace three-dimensional world which we cannot know is out there; but we nevertheless can use it safely in the routine of daily life. The poetic imagination constructs a personal idiosyncratic world which, if it is purely subjective and is only the artist's, still helps us to see beyond the merely instrumental world of the everyday imagination. The scientific imagination hypothesizes a purely mechanical world which is necessary if the scientist is to proceed as scientist.

But, for all we know, these three worlds are equally mythical, however useful they may be. And, as I have suggested before, if James takes seriously his conception of the "given," which after all allows these worlds their independent and equally valid (or invalid) status, then they may all be sheer nonsense. Their value would lie in the satisfaction they grant to man as myth-maker and in the activities they make possible for him. But we cannot judge between or among these worlds, since the only common outside factor in terms of which they could be judged—the sense data which is given—would equally allow, or rather disallow, each of them. We seem in effect to be back to Richards and his impulses (against which theory, incidentally, James argues very effectively), except that science has now been thrown into the emotive pot as well.

On the aesthetic level James is filled with inadequacies, because, in order to find all of man's activities imaginative, he has had to make the imagination so common a common denominator that, when he comes to discuss poetry in terms of the imagination only, he is unable to handle any of the really complex problems involved.[20] He is completely unable to speak in terms of poetic form, since nothing he says about the imagination allows him to account for varying mediums. The poet's mental constructions, rather than his writing, are what count for him. I have shown that Hulme, who shares with James the interest in the poet's way of seeing (although Hulme opposes intuition to stock recognition as James can never do), insists that the poet has a language problem which is involved with the perceptual one. If James could view the primary imagination as involved only in true perception (as contrasted with mere recognition), then he could reserve for the secondary imagination the urge to create art, to symbolize the perceptions of the primary by submitting them to the transforming and creative agency of the medium. Then he could handle more adequately the place of imagination in completed poems. But then too he could no longer treat the poetic, scientific, and everyday imaginations as being so similar.

As it is, James' imagination does its constructive work on individual objects in the world, so that in poetry all that can be discussed is the way in which the described object is perceived by the poet. But the description of a given, or rather a constructed, object does not constitute the poem any more than the representation of an object constitutes a painting. Through a formal structure allowed by the objectivity and communicability of the medium, the art product transcends any single object represented within it. This structure, which allows art to exceed imitation, is an aspect about which James has the right to say very little. For James' imagination is an independent, self-sustaining faculty whose perceptions are fully formed before the poet undertakes their translation into poetry. James' weakness in handling formal poetic properties springs from this inadequacy. Indeed, he cannot differentiate the artist from the rest of us or tell us why the poet chooses the particular art form he does, so divorced is James from any technical considerations. Thus we find him discussing Shakespeare with Wordsworth or Shelley, oblivious of the need to differentiate among them.[21]

In these discussions too, it is apparent that he cannot make the all-important distinction between fancy and the imagination as significant critically as it was for Coleridge. The one difference between them, he tells us in the only passage concerned with the two, is that the imagination is serious and fancy trivial, that the imagination constructs a world in which it believes and the fancy plays with one about which it does not much care.[22] Now this is rather similar to Ruskin's definition of the two faculties. Like Ruskin's, it is very far and unfortunately far from Coleridge's distinction, which has been so crucial for modern criticism in differentiating symbolism from allegory, analogy from metaphor. Imagination is frequently seen today, as apparently it was by Coleridge, as the agency that allows the creative and organic unity the successful poet imparts to his work. It is thus opposed to fancy, the faculty that sponsors the mere associative comparisons of the philosopher or scientist who wants to sound like a poet; the faculty that may be characterized, in the words Tate quotes from Yeats, as "the will trying to do the work of the imagination." [23] James cannot admit this distinction since to do so would bring him to the poetry-science dichotomy he wants to avoid.

Thus James can equate the poetry of statement with the poetry of dramatic context, although, perhaps sensing his inadequacy here, he does make a qualification which finds no substantiation in his system.

Of course, if a poet can convey his "work" without explicit expression of belief, he should most certainly do so. But clearly there is a large class of poems in which this is impossible. Poetry should show and not say; expression of belief in poetry is justified only when it is unavoidable.[24]

This ambiguous statement, with all the questions it raises, is left undeveloped and is relegated to a footnote. Why one method is better than the other we are not told, and indeed James' subsequent criticism shows little awareness of this problem in evaluation. Since the one requirement of the imagination, according to James, is that it be "vital," eventually the only mark of the poetic imagination is to be found in the animism which Ruskin termed the "pathetic fallacy." [25] James' discussion shows that here too there is no apparent way to judge, since he does not distinguish between the personification in which the object really takes on a new life and the stale cliché which has long lost any figurative power. For him the leaping of water, the dashing of seas against rocks, the drooping of day—these have as much claim to be called poetically imaginative as has the best of Shakespeare.[26]

We may ask how, then, the critic can establish poetic value. In the chapters on Wordsworth, Keats, and Shakespeare we receive a single answer. And it is an answer which, far from being applicable to any text as poetry, is very largely biographical, since it is based on the poet's mind and the fullness and breadth of its development. The success or failure is a success or failure of the poet's idiosyncratic imaginative world as it may be constructed from all his work. And the criterion is a curiously vitalistic one. Poets fail who cannot include harmoniously all the elements of life.

. . . in poetry the enjoyment of poetic experience of any part of the world is fraught with the necessity of discovering a wider and more inclusive imaginative apprehension, in which more and more elements in experience are caught up and incorporated. The imagination of the great poet at least never rests from this momentous labour which endeavours to encompass the whole of life, and to achieve a comprehensive unity of imaginative pattern.[27]

Thus Wordsworth's is a "failure to co-ordinate scientific inquiry into his total view of human experience." [28] We begin to see why James refuses to separate science from poetry. His humanistic vitalism, with its emphasis on inclusiveness, demands their union.

In making this biographical judgment of the man (James seems hardly concerned with an aesthetic judgment of the artist), we are to read the poetry, without regard for context, for its philosophical import; and the poet's personal effects, where they are available, are equally useful. But is this not the kind of judgment we should expect to spring from a theory that is so completely involved in the poet's perception and so completely negligent of the means of expression?

It should be noted too that James overlooks the important problem of the aesthetic control of the reader by the poem. But how, with his idea of the "given," can he do otherwise? For the art object itself can consist only of sense data, and it is up to each spectator to construct it imaginatively, and therefore mythically, for himself. Not only is there no possibility here for any objectivity of judgment, but we cannot describe any quality as existing in the object. Thus it is we, as spectators, who create the object's unity.[29] What, then, is the artist's responsibility? James tells us, "the act of awareness is a creative act which may require for its occurrence the presence of certain physical factors, but which cannot be reduced to them." [30] In a fuller discussion he states:

We must therefore realize that the total object is an object to the imagination; and that what of the world is "discoverable" is a world eviscerated of imaginative content, if indeed it can be called a world at all. The sensory elements which we describe as "given" to the mind are not therefore, in the strictest sense, "given"; for they are changed by the imagination which creatively integrates them into the unity of the imagined object. And the total object is "created" by the imagination; for as a totality it certainly is not given but is at once made and contemplated by the imagination. Because this is so, the poet may seek to compel us to imaginative creation either by the use of sensuous description or suggestion (as in onomatopoeia), or on the other hand by more directly suggesting the inner vital quality of an object (as by metaphor).[31]

The aesthetic experience, then, is completely analogous to the creative act, and the created poem can no more control our responses, can no more prevent us from going beyond it, than can any other sense data in the physical world of which the poem is a part. And again, because of his insistence on maintaining his skeptical "given," James is reduced against his will to the crude subjectivism of his enemy, I. A. Richards. Nor can his belated plea for religious dogma and institutionalized morality extricate him from this charge, since he can advocate these only as useful imaginative constructs (that is, inclusive or comprehensive ones) which have no relation to knowledge.[32]

I have perhaps been too long in refuting this position. If at times I have strayed from the creative act, it has been, I hope, only to return to it with greater clarity. It seemed generally important to reveal in full the dangers inherent in the extreme constructivist position, which would have the poet, the scientist, and the layman standing at the same remove from an unknowable reality, each with a vision measurable only in terms of its coherence, since there is nothing known to which it may or may not correspond. In this case, the intra-systematic character of all discourse—each mode conditioned only by the purpose for which it is conducted—would make all of them equally autonomous to the point where there could be no poetics, or very much non-poetics either.

Moreover it seemed aesthetically important, if I may generalize from this single instance, to point out the grave theoretical difficulties involved in an attempt to break down, on the analytical level, the useful distinctions in kind which may be drawn among man's various activities, particularly, in view of my purpose here, between the aesthetic on the one hand and the theoretical and practical on the other. The denial of these distinctions arises out of a basis for similarity which is so broad that it prevents us from characterizing any of them individually; one which, with respect to the aesthetic, fails to provide for the manipulations of the medium which make possible the existence of this mode of activity. It would seem profitable to maintain the distinction between cognitive and moral activity on the one hand and imaginative creativity on the other *—a distinction which characterizes much contemporary criticism—provided that, as was suggested earlier, the distinction is seen in more than linguistic terms. Yet this is not to transfer it to faculty psychology or to transcendental metaphysics, since language is not to be neglected either. If the precise formulation of this distinction still eludes us, this ought not to lead us to abandon a perhaps fruitful approach for one which, while more clearly defined, reveals itself to be barren.

It would be less than adequate also not to go part of the way with James and grant that the primary imagination may function outside the realm of art. But it is as true perception, as contemplation for contemplation's sake, rather than as mere recognition, that it would so function. Where this momentary imaginative grasp strives to symbolize itself, where it fights for form, it will,

* Once more (see note on p. 91) I am anxious to make it clear that I do not mean blindly to lump cognitive and moral activity together in distinguishing them from aesthetic activity. It is rather that the difficult business of distinguishing between them here would not be to my purpose. And since, as I have said, our critics have often carelessly collapsed cognitive and moral activity in their science-poetry or prose-poetry dichotomy, I think it permissible for us not to triangulate our consideration, provided we are aware of what we are doing.

via the secondary imagination, refer itself to, will control and in turn will be controlled by, a medium. Imagination, then, may very well be applied to a range of activities broader than that of the artist practicing his craft, but only when the other activity (science, moral philosophy, or bricklaying) for the moment is seen as autonomous and, therefore, as itself aesthetic.

*❧ SECTION II*

*THE AESTHETIC OBJECT:*
*SCIENCE, POETRY, AND LANGUAGE*

# Chapter 7

# I. A. Richards: SOME TOOLS FOR AN ORGANIC CRITICISM

WE SHOULD now be in a position to examine more precisely the kind of aesthetic object the poem is which we, via our critics, have for so long observed in the process of being made. I have shown that most of the theorists examined so far fall into a common error of inconsistency: on the one hand they want an organically unified object whose meaning is untranslatable, or *sui generis*, and on the other hand they set forth a concept of the creative act which often seems to allow only an object with a separable content and an embellishing form. They claim the work has an independent status—that there is a formal barrier which cuts it off as a separate and complete world from any simple one-to-one relationships to its author or its society—and yet they see the poet as having a coherent idea of what he means to say before he says it in his poem, as having something that is fully formed before it has taken any form. This is more or less equally true of Eliot's emotion, Richards' experience, Ransom's determinate meaning, Tate's extension, and Winters' rational statement, although these theorists also seem concerned, even at the cost of inconsistency, with saving their systems from the consequences of these mechanistic assumptions.[1] My task thus far has been to set forth the requirements to be met by a concept of the creative process for which there would be some authorization in the work of these critics and in which their inconsistencies could be systematically resolved.

## The Aesthetic Object

It would seem initially that, in dealing with the way in which they conceive of the poem as aesthetic object, I can forget about these difficulties, since about the poem itself each seems to be much more consistent and all seem to be much more of a single mind. The major property most of them insist upon is, of course, organic unity with its corollary that no translation of the poem into any other symbols can preserve its complete meaning, that no analysis can exhaust all that it says. It is this concept I shall have to examine closely, principally with an eye to determining why it is that they should need it and how it serves the aesthetic toward which I am here trying to lead them. In other words I must determine precisely what this concept means in a full and systematic sense; for the claim of organic unity is hardly a new one in the history of aesthetics and literary criticism. But modern poetics has made perhaps its greatest contribution to literary study in the specific and workable extension it has given this concept of organic unity—a concept which in the past had so frequently served as facile analogy and thus as impressive but not very usable verbal camouflage.

It should be profitable to begin the discussion by returning to I. A. Richards. Although the tone of those modern critics in whom I am interested is completely different from that of his materialistic psychologizing, we must recognize that it was upon his insistence on the importance of context that the more sophisticated modern theories were to be built. If we review Richards' theory, extending it beyond what was said earlier for purposes of the previous section, we should discover what later critics found useful and what they had to modify in order to construct a sound objective theory. We saw earlier the physiological basis from which Richards' theory proceeds and noticed particularly the deleterious effects this basis has on his conception of the creative act. These weaknesses infect also his theory of aesthetic value and his definition of the poem concerning which this value is predicated.

Richards' theory of value is implicit in the parts of his work already examined. It should already be clear why for Richards there can be no value in any object. The value of an aesthetic object can only be instrumental; that is, the work has value, is a good, insofar as the experience it communicates allows a complex organization of impulses in the "right" reader—the fellow Richards invents in order, as he thinks, to escape an unqualified subjectivism.[2] As I showed, the broader the range of impulses which are reconciled, the better the work of art.* Thus the work has no real mode of existence beyond that of any sensory stimulus until it makes contact with a reader. This concept allows Richards to formulate a criticism based on the interaction of contexts.[3] And this interaction of contexts is the basis for Richards' semantic approach to the work of art. With some care Richards sets forth a theory of association which is contextual rather than linear. Instead of undergoing a stream of association, we recall entire contexts which surround words every time we meet them.[4] Thus the reader brings his own set of contexts—necessarily not controllable by any author—to the work. These interact continually with the contexts which contain the words of a literary work. The latter, of course, are controllable by the author.[5] It is this interaction of contexts that prevents the reader from having exactly the same experience as the author or as other readers.

What, then, and where is the poem? Richards is in difficulty here because the interaction of contexts makes the poem so different for each reader and, thus, because he cannot give the poem an existence as an objective structure. The poem must exist as a single experience or a mere addition of single experiences. It cannot be a truly normative structure for him.[6] Therefore he compromises by defining the poem as that class of readers' experiences which are to a certain degree similar to the experience of the author.† Again we must notice that there is no reference in the

---

* This can be compared with Coleridge's claim that poetry brings the entire soul of man into activity. But Richards has converted this statement of a transcendental epistemology into naturalistic psychological terms.

† *Principles*, pp. 223–27. Whether Richards means by the poet's experience the experience that led him to write the poem or his experience when reading the completed poem depends upon which passage in *Principles* one wishes to cite. See pp. 180–85, 190–206, 226, and the note to p. 227 for the former definition and p. 227 for the latter. Richards is about equally open to criticism, whichever definition one attributes to him. The rest of my paragraph is directed

definition to the literary medium. And we have seen also how amorphous an affair the author's experience is. Yet this experience is to be the norm that defines the poem. Richards will allow a norm on this level because the author's experience is an act in time. Any less obviously experiential a norm would dictate that there be qualities in the work itself.

Richards attacks those who see structure and values as belonging to the object, insisting that these people can say nothing analytically about them.[7] All such critics, he insists, are Idealists who privately intuit qualities in the object but who cannot describe these intuitions. Therefore, identifying these critics with the impressionists (and we may grant that he had some historical justification in so doing), he denies that they can say anything worth while in theoretical or practical criticism. According to Richards, then, either we deny the existence of qualities in the object or we are self-willed, mute Idealists; either we indulge in Richards' mechanistic psychological analysis or we cannot analyze at all.

In many of those influenced by Richards we have a workable position that skirts his disjunctive. These would claim that, while a work of art may have an infinite number of values of different kinds, it functions primarily as an aesthetic object and must first be experienced and valued as such. The work has within it a "discriminable structure" [8] or a "system of norms" [9] which is open to inspection. The qualities *of* the work and *in* the work are phenomenally "anchored" [10] to this structure or these norms. But the reader *discovers* these qualities (which exist prior to his interest); he does not *create* them. They are in the object because he can talk about the structure which contains them.[11] A value that is not anchored or is not seen as anchored cannot be talked about and remains essentially the kind of unsupported intuition that Richards disparages. But the capable critic must not allow himself

mainly against the first of these definitions. If Richards means the second definition—"the relevant experience of the poet when contemplating the completed composition"—then we may ask why the poet, as spectator, should necessarily be any more reliable than any other reader. On the contrary, his personal interest may make his experience of the poem utterly idiosyncratic (as Richards in effect admits in his note to p. 227).

such evasion and must argue his every claim for value. While no critic may be correct, yet every evaluation is corrigible by an appeal to the structure. The give-and-take of critical discussion seeks to eliminate what is idiosyncratic in order to establish more and more successfully what is in the object.

This idea of norm, of corrigibility, of the elimination of the idiosyncratic, is not to be confused with Richards' attempt to define a norm: the class of experiences relatively close to the author's. For in the latter case the norm is hardly capable of being described, nor the relations of its parts calculated, however roughly. This standard advanced by Richards, then, is not normative at all. It can hardly exist as a corrective. It is merely the regulator of the lowest denominators ranged about it. Such a standard dictates not how much a work may mean or be worth, but how little it can mean and still be relevant to the work. It is significant to note here that the scientism of Richards becomes far less empirical and demonstrable than the so-called "Idealism" of his opponents.

The enormous differences between the position of Richards and the others being discussed here stem from the problem of the medium. My conclusions about the creative act indicate that the need to recognize the artist's struggle with his material prompts these later theorists to their claims about objectivity. There is no preformed experience to be talked about critically. And it is not the capability for complex experience that characterizes the artist, but rather his ability so to shape his material that a significant organization of it, containing value, emerges. The interaction between artist and material produces the art object; this object is not predictable by the artist before the give-and-take of the creative process. For this reason the object's value can never be attributed to anything but the formal organization which is the object. The artist's experience that counts for the reader, after all, is the act of composition itself. Obviously, then, the reader's experience is not to approximate the artist's.

Once we concede these things, we are enabled to investigate innumerable technical problems that Richards cannot consider as central to the problem of value. Here we have a paradox. Richards, the semanticist and would-be scientist, cannot account for the material aspect of a work, while some whom he treats as inarticulate Idealists apparently can. In fact, far from resting in any intangible theory of intuition, the latter have produced an analysis infinitely more adequate scientifically than is that of Richards. Indeed it seems to be an amazing feat on the part of those of the new critics who spring from Richards that, with a theory so inadequate on the level of technique, they (and, for that matter, Richards himself) have been able to produce so much excellent criticism.

However, it is the division of language into the "emotive" and the "referential" that helps Richards to transform so flimsy a theory into one that has proved to be so useful in its insistence on total context.[12] This is not for him an *ad hoc* distinction; it is rather demanded by the nature of his assumptions. I have discussed the interaction of contexts, the contention that while sensation may depend solely on an external stimulus, emotional states depend equally on the reader's internal condition at the time of the stimulus. With this concept Richards denies the idea, so currently popular in critical theory, that the reader must enter the autonomous world of the artistic probability created by the author, leaving his real world behind. Richards will not grant this much to aesthetic contemplation. Remembering Richards' claim that the witnessing of art is different only in degree—that is, only quantitatively—from any other experience, we should understand that the interaction of contexts demands that the reader cannot and should not lose hold of his own world. Yet Richards is too sophisticated to ask that we read only works whose "world" is philosophically congenial to our own. Thus the creation of two languages, that of science or knowledge and that of poetry or myth, allows the reader to make a "provisional acceptance" of the beliefs involved in the poem, since they are not really offered as knowledge.*

The distinction he makes within language, despite crucial short-

* Richards makes another and more insidious use of this distinction. Whenever he wants to dispose of a non-naturalistic philosophy, he merely dismisses it by calling it mythic (that is, emotive) rather than allowing it to be a serious attempt to arrive at knowledge.

comings in its unqualified denial of meaning to poetry, has been extremely useful to criticism. The aim of art, he claims, is to organize our impulses on as broad a basis as possible. This would mean the simultaneous satisfaction of equally intense and opposed impulses, inducing an equilibrium or detachment—a blockage of the tendency to action. For the impulses are satisfied by being translated into "attitudes" ("incipient actions") rather than into actions themselves. Since opposed impulses are simultaneously satisfied by the arousal of opposed attitudes, none of the impulses, which have fulfilled themselves as attitudes, can spill over into overt action.[13] The better the experience, the broader the organization of attitudes and the less tendency there is for action. Here is the ground for the recommendation by Richards, and later by Brooks, of a "poetry of inclusion," with value being assigned in proportion to its inclusiveness.

It should be obvious that nothing so straightforward and unemotional as scientific truth (the only kind of truth there is for Richards, since the rest is mythic) can satisfy the demands made of artistic contemplation. To repeat, for Richards the end of all experience is the arousal of attitudes, the success of the experience depending on the extent of complexity in the cluster of attitudes. In the ideal poem we should not have even a tendency to incipient action in any single direction. Here impersonality would equal complete involvement. Emotive language, in which words are exploited for much more than their unimpassioned referential significance, is for Richards the means to this end. Thus we have a theoretical justification for exposing the fallacy of judging a poem as a philosophical statement. The separation of propositional truth from poetic value, so important to modern critics, is here made in the context of Richards' impulse psychology. For it is not the truth-value of any experience which determines its worth, but rather its efficiency as an organizer of impulses. We must be physiologically contained by the poem.

It is, then, the "total effect" of a work which brings these varied impulses into play. No single aspect of the poem can receive our attention as an isolated phenomenon, since it is the interrelation of all of the aspects which touches the impulses. Thus meter, rhyme, or any other element functions in a total context rather than independently. Only this context can furnish any control over the reader as it interacts with the contexts he brings to the work. The usefulness of elements must lie in their totality, since the value of the reader's response exists only in the totality of impulses that are activated. And this totality must be more than the sum of its parts. This organic concept of "total effect" leading to "total response" would seem to deny the content-form dichotomy which we saw at work before, undermining Richards' critical theory. And of course, Richards himself expresses only contempt for content-form theories. Yet there seems to be no way of circumventing this contradiction; for, as Chapter 3 has shown, in distinguishing between the "critical" and the "technical" parts of the poem and consequently in allowing as the sole ground for judgment the poet's experience prior to the act of creation, Richards seems unmistakably to be viewing content and form as separate entities in the poem.

It is now possible to summarize the more useful aspects of Richards' position. First, his is a critical position which, if grounded on different philosophical assumptions, could provide the poem with a uniquely independent status. But secondly, this status could be justified only by a purely linguistic critic, who could use Richards' emotive-referential dichotomy to show that the poem, having other than referential interests, must not point directly beyond itself. We saw that Richards proposes an impulse-psychology which poetry serves by organizing simultaneously as many impulses as possible. And since only poetry can satisfy many impulses which would normally be incompatible with each other, that is its justification.

How can poetry accomplish this? If poetry is single-minded, if it appeals only to one set of impulses—if, in other words, it is in any sense partisan—then the number of impulses it can organize is severely limited. In this case, there is no need for poetry at all, since in our normal response to the demands for action made by everyday life only one set of impulses can be satisfied at one time, at the cost of other sets. If the organization or equilibrium of impulses is poetry's sole objective, then it must do better.

The answer lies in irony, which will allow opposing impulses to be aroused simultaneously. But this of course calls for a definition of "irony" utterly different from what is normally meant by the term. Conventionally "irony" is thought of as a single-minded device whereby an author seems to be saying one thing while making it perfectly clear that he means precisely the opposite. It is thus a simple inversion, which allows us to see what is really meant through what is apparently said. But Richards' conception of irony, closer to that of German romanticism, would seem to demand that the poem, while stating one view (though, since it is emotive, not offering it as truth), should by ambiguity or some other device present the opposite view at the same time. Yet it should not show one up at the cost of the other. It should refrain from judging between them, so that it may organize the opposing sets of impulses at the same time.

Irony in this sense consists in the bringing in of the opposite, the complementary impulses; that is why poetry which is exposed to it is not of the highest order, and why irony itself is so constantly a characteristic of poetry which is.[14]

Here we have the basis for a favorite insistence of many new critics: that a poem can make itself invulnerable to the reader's irony only by being itself ironic. But the temptation to bestow qualities upon the poem must be resisted by the psychologistic Richards if he is to remain true to his epistemology. Thus his realization of the demands made by the subjectivistic nature of his system prevents him from consistently treating irony as an objective feature of the poem. It is true that in the above quotation he speaks of irony as "a characteristic of poetry" that is "of the highest order." But elsewhere, in speaking of "balanced poise" (apparently another phrase used to describe the effects of irony), Richards says,

It is a general characteristic of all the most valuable experiences of the arts . . . We must resist the temptation to analyse its cause into sets of opposed characters in the object. As a rule no such analysis can be made. The balance is not in the structure of the stimulating object, it is in the response. By remembering this we escape the danger of supposing that we have found a formula for Beauty.[15]

Of course theorists like Brooks, who have been influenced by Richards but who are not, like Richards, committed to subjectivism, have, perhaps fortunately, gone a long way toward converting this concept into the "formula for Beauty" against which he warned.

# Chapter 8

# The Transformation of Richards:

## A CONTEXTUAL THEORY OF THE
## AESTHETIC OBJECT

EVEN as Richards inadvertently paved the way for the study of poems as independent structures—by which I mean, as he did not, that they cannot in any way be reduced to the psychology of the poet in one direction or to the psychology of the audience in the other [1]—he created, as he meant to, several obstacles which his followers had to overcome in order to earn this position. It is impossible to conceive of the work itself as a self-contained entity when it is relegated to being a shadowy middleman that merely reflects the psychology of the two people who have to do with it, the poet and the reader. And it is reduced precisely to this status when Richards defines it solely in terms of the experiences of its readers and the experience of its author. So long as Richards maintains his concept of the interaction of contexts, so that the reader's life outside the poem is as crucial a factor in his aesthetic experience as is the life he discovers in the poem, he has left us a good distance from a consideration of the poem as a separate world. And if the poem is allowed to be no more than an almost featureless stimulus—which is all it can be if irony is not consistently treated as a characteristic of the poem rather than of the reader and if "a carpet or a pot or . . . a gesture" can be adequate substitutes for the poem [2]—then any attempt at criticism, organic or otherwise, seems pointless. Certainly many transformations had to be worked in the theory if its useful features were to be applied soundly.

## The Aesthetic Object

As an aid in these needed transformations, fortunately, the later critics had available a second kind of influence which accompanied that of Richards. It was the sense of absolutistic orthodoxy and traditionalism which, stemming from Hulme through Eliot, allowed them to fashion the alien positivism of Richards into workable objective criticism.

Although it was Richards who made familiar the concept of irony as such, it is implicit also in Eliot's early work in which he asks that poetry be once again the product of those who have a "unity of sensibility." In his defense of and plea for a poetry of "wit," a truly "intellectual," rather than a self-consciously "reflective" poetry (not unlike Hulme's defense of and plea for a crisp poetry of fancy rather than a spongy poetry of imagination), Eliot seems clearly to be calling for serious subjects to be understated, and "wittily" understated, in order for the fullest degree of their true seriousness to be exploited. It was the lack of this, he tells us, that ruined Milton.[3] In his "The Metaphysical Poets" he couples this call for a poetry of wit with one for a difficult poetry. Now of course this idea of poetry as being difficult, as requiring tremendous effort on the part of the reader, is a new one in criticism and one that would clearly lend itself to incorporation with Richards' claims about irony. Thus, as the work of Cleanth Brooks testifies, the divergent positions of Richards and Eliot meet at several crucial points.

While absorbing the more traditionalistic claims of Eliot, the modern critics who have been influenced by Richards have continued to distinguish between science and poetry on the linguistic level. However, in order to perform the act of rigorous criticism which they proposed to themselves, they had to free themselves from the critical paralysis which the logical extension of Richards' affective psychologism would force upon them. Thus they had to consider aesthetic qualities as objectively structured. But, once freed from defining poetry in terms of impulses, they had to find a new function for it, one that would still keep it distinct from science or the purely referential and yet be based on language, since they had to utilize the valuable linguistic tools given them by Richards. Therefore they began to think of poetry ontologically, as Ransom might put it, to regard the poem as an objective structure which is a separate world of meanings, which has its own mode of existence.

In a critic like Cleanth Brooks [4] and to a lesser degree, in William Empson, particularly in his *Seven Types of Ambiguity*,[5] the fusion of the opposed metaphysics of Eliot and Richards into a methodology which, strangely, is at once heterogeneous and effective, can best be observed. We have seen that, despite the extremely antithetic philosophical positions of Richards and Eliot, they somehow have several points of contact on the critical level. And since modern critics for the most part are content to theorize without too much thought about philosophic and aesthetic presuppositions, such amalgamations as these are to be expected, and, indeed, despite the contradictions on the philosophical level these amalgamations have done much to further the value of modern criticism.[6]

Irony, paradox, and ambiguity are as valuable to Brooks as they are to Richards, from whom he seems to have inherited them. But Brooks' interest is literary rather than psychological and his value-theory objective rather than subjectivistic. Thus irony for him is a quality which is structured in the poem and which makes the poem valuable objectively. But if Brooks' interest is not psychological, how does irony come to be valuable for him? For Richards justified irony in terms of the greater number of impulses that could be organized. The value of irony arises for him out of the belief that such ambivalences of attitudes lead to the satisfaction of many impulses with a minimum of frustration. The poem does not allow the reader a commitment, or even an incipient action, in any single direction.

Brooks justifies irony in two ways.[7] First, in terms of the relation between the poem and the reader—the relation about which Richards talks—Brooks invokes Hulme's insistence on freshness in poetic expression, on the avoidance of stock expressions which produce stock responses. But, secondly, he justifies irony even more significantly by transferring Richards' discussion from the relation between the poem and the reader to one between the poem and reality, a relation which Richards was forced to deny. To go too deeply into this second relation here would be to anticipate much of the final section of this essay. Suffice it then to say that Brooks considers our actual experience in the world to be infinitely complex. No single abstract moral or scientific system can do justice to all the data. No one position can preclude, on the level of abstraction, other possible interpretations which also have their merits. Only the poet is able to handle this complexity, the complete texture of reality, with any real fairness. Like Ransom, Brooks would claim that poetry restores "the world's body" which more purely referential discourse, using only its skeleton, must ignore.[8] The poet may begin by expressing one viewpoint, but by various devices like irony he should imply the equal tenability of conflicting viewpoints (and, as with Richards, one must assume the more viewpoints and the more conflicting they are, the better). The poet must not choose among these positions but rather must continue to see all around the problem without sacrificing the total view to a partial insight. Only the poet's "unity of sensibility," given him by his tradition, can struggle with all these recalcitrant elements and lose none of them in the organism which is the created poem. As Brooks points out, this "balance or reconciliation of opposite or discordant qualities" is precisely Coleridge's definition of imagination.[9] Thus when Brooks calls maturity one of the criteria of great poetry, he means by it the ability to see problems in their true complexity. We might say that what Brooks requires of the poet, if I may distort Coleridge's famous dictum, is a "suspension of belief."

It is clear, then, that Brooks, who has done the most with the concept of irony, so as to make more useful to practical criticism Richards' concept of equilibrium, was forced to tear this insight from the physiological context given it by Richards; in order to make it critically workable, Brooks had to free irony from its bondage to the reader's mechanism and make it part of the structure of the work itself. It should be re-emphasized that he made two changes which allowed him to develop the concept of irony out of the critical paralysis that strict adherence to Richards' theory would involve. First, he transferred irony from the mind to the poem, and in so doing he was able to talk about freshness of poetic context instead of being restricted to organizations of impulses. Secondly, as we shall see more clearly in the final section of this essay, by claiming for the poem some kind of meaning in terms of the world around it, he was able to make the concept of irony serve a profound and crucial belief that the role of poetry is a unique and indispensable one.

While many objections may be raised to the uses he makes of irony, so that it may be claimed, for example, that the theory either leaves out of account many fine simple or (in Tillyard's phrase [10]) "direct" poems of single meanings or else tries to assimilate them to the theory by completely distorting the poems in an over-ingenious manner that is little less than sacrilege—while these and other objections may be urged against his use of the concept, nevertheless it must be admitted that his version has helped in many individual explications of poems and has advanced us along the way to an effective poetic theory which would do justice to the peculiar function of the art. And none of this would have been possible unless the word had been taken out of the universe of discourse provided for it by Richards and put into one that can more effectively deal with purely literary problems. But despite this transfer and despite the fact that Brooks confers upon poetry a real and important relationship to the structure of reality, he remains at one with Richards in keeping the distinction between science and poetry and keeping it on the linguistic level.

My central concern in this section, however, is not with the relation of poetry to reality but rather with the poem in its function as aesthetic object with respect to its reader. Thus I am here interested in the first rather than the second of Brooks' transformations of Richards' theory. In transferring irony from the reader's mind to the poem so that he can talk of the freshness and complexity of the poetic phrase, how can Brooks arrive at a theory of context that allows the successful poem to be an inescapable and fully realized world of meanings and values and consequently to control the reader's attention completely? For Brooks may seem to have negated the force of Richards' referential-emotive dichotomy by insisting that poetry does tell us about experience. How, then, is poetry kept from becoming, in its nature and in its function, as referential as is science and therefore from leading us, in our experience of it, as immediately away from itself as does scientific discourse?

Fairly uniform answers to these questions are given us by Brooks; by Allen Tate, who holds a somewhat similar, if less extreme, theory; and by Robert Penn Warren, who has theorized in writing less often.[11] The transformation of Richards' formulas is clear in all of these. To begin with, they all assume a distinction between science and poetry on the level of language. But while all of them classify scientific language as immediately referential, none would restrict poetic language to the emotive. Since poetry, like science, consists of verbal symbols, what allows poetic language to be more than simply referential in the relation between symbol and thing symbolized? For these writers the answer is found in poetry's formally controlled complexity. In the terminology of Charles W. Morris, whom some of these critics discuss although they must ultimately disagree with his views on poetic meaning and value,[12] poetic language receives its sanction primarily from the syntactic function of language, scientific language from the semantic function.[13] In other words, the language of what might more generically be called prose discourse (with fiction, of course, excepted since we are here using *poetry* in its broadest or Aristotelian sense [14]) functions only as a signifier. It points directly to the world outside language and is effective to the extent that it points unambiguously, to the extent that the sign and the thing for which it stands have a one-to-one relationship to each other. We must never be lost or trapped in discourse but must be immediately led at each point to the referents of the words. Thus prose discourse is thin, indeed transparent: we are to see directly through it to the objects (and the relationships among objects) for which it is a counter.

Poetic discourse is another thing entirely. In it we are ideally to be trapped, never to escape for the poem's duration. But the poem does consist of words and words have meanings—the same meanings they have in prose discourse, since the emotive claims of Richards have been rejected. These critics, after all, are not writing a theory of nonsense, the only possible kind of discourse in which the referential aspect of language could be utterly neglected. Obviously, then, the poet must recognize the threat which exists to his attempt to force us into an aesthetic experience: the threat that the designating character of language may lead us out of his poem at any moment or may, indeed, prevent us from ever getting enmeshed in it.

At this point it should be profitable to pause a bit and consider the concept of the aesthetic experience these critics ought to have in mind if they are to advance this theory with any consistency. Of course, as critics they are concerned with justifying their methods of operating discursively on the poem rather than with justifying their pure experience of it. Consequently, I must concede, they do not betray any awareness that to get systematically at a theoretical account of the aesthetic object they should come by way of the reader's aesthetic experience as well as by way of the poet's creative act. Nevertheless it seems clear that the kind of aesthetic experience which would be consistent with their claims about the poem as aesthetic object would be one much like that defined by Eliseo Vivas.[15] Vivas characterizes the aesthetic experience as a state of "intransitive rapt attention" upon the object. Whatever meanings and values are in the object must, during the experience, function reflexively; they must be seen as lying immanently within the object rather than as transcending the object and thereby leading the spectator back to the world. The symbols upon which he focuses must be *intra-referential* only, lest his attention be diverted from the self-sufficient system constituted by these symbols.

Now since this state of attentiveness is a psychological phenomenon and therefore lends itself to descriptive study only, we must refrain from saying just what kind of object ought to bring the spectator to this state. Nor can we maintain, short of further evidence which is not likely to be forthcoming to support so improbable a claim, that only a work of art can arouse this state in him. The state will occur when it will occur, and to deny, for example, the power of nature to produce it would be to fly in the face of overwhelming testimony. But this definition of the aesthetic state does require that the object, natural or man-made, exercise some control over him and over the tendency in him to escape to his worldly interests. If it is a natural object to which he responds aesthetically, then either it has been given a form which can so control him or he, thanks perhaps to the habits acquired in his commerce with art, projects such a form upon it and becomes an artist himself. Which of these two is the more likely possibility I leave for metaphysicians to dispute.

If it is a man-made object to which the spectator responds aesthetically, then again the control must be attributed either to the object or to his powers of projection. But to choose one of these alternatives is the delicate task of the critic and therefore becomes our problem. For the choice will vary with each object; and on our decision will depend whether or not we attribute aesthetic value to an object. For if we cannot find in this object the control needed to give rise to an aesthetic experience in the spectator of normal awareness, then we must assume that the spectator has been the artist, that he has cast a form upon the object of his perception, a form to whose control he has himself fallen prey. And although, as psychologists, we must refrain from saying whether this aesthetic experience is more or less valuable than that in which the spectator submits to controls in the object, we can make a normative judgment about the capacity of the object to produce this experience generally. For if the controls are in the object, we should expect an aesthetic experience to be produced and should blame the spectator's distractions or peculiarities if it is not; but if the controls are not in the object, so that an aesthetic experience must be attributed to the spectator's powers of projection, then this response is one that is idiosyncratic and that we cannot expect to be repeated. If, as practical critics, we are to establish aesthetic value in the case of the individual poem, we must look continually at the object—not at the reader—and try to discover what experiences its observable features may justly allow.

In terms of this definition of the aesthetic experience, we must note that, while the aesthetic object is not the only kind of object in whose presence the spectator may undergo an aesthetic experience, it is the one kind which is so constructed as to facilitate that experience, in a sense to force it upon him. Armed with this systematic view of the aesthetic object, a view which clearly follows from the description given earlier of the process which created this object, we can return to the critics who, consciously or unconsciously working in terms of this view, try to establish the uniqueness of the poetic object. They were struggling with a most crucial problem: if the language of poetry is not, as Richards called it, emotive, then it must share with prose discourse certain referential characteristics; if it does function referentially, or transitively, as Vivas would say, thus pointing away from itself, how can it at the same time function as aesthetic object and enclose us in an aesthetic experience as I have defined the term?

These critics unanimously affirm that, while the words of a poem, considered atomistically, may function referentially, the poetic structure of words, considered contextually, prevents the individual words from so functioning. The poet knows the inherent danger in his medium: that words struggle to mean things. He must, by the formal context he imposes on them, prevent them from achieving their natural (that is, their nonpoetic) function. He must use every device at his command to block their direct pointing or he does not produce an aesthetic object.

Here some of the tools given these critics by Richards are put to effective use. Such insights as Richards' introduction of irony serve to bring them to the doctrine of contextual complexity. The poet prevents his poem from competing with science or philosophy—that is, from yielding any propositional statement which can be extracted from it without loss of meaning—by making his context inviolable. As prose discourse was to be unambiguous, thin, transparent; so poetic discourse is to be purposely ambiguous, dense, opaque and indeed reflective. If there is within the poem any possible proposition, it is so laden by its context with qualifications, double meanings, and ironic contradictions that it can no longer stand as a proposition. It is too ambiguous, too confounded for the realm of logic. Hence arises the demand from these critics that poetry be "mature," that it see all around any experience and not cheat our life of its complexity, our world of its body. So completely have these critics absorbed what they could use of Richards that we find Brooks putting forth this demand in the words of Richards by calling for a "poetry of inclusion" rather than a "poetry of exclusion." [16] He even proposes a scale of poetic value which is to move from the low or exclusion end to the high or inclusion end. Of course, as Brooks makes clear, he means by this something quite different from what Richards could mean, restricted as the latter was by his physiological assumptions.

But unfortunately Brooks, despite his transformations of Richards' ideas, has not completely shaken off what Vivas calls Richards' "vitalism." [17] Thus we are led to imply that the more complexity the better, so that this theory easily lends itself to the sanctioning of complexity for complexity's sake. We may fear that we are given the unhappy alternatives of being deprived of some fine relatively simple poems or of being shown by reckless over-ingenuity that they really are no simpler than Donne's. And, fearing also that we may be given as works of poetic art complete jumbles which attempt uninhibitedly to reproduce unaltered the chaos of our world in order to reach the ultimate of inclusion, we may justly ask how much inclusion there can be before there is too much, before we lose art altogether?

Of course, on the other hand, we should appreciate the value of this theory both in its distinguishing of poetry from science and philosophy so that it can allow an aesthetic experience and in its refraining from denying poetry's intimate relations with reality. It should be apparent, for example, how much this doctrine improves upon Eliot's crude dichotomy (not unlike the old form-content dichotomy, we observed) between poetry and beliefs.[18] According to Eliot, it will be remembered, a poet gives us no new interpretation of reality. He rather borrows his beliefs from his environment and shows us in his poem, via the objective correlative, how it feels to hold these beliefs. So long as these beliefs are fairly mature they will not interfere with our reading of the poem even if we do not agree with them. Thus the most important function of beliefs in poetry is the rather negative one of staying out of the way so that we can enjoy the poetry, the emotional equivalent of the beliefs. The closeness of this theory to Richards' and, consequently, to the reduction of poetry to the emotive are obvious even if they are surprising in a theorist with the convictions of Eliot.[19] Thus, Eliot tells us, when we read Shelley the beliefs get in the way because of their puerility and as a result we are blocked in our attempt to read and judge the poetry sympathetically as poetry. All this is far from an organic consideration of the poem in terms of the definition of the aesthetic experience which I have been using.

Critics like Brooks and Tate, however, must treat the problem differently. Shelley's weakness as poet, they must claim, is not so much the poverty of his ideas as it is his failure to hold them in the formal context of the poem.[20] As a result they present themselves out of context as ideas; they leap forth as ideas and plead to be judged as true or false much as we would judge a scientific or philosophic idea. If they were held in the context they would never so present themselves. Of course, it might very well be argued, if Shelley were to hold his ideas in the poem's context in the manner suggested by these critics, he would perforce have to give them depth and complexity so that they would no longer betray the puerility with which Eliot charged them.

Is there, then, any but a verbal difference between the two complaints? On the systematic level there is a great difference. While Eliot's objection is aimed at the content side of a form-content dichotomy, the other objection is aimed at a weakness in the unified context which should combine these two elements organically. Our agreement with Eliot's objection would depend upon whether or not we thought Shelley's ideas to be puerile;

and this is hardly a literary problem or one that could be resolved by reference to the objective features of the work. Our agreement with the other criticism would depend on how similar our analysis of the poem would be to that of those making the charge. This is a literary problem which could be solved only by a constant appeal to the objective features of the work. We should have simply to decide, although in practice it is not usually quite so simple, whether or not Shelley's poem was functioning as an aesthetic object such as is required by the conception of the aesthetic experience I have set forth; to decide, in other words, whether the statements in the poem were functioning as prose discourse—that is merely referentially or allegorically—or whether they were functioning in terms of a self-contained context.[21]

Granting the value of this theory, I must return to the major question that confronts it: how much complexity and how much inclusion before there is too much? Or, to ask the prior question, should a Brooks borrow uncritically from Richards the claim that a poem is valuable in proportion to its complexity and that there is no limit set to the extent of its possible inclusiveness? The critical sensitivity of Brooks protects him from the more extreme implications of this theory, even as this sensitivity probably prevents him from intending these implications to be drawn from it; nevertheless the theory seems to lend itself to these more dangerous interpretations and thus to sanction the romanticism such interpretations would sponsor. For despite his anti-romantic orientation, Brooks, in rushing headlong toward an ever-increasing multiplication of complexities in order to move poetry farther and farther toward the maximum of inclusiveness (the maximum being, I would suppose, the unrefracted chaos of actual experience), seems to be fleeing from the virtue of classic control; in his flight from the "heresy of paraphrase" he is fleeing also from what Ransom or Winters would think of as rational order. As we shall shortly see, Tate, in taking up a less irrationalistic position, tempers considerably these extravagant claims about complexity. But in the hands of Brooks, the theory, ironically, would seem itself to be highly romantic in its emphasis on illogicality.

[ 134 ]

Within much the same conception of the aesthetic experience and the aesthetic object, this theory must somehow be modified to one which would still see the poetic context as blocking the tendency of its individual words to point immediately beyond it and yet as resisting the extremes of confusion. But an unyielding dilemma must be evaded if this compromise position is to be attained.

On the one hand there is the need to maintain the context as self-contained; that is, the need to keep out any meaning not necessitated by the organic and closed system of mutual inter-relations among the terms which make up the context. If the terms have a simple referential responsibility or if the relation-ships among them have a logical responsibility, then the context has been violated by dictates which do not grow from within but are imposed from without—in the former case from the general world of meanings which existed prior to, and still exists inde-pendently of, the growth of this unique system; and in the latter case from abstract procedures which relentlessly force the com-pliance of all discourse with equal indifference, unmindful of the exceptional needs of any one of them. The context can no longer prevent even the submissive reader from wrenching out parts of it and treating them atomistically by referring them to the stand-ards of other realms. Its god now transcendent rather than imma-nent, the context can no longer control the reader by containment. Thus it is that the context, if it is to maintain the organic quality which brings it into existence, cannot contract any obligation which is not intramural. Otherwise at best the poem is not Yvor Winters' "new word" but merely a pretty synonym for old ones.

On the other hand, however, there is the difficulty—indeed, if language is considered primarily as referential, the impossibility—of consistently maintaining an unqualified organicism. I have already pointed out the danger involved in the insistence upon a self-contained context which seals itself off by the unchecked mul-tiplication of complexities, hell-bent for chaos. And there are fur-ther problems. Our literary history continually reveals the enabling power which a vital literary tradition works upon the individual poet; our great critics, with their once-removed discourse about poems, have surely managed now and then to illuminate them for the rest of us; yet, in spite of all the evidence, the organicist must claim that the completely autonomous poetic context, one whose meaning is unique, *sui generis*, is also one that is utterly cut off from literary history as well as from literary criticism.* That is, it declares itself to be beyond comparison with all other poetic contexts and invulnerable to the commentary of the critic: if the critic is to do more than merely repeat the words of the poem, he must be forced into a language which is necessarily derived from a system of meanings other than that of the poetic context. Indeed "the heresy of paraphrase," [22] with which contextual critics have commonly charged their less new-critical colleagues, may seem justly applicable to anyone—even a self-styled contextual critic—who tries to analyze a context using, as he must, a language drawn from outside this context.

But if we overlook evidences to the contrary, the outlawing of essential historical relationships in literature and of effective literary criticism, while surely posing some serious inconveniences, is not itself sufficient warrant to reject an aesthetic which so legislates. Is it not, however, also likely that an utterly self-contained poetic context is cut off even from its potential reader? For he comes to this unique system, to the "new word," armed only with old words which can hardly be expected to pierce through to its untranslatable, incomparable meaning. How, with his old meanings, is he successfully to explore the new world of meanings which the poetic context supposedly encloses? And if a theory cannot allow us our full experience of the poem, then indeed it would seem to be in serious difficulty.

It may be tempting to argue that the contextualist does not mean to maintain so extreme, and thus so self-defeating, an organicism. But it is difficult to see how he can qualify it so long as he insists on the poem's autonomy, so long as he charges any

---

* Just as recent contextual theorists are, ironically, those who place so much faith in the rigorous critical act, so too—and again ironically—it is they who are especially concerned about the place of tradition in poetry. But it should by now be apparent that their theoretical difficulties hardly begin or end here.

translation, however cautious, of the terms in the context with "the heresy of paraphrase." It is indeed instructive to look at the work of Croce in this connection, since he is an organicist who unflinchingly accepts the consequences to which his organic claims commit him.[23] The Crocean critic, it is true, can, by an act of intuition similar to that of the poet if not spiritually identical with it, "reproduce" the work in himself.[24] To the extent, however, that he is a judge discoursing about the aesthetic efficacy with which the parts contribute to the work's totality, the critic, if he is to be consistently Crocean, can only stand in speechless admiration before the successful poem—one in which there is no "non-poetry" to be separated in Coleridgean fashion from the "poetry." For he knows he can use no words of his own without abusing the language of the poem's context.* Yet this dead end of practical criticism seems hardly to be the aim of the more contextual of modern critics whose work has been distinguished by its painstaking detail of scrupulous verbal analysis. In contrast to their impressionistic predecessors, they have insisted that literary greatness is something to be talked about and to be demonstrated objectively—if, that is, we can say what literary greatness might consist in, when ideally every poem must work for a greatness of a different kind, of its own kind.

There are, of course, those of them who are more aware of the critical limitations imposed by their position. These may claim that they always maintain a special alertness to the difference between the work of art and the work of criticism so that the latter

* It would seem possible for the organicist to say that his theory—in setting ideal requirements for the perfect poem, one which can never exist really—does not frown upon the chances for aesthetic experience or even on the prospects for criticism. For in dealing with an actual poem we could be allowed entry via those imperfections which, in restoring to language its normal duality, break open the closed contextual system that might have been. But a Croce could never take this way out. Within the terms of his Coleridgean distinction between the poetry and the non-poetry in the poem, he can never permit the duality of the latter to offer a way into the integrity of the former. The critical task must end when the non-poetry is revealed for what it is and the poetry is left in the glory of its untouchable purity. Recent contextualists are equally disdainful of imperfections and would hardly tolerate them to be indispensable to critical discourse or aesthetic experience. And thus the problem of even experiencing the poetry remains for them what it has been claimed to be above.

is never taken to be an easy substitute for the former. Rather the work of criticism is to be offered tentatively and with humility as a well-meaning guide through the well-plotted maze to which it points. It merely is to indicate rewarding configurations among the poem's internal relations since it dare do little more about them. If these critics are told that this is not a very satisfying objective for criticism, then they can only insist meekly that it is the best they can do without violating the art which is in their keeping.[25] In practice, however, even the more modest of them seem to go considerably beyond the severe boundaries of critical discourse to which their contextual theory ought to restrict them.

The contextual theory, then, felt by many modern critics to be utterly indispensable if they are adequately to explain their experience of poetry, would seem to carry with it many weighty burdens. Not the least of these, if one with the courage of Croce is content to follow where his theory leads, is that it denies him the right to engage in the one activity for whose sake he bothers about theorizing: the detailed technical analysis and criticism of specific works. Indeed, such a theory makes it difficult for him to see how he can even experience these works fully. But the only alternative would be to break open the context; and this, we have seen, would be at least as costly since it would end even more obviously in destroying the possibility for an aesthetic experience to be produced by the poem. Once open, the poetic context would be prey to an indiscriminate host of arbitrary meanings derived from other contexts. Poetry could no longer hold itself aloof from paraphrase; and thus, no longer free of the ordinary demands of reference, it would lose the one characteristic that could set it off from other modes of discourse.

It should now be clear that, if Brooks' tendency toward unbridled complexity is to be modified in the more classic direction of greater order and control, we must effect the transformation only while remaining alert to the threat to the integrity of the context posed by any attempt to constrict it from the outside. Yet respect for those sound aesthetic objectives that prompt a critic like Brooks does not alter the need to qualify the reckless implications of his theory. How one can mediate between the two unsatisfactory alternatives without seizing upon an irresponsible eclecticism is another problem to worry future theorists in this tradition.

But surely complexity need not be cherished for itself; nor need we suppose that the more complexity a poem has, the better it is. Indeed to make such a demand, as Brooks seems to, is to set up complexity as a mechanical demand, one that would violate the integrity of the poem as much as would other mechanical demands which Brooks would abhor.[26] Complexity must rather be seen as subordinate to and limited by the formed and orderly entity which is the total poem. The degree of complexity to be required for successful poetry should vary with the special needs of each poem. And what should determine the needs of the poem—as along with its poet it strives to establish the integrity of its context—is something other than complexity, which, however, may very well be said to serve the poem and its peculiar needs. In making complexity an end in itself, Brooks seems unwittingly to be submitting the poem and the imagination which in part controls it to the whimsies of self-animated words. And this is pretty much what he was suspected of doing in my earlier consideration of him.

# Chapter 9

# The Contextual Theory:

## FURTHER QUALIFICATIONS AND COUNTER-QUALIFICATIONS

THE dangers, the tendencies toward reckless romanticism, which unless it is to be carefully qualified, the complexity theory involves, ought now to be apparent. It is not strange that it should have these tendencies since the science-poetry dichotomy out of which this theory grows was originally a romantic one, and as such contained many elements of irrationalism, some few of which Brooks seems still to maintain. Of course those modern critics who, following Richards, distinguish between poetry and science on the linguistic level, have been aware of the irrational elements of the original distinction. And since they have been in agreement in their condemnation of the romantic irrationalism, they have not been totally unaware of the paradox involved in their use of a dichotomy which springs from so suspect a source. They have accordingly tried to transform the distinction between science and poetry into one which could justify an anti-romantic approach to poetry.

To certain romantic poets and theorists [1] scientific language or reason meant denotative adequacy, logicality, precision, truth to particular reality. Therefore, by way of contrast, poetic language, if it was to allow a unique function to poetry, needed to be characterized by unbridled connotation, the lack of argumentative progression, [2] vagueness, truth to the ideal and universal. In other words, they made an absolute distinction between intellect and imagination or intuition, between reason and emotion; and poetry, the revelation of the highest truths, had to be purely emotional and intuitive.

It may well have been this dichotomy that led to the very aspects of romantic poetry which the modern critic most abhors. Consequently this critic finds that the romantic, in his poetry, failed to avoid those pitfalls of scientific discourse against which his theory was directed. For vagueness, lack of denotative precision, and idealism usually stray into the realm of generality and abstraction. And the poet who employs this kind of language just to avoid science only succeeds, because of his abstractions, in producing that "Platonic poetry" which is but a weak imitation of science. For, as we have seen Tate point out, because of the romantic's emphasis on emotion without his attempting to justify the emotion contextually, his rhetorical argument by example can never be as convincing—which is what the romantic poet wants to be—as the rigor of scientific or philosophical demonstration. Because this poet allows himself a lack of contextual justification such as characterizes prose discourse, he competes with science and is badly shown up by science since his methods are so much less exact. Further, his generalities can capture no more of what Ransom would call the particularities of the world's body than can the more rigorous generalities of science.

Our critics, then, equally anxious to distinguish science from poetry, have recognized, first, that the intellectual cannot be eliminated from poetry and, secondly, that in distinguishing poetry from science it is not poetry which has to be abstract and science concrete, but quite the other way around. They cannot argue against the insistence that the language of science is referential. But this is the very quality that allows them to consider science as abstract, since they do not equate denotation and concreteness in the way the romantics did. Furthermore, by changing the direction of the argument, they can use the connotative element of poetic discourse to reinforce concreteness.

The key to their distinction between science and poetry lies in the doctrine of poetic context which I have been examining. In scientific discourse, they claim, the point-by-point reference of words to things and their relationships should be as exact as possible, to avoid misunderstanding. Thus no modifications of the surrounding context can take a hand. But this, they would insist, is to assume a completely systematized, unambiguous world—a world, in other words, in which the sensitive and fully human being has never found himself. The poetic context, however, can promote the modifications, shades of meaning, and paradoxes which characterize reality below the level of scientific or philosophic abstractions. While keeping the need for a science-poetry distinction, these critics have shown that although both poetry and science can share the common language of specificity, only poetry can so control it as to make its statements concrete and yet nonreferential—that is, concrete only because they are cross-referential, because they point to each other rather than point atomistically to the outside world. For even specifically denotative words are at best generic unless highly controlled contextual interrelations force them to assume a unique particularity.

This realization, that poetry and science share what is essentially a common language, is reflected in the less anti-intellectual theories of modern critics. Here again they have had to go somewhat beyond Richards, whose distinction, in its extreme form, is essentially not far from that of the romantics. Richards calls the nonreferential "emotive" and, having consigned the ideal world in which the romantics believed to the realm of myth, he joins them in denying to poetry truth to specific reality. This complete denial to poetry of the rational and meaningful allows Richards to advocate unchecked inclusiveness as a poetic criterion. While this is not the criterion established by the romantics, it shares with them a neglect of those restraining elements that help produce order.

Brooks, in his failure to modify Richards' criterion of inclusiveness, may seem to join Richards and the romantics. But on the other hand, since poetry is meaningful for him as it is not for Richards, Brooks—anti-romantic that he does remain—theorizes largely to insist that some rational checks must be provided to prevent emotion from running away with itself into sentimentality. And there are further concessions to reasonableness in the particular twist he gives to Richards' concept of irony: that any emotion or attitude be justified intellectually by the specific and coldly considered objective situation in the poetic context; * or, as his colleague Robert Penn Warren so effectively puts it, that every emotional attitude in a work "must come to terms with Mercutio." [3] However, while Brooks may in this way provide rational checks for runaway romantic emotions, his theory, as we have seen it in its implications, fails consistently to provide them for the runaway complexities created by his hardheaded corrective for romanticism.

Other critics in this group, perhaps sensing that a theory like Brooks' does not forcefully enough outlaw romantic tendencies, have given more ground to the rational or paraphrasable content of poetry. The metaphysical poets seem to have shown them—as they showed Brooks, who did not wish to carry their lessons in this direction—that apparently severe rationality and denotation could be turned into the most poetic (that is, contextual) complexities. Thus Ransom speaks of the necessity that all poetry have a logical structure in terms of which poetic texture may diverge. Tate's criterion of "tension," in a like fashion, would call for a solid base of "extension" or denotation on which "intension" or connotation can build poetically. And the distinction made by Winters between conceptual content and emotional content or between rational motive and resulting emotion indicates a similar line of thought. These critics emphasize more than does Brooks the rational and denotative aspect of poetry which the romantics ignore. They may seem often to concentrate on the breakdown of rational and emotional elements in the poem while Brooks seems to concentrate on their fusion, since he refuses to concede that they can be spoken of separately or that logic or denotation ever exists as such in the poem.

* Of course this doctrine also seems to be indebted to Eliot's objective correlative, in accordance with which an emotion must not be "in excess of the facts as they appear."

Yet, aside from the free rein Brooks seems to give to complexity, these critics may seem to be stressing the negative or analytic side of much the same thesis as that whose positive or synthetic side Brooks is stressing. For example, Brooks and Ransom have disagreed, so that Brooks claims that Ransom, in insisting upon "logical structure," has committed "the heresy of paraphrase" and Ransom claims that Brooks, in denying "logical structure," has retreated to the anti-rationality of romanticism.[4] But Ransom, while stressing the rational waywardness of texture still maintains, at least at one point in his writings, that it is this texture which transforms the structure into poetry; that what differentiates the poem as poem is the new—and the other than logical—criterion of relevance which the texture enables it to achieve, thus putting it beyond the possibility of logical paraphrase. And this is precisely the claim of Brooks. Since Winters similarly claims that the final, unique judgment, which is the poem, cannot be contained in its rational paraphrase, Brooks' complaint against him is not unqualifiedly justified any more than is his criticism of Ransom.[5] And as for Winters' vehement attack on Ransom,[6] there would seem to be insufficient difference, on the methodological level, to warrant it. Finally Tate, in seeing tension as that which fuses the poem's extensive and intensive elements into a new and integral mode of discourse, ends up, in spite of his rational interest in extension, not so far from Brooks as the latter might believe him to be.

It should be added that Ransom's notion about "the precious object," springing strangely from his interest in Freud, paradoxically brings him even closer to Winters' theory. For Ransom here seems to be identifying texture with feeling, as does Winters.[7] In any case, Ransom and Winters seem, where they are not making organic claims for poetry, to agree in distinguishing reason from emotion in the poem, despite the differences between them which would arise out of Ransom's naturalistic affiliations. In restricting the element which distinguishes the poem from the logical paraphrase (and thus from nonpoetic discourse) to feelings only, both Ransom and Winters seem to be retreating from an ontological conception of poetry (which Ransom called for in his *The New*

*Criticism*) and thus to be nullifying the advances made by modern criticism from the science-poetry distinction left them by the romantics and by I. A. Richards.

It should be observed, then, that as Brooks can maintain the complete integrity of the poetic context only at the price of romantic irrationalism, so our other critics can maintain that there is rational control over the poem's complexities only by losing for the poem its organic unity. The "rational" elements of Winters, the "structure" of Ransom, the "extension" of Tate seem frequently to be viewed too separately as actual entities in the poem. But for the contextualist, there can be no logic or denotation as such in the poetic context, although, as we have seen, it may be in terms of these nonpoetic demands and in terms of the deviations from them that this context has come to be formed. Thus these theorists may seem to be setting up a form-content dichotomy despite their attempts to prevent it by claiming that the poem is more than the paraphrase, that there is ultimately an inviolable unity achieved. This dichotomy may be an outgrowth of what I showed to be a common weakness in modern conceptions of the creative act: the failure to account for the essential difference between the poet's idea of what he means to say before he begins to work in language and what is actually said in the completed poem.

It was maintained earlier with respect to the creative act that a position must be found between one which claims that the poet uses language as a tool to serve his prior conceptions and one which would have words determining themselves; so with respect to the poem a position must be found between one which sees the rational and denotative element as a separable factor and one which dispenses with rationality and meaning altogether. Such a position is a necessary one if we are theoretically to hold the poem together and yet not run to romantic extravagances. To arrive at such a position we would have to begin with the insights of Brooks and, without falling victim to the inconsistencies which plague eclecticism, somehow modify them in the healthy direction indicated by Ransom, Winters, and Tate. But we should have to stop short of their bifurcation of the poem. For, as has been intimated above, the attempt to avoid romanticism by establishing the rational as an important and independent element ironically returns these theories to their romantic forebears, just as, according to Tate and others, the attempt by the romantics to escape science only led them to compete with it. Once the rational is made an element in the poem it seems inevitable that the other element somehow be connected with emotion. And if the rational is the element that poetry has in common with prose, then it must be the emotion that transforms the statement into poetry. The difference between science and poetry then would be that, in the latter, emotion has been added to the statement and has somehow transformed it into another mode of discourse. And there is considerable agreement between this conclusion and that of the romantics as well as of I. A. Richards. The possibility of distinguishing between poetic and prose discourse in terms of what has been said about the aesthetic experience—that is, in terms of context—has been left far behind. But if these theories, because of the place they give to prose statement, tend eventually to collapse the distinction between poetic and prose discourse, Brooks, because of his failure to check complexities, tends to collapse the distinction between poetry and chaos. It is necessary, then, to go beyond Brooks by imposing certain orderly and restraining demands and yet to stop short of converting these demands into separable elements which find a place in the poem.

This position would have also to straighten out a confusion common to the theories of Brooks and of the others examined here. It is a confusion springing from an inadequate conception of language, and although the difficulties to which it may lead will be more apparent in my final section, it tends also to obfuscate the linguistic analysis of the poetic object. These critics all seem to have collapsed what I will call the structural or systematic properties of prose discourse into its semantic properties. When they speak of the rational element of language they seem to mean by it sometimes its referential quality, sometimes its logical structure, and sometimes both at once. Somehow science, denotation, and abstract logical relationships are all to be comprehended by the single term "rational" or "logical." Thus Winters differentiates reason from emotion by using a primitive linguistic distinction; that is, by referring respectively to the denotative and connotative power of words.[8] Yet the rational element of his poem is to reveal itself in a logical structure. Why the semantic properties of language must in any way dictate that the structural properties of language necessarily form a logical pattern Winters does not say. Ransom seems equally uncertain whether his "structure" is prosaic because it is logical in systematic pattern or because it is paraphrasable or translatable semantically at every point. Again, Tate uses the logical terms "extension" and "intension," although in his discussion it is obvious that the poem's extension concerns the precision of its denotations as well as the inevitable pattern of its logical relations and that the poem's intension involves equally the sacrifice of both. And when Brooks complains about what logical demands would do to a poem, what bothers him is that the referential function of prose discourse would not allow a word to be controlled by its context. Like the others, he concentrates on the semantic dimension of prose discourse, supposing wrongly that its structural dimension somehow operates within it.

It should be clear, then, that two very different problems of language are here confusedly collapsed into one. First, there is the semantic problem, the problem of the denotative power of the word. Secondly, there is the structural problem, the problem of permissible relations among terms and propositions. The first is the problem of truth, of correspondence; the second the problem of validity, of coherence. If the second problem is subsumed by the first, as these critics indicate, then it is clear that the sole distinction between prose and poetry may be found in the referential character of the former as against the self-contained, contextual character of the latter. But if the logical problem is properly seen as separate from the semantic problem, then indeed the foundations of the prose-poetry distinction based on referentiality, upon which modern criticism is built, are seriously shaken. For then the terms of prose discourse are seen as also deriving their meanings from a controlling context, in this case a logical context. They are no longer free to point uninhibitedly any more than are the terms of poetic discourse which are contained by a unique, formal context. Thus prose discourse can no longer be defined so simply, as purely referential discourse; and consequently poetry can no longer be so simply distinguished from it on the basis of being contextual or cross-referential.

A theorist can still maintain that, while the context operates in both prose and poetry, in poetry it operates far more intensely at the expense of simple reference: in short, that poetry differs from prose only in degree. But the line of theory I have been tracing cannot manage this pleasant compromise. Our critics, properly, have not spoken of more-or-less as concerns the legitimacy of paraphrase or the uniqueness of the poetic mode of discourse, its absolute status. For uniqueness either is or is not; it is a matter of kind, not of degree. Yet I have shown that a more cautious view of language evaporates any qualitative distinction between prose and poetry based on a distinction between reference and context. It may be that if a theorist could see more clearly into the nature of the contexts operating in prose and in poetry, he would be able to locate, in the difference between the restricting—and yet enabling—operations of logic and of organic form, a distinction in kind which would not depend on the false reduction of the problems of language to the one which concerns the reckless semanticist.

The Chicago neo-Aristotelians make a similar objection to the theory of language which underlies the referential-contextual distinction as they try to define poetry in other terms.[9] In order to make effective their general attack on linguistically based criticism, they seize upon the alleged failure of our critics to see any but the semantic properties in prose discourse.[10] The Aristotelians claim that the distinction between prose and poetry cannot be made in terms of language since language is "one only of the several antecedent causes of poems, and the cause which they have most in common with all other literary productions." Thus, they claim, our critics "deal only with one of the necessary, and never with any of the sufficient or distinguishing, conditions of poetic works." [11] And recognizing that through the structural properties of all language contextual qualifications enter prose as well as poetry, the Aristotelians claim that the prose-poetry distinction based on language must break down. Thus Crane insists that our critics, being concerned with only one, and this the least important, of the four causes inhering in literary production, can indicate only the similarities but not the differentiae among various kinds of poems. And more important, he insists further, if we grant that the problem of context is not unique to poetry, these critics can indicate only the similarities but not the differentiae between poetry and other forms of discourse. Whatever single quality the critic may be looking for in poetry (and Crane must maintain that each of these qualities may occur in prose as well), whether it be the irony of Brooks, the tension of Tate, or the texture of Ransom, his analysis can deal only with examples of this quality in various works and his judgment must rest on the amount of this quality he discovers. As a result the new criticism generally, the Aristotelians insist, is a "Platonic" rather than an Aristotelian criticism; that is, it is one which is concerned with likeness rather than difference, one based on a priori assumptions rather than inductive method.[12]

I have tentatively agreed earlier with the Aristotelians that perhaps certain of our critics may tend to reduce the poem too completely to the behavior of words. But on the other hand I have objected even more vigorously to the tendency of the Aristotelians to deny a primary importance to language and rather to emphasize a separable and pre-existing plot-synopsis. Similarly, I have here agreed that the definition of poetry as contextual, in addition to raising many serious difficulties, is too simple; that it is shown by a more adequate view of language not to distinguish poetry in kind from prose. But I have still left open to abler theorists the possibility of defining poetry in terms of language, as a special mode of discourse, provided the definition does justice to the dimensions operative in prose discourse. For it is probably in terms of the differing kinds of contexts that a prose-poetry distinction should be drawn. And as for having a priori assumptions, is it possible to have an aesthetically responsible theory without them? This is as much as can be said here to defend the theories I have been discussing against the charge of being "Platonic." Can the Aristotelians do better by their theory?

Let us trace this theory. At the outset of their theorizing the Aristotelians doubtlessly had an inductive theory, if indeed it was a theory at all in terms of the requirements a systematic philosophy of art would set upon critical theory.[13] For it was a theory that seemed to deny the possibility of theory. This early criticism was distinguished only by its structural investigation of the orderly relation of the parts to the whole in the individual poem. The critic examined each work without any preconceptions in order to reveal precisely what unique formal structure was involved in it. There was no possibility for carrying over what one might have thought he learned about poetry in general from one work to an investigation of the next. For there was no poetry in general; there were only unique individual works. To attempt to apply any insights gleaned from an analysis of one work to an analysis of another would have made the critic aprioristic and therefore a Platonist rather than an Aristotelian.* Thus neither could there be at this stage any interest in poetic species.

But while these critics had induction at this stage they had little else that could be called a theory. Indeed it is instructive to note that this earlier work is not included in their recent anthological record of the school's achievement, *Critics and Criticism*. Apparently their individual analyses as well as new interpretations of the *Poetics* led them to see the possibility of developing a general theory of poetry. And in their more recent work there is a systematic aesthetic stemming from the *Poetics* and the extensions they claim to have made in its spirit.[14] As its first principle the system assumes imaginative literature to be an imitation of nature having

---

* I have already examined at length a similar failure to permit any comparisons between works or any carry-over from one work to the next in the unqualified version of the contextual theory. But, as the neo-Aristotelians are only too quick to point out, our critics, despite this theoretical orientation, do find some qualities to attribute to the nature of poetry in general.

pleasure as its end. The key to this approach is found in its scholastic division of literary works into species, each of which is defined
by the peculiar effect it is to arouse. Thus, in terms of their
strikingly obsolete psychology, if we may discover inductively
in a work the intention of arousing pity and fear, we know we
are dealing with tragedy; if amusement without pain, comedy (or
the "lout-comic"); if revenge, either serious or comic punitive
(or the "rogue-comic") depending on other factors. And so it
goes on into other species. All poetry aside from narrative and
dramatic is classified as lyric, and the lyric is further subdivided
according to its intended effect and its object of imitation.

These divisions are more than merely descriptive ones. It is
the determination of the species, according to the effect to be
aroused, that enables criticism to begin. The basic criteria for
all beauty are order and magnitude. Now Aristotle says of drama
that "the proper magnitude is comprised within such limits, that
the sequence of events, according to the law of probability or
necessity, will admit of a change from bad fortune to good, or from
good fortune to bad"; thus probability becomes a principal criterion. Of course probability is not to be taken in any simple
sense: it is not simply to be referred to life. If it were, it would
be mere possibility. But, on a more sophisticated level, artistic
probability is to be considered in terms of the fable created by
the author, in terms of his world. In an effective plot, concurrent
with probability and yet always consistent with it should be the
element of surprise, which may come in the form of such devices
as reversal of intention or discovery. The former and more effective
of these involves a result which is the opposite of what the actor
intended and which is brought about only by his intending its
opposite. Here is a concept which seems similar to the irony of
Richards or Brooks, except that it is founded on structure rather
than language. Since probability is the criterion by which all parts
of the work are to be judged, then the examination of the sets of
probabilities, long- and short-range, in terms of the final effect,
is the key to the determination of the species of any work and to
the judgment of its value as an example of that species. Despite

what may seem to be its affective orientation, this approach restricts itself completely to the poetic text. Specific attributes of the audience, considered as universal, may be ignored; and the intention, being the artistic intention, involves no personal reference to the author.

The system consistently adheres to Aristotle's four causes. Although Aristotle does not explicitly use this exhaustive analysis in the *Poetics*, his modern interpreters have introduced it into his definition of tragedy. The most important aspect of intended effect is the final cause, while the object of imitation is the formal cause, the manner of imitation (our modern "point of view") the efficient cause, and the means or medium of imitation (language) the lowly material cause. The object of imitation is of the greatest importance in determining the final effect; and we are always to assume that, except in lyric poetry, it is an *action* involving certain types of characters which is being imitated and which arouses the intended effect. In lyric poetry the object of imitation may be a character engaged in moral reflection, or a character in a state of passion as well as in action, but these alternatives are treated in an analogous fashion. It is perhaps this focus on action which has persuaded the system to be so completely absorbed in the structure of the incidents, that is to say, the progression of any work. The problem of manner or point of view enters the appraisal of a work with the question of what the author has chosen to include and what to omit, what to have shown and what merely reported to the audience. Problems of the "means," language in all literature, of course, are somewhat slighted as secondary matters which are merely to conform to the structural discoveries. But, except for the required fitness, diction is not made an important factor in our appreciation and judgment.

There may seem to be something circular in a system that first demands from each work a peculiar emotional effect, searches it out from the work's structure, and then judges the work by its conformity to this effect, which the systematic critic may very well have read into it.* But looking beyond the problem of logical

* This circularity as the critic moves from theory to practice is perhaps no

validity to that of aesthetic adequacy, we see that the system is a purely formalistic one in its restricted emphasis on the relation of the parts to the whole, in its disdain of questions about theme or meaning;[15] in its insistence, in other words, that the arousal of a peculiar kind of pleasure is the sufficient as well as a necessary cause of a literary product.

This exposition of the theory should make it clear that these critics can no longer claim the induction they have denied to other systematic critics. We have been told that all criticism is Platonic which sets forth an a priori ideal toward which all poetry must strive and then judges the work according to its approximation of this ideal. Thus this criticism deals not with the poem as poem but rather with the poem in relation to an extrapoetic conception. On the other hand, Aristotelian criticism is to be purely inductive, assigning all the nonpoetic properties of a work to other fields of discourse, so that questions of "thought," for example, not properly the business of *Poetics*, are to be turned over to *Rhetoric* for appropriate action, thereby allowing the Aristotelian a pleasant evasion of the thorny problem which concerns the meaning of poetry. Aristotelian criticism, then, in talking about poems, is to deal with their differentiae rather than their similarities. This may very well have been true of the earlier criticism of these neo-Aristotelians, which never did more than carry out structural analyses of individual poems. But as the Aristotelians have developed their general poetic theory, they have added the all-important aspect of final effect, toward which the formal properties are directed and in which the problem of species is resolved. If, as they sometimes seem to,[16] they still claim for the work, as a member of a species, the absolutely unique structure they spoke of in their earlier writings, they can now do it only at the price of inconsistency. Thus, while their system is as highly formalistic as I have observed it to be, it nevertheless rests on the primary assumption that the end of art is pleasure. And since

more evident here than it is with any of our critics or, indeed, with any critics who fit into the Chicagoans' "Platonic" category. But I am here trying primarily to show that the so-called Aristotelian is no longer any less essentially "Platonic" than are those he attacks.

the arousal of this peculiar pleasure is the key to judgment, then their system also depends on the adherence of literature to an extrapoetic ideal;* in terms of their critique of other theorists, it also is incapable of distinguishing poems from each other or poetry from other forms of discourse. It also, in short, must be placed in their category of the Platonic. Ransom sees a similar confusion in the claims of the Aristotelians. He observes the unqualified use of logical paraphrase in Elder Olson's analysis of "Sailing to Byzantium" coupled with a rejection of all extrapoetic "commonplaces." He asks,

How is Dr. Olson going to determine the logical organization of "Sailing to Byzantium" without applying the commonplaces of logic? And if he applies the logical commonplaces—as he does— what is the objection to the moral ones? [17]

It would seem, then, that little is to be gained, even in the face of the dead ends to which contextualism may lead us, by abandoning an interest in language for a non-linguistic interest in a disembodied structure; that we cannot hope to distinguish poetry from other forms of discourse effectively enough to allow a workable critical theory unless we concentrate on the primary importance of the poet's medium. The Aristotelians have helped to show us, however, that all discourse—prose as well as poetry—is characterized and in part determined by a systematic context. They have shown us also the value of supplementing the linguistic analysis of poetry with an analysis that takes into account certain

* The affective interests of the Aristotelians may seem to rest on a psychology which can hardly claim support from current empirical approaches to this science. To their obsolete psychologizing they may wish to add the common but questionable belief that the poetic pleasure is unique in its kind, so that poems in the service of this end are not in the service of an objective broader than poetry. We find Aristotle himself arguing for the claim that pleasures differ in kind one from another ("Nichomachean Ethics," *The Basic Works of Aristotle*, ed. Richard McKeon, New York, 1941, pp. 1097–1102). But some psychologists (and I assume that pleasure is their business) would be quick to point out that it would be hard indeed to demonstrate that pleasures themselves, in abstraction from the objects that produce them, differ in kind. Rather it would seem that what defines the specific felt character of a pleasure is the object that arouses it, so that pleasure qua pleasure, as a subjective phenomenon, varies only in the degree of its intensity. According to this view, the pleasure of a poem differs from the pleasure of something else—a quintet

traditional formal patterns. That is, they have helped us to see that these conventional patterns, which are, after all, a significant aspect of the literary medium, are structural affairs of genre as well as linguistic affairs of meter and rhyme.* Thus, if we are to improve upon the prose-poetry distinction examined in this section, we must work toward a theory which, still linguistic in its focus, adds an interest in the structure of all discourse and in the traditional formal structures of poetic discourse to the restricted interest in semantics which has characterized the work of those critics who have thought of the referential and the contextual, respectively, as distinguishing prose and poetry.[18]

or a ball game—by virtue of the difference between the poem and the something else: a poetic pleasure is no more than a pleasure produced by poetry rather than by something else. And to dedicate poetry to this end is hardly to remain within a poetic ideal. Further, the problem of distinguishing between the pleasure-producing objects, the poem and the something else—apart from their subjective effects—still remains unsolved by the Aristotelian. (See my similar discussion of Eliot's concern with aesthetic emotions in the notes on pp. 49 and 50.)

* It should be needless to add that the neo-Aristotelians would hardly assent to my translating their idea of species into the mechanical recognition of conventional formal patterns. I realize how violently I am wrenching this idea from *their* systematic context. But at this late point I am no longer trying to do justice to their theory, since I have already (and I hope with justice) rejected it. I am rather trying only to appropriate from their approach what hints I can, for aid in the finding of a direction to be explored by contextual theorists who feel as I do the need for a new access to their problems, but one which will not force them to abandon their orientation.

# Chapter 10

# A Note on the Objectivity of Value

THE theory of the poetic object entered upon in this section presupposes that, as aesthetic object, the poem is an independent entity containing aesthetic value. The definition of the aesthetic experience, advanced above, formed the basis on which it was possible to conceive what the poem ought to be in order to force this experience upon the reader whom it was trying to bring under its control. Thus the objectivity of value, hardly a universally accepted view today, has been assumed. And I do not want here to enter the highly technical realms of value-theory and epistemology in order to argue for this assumption and thus to defend the philosophical validity of an objective theory. Rather, in concluding this section I should like to examine, in light of the claims which have been lodged against its practicality and adequacy, the advantages of an objective theory to criticism in general and in particular to the kind of criticism being pursued by the critics here under study.

The various modern modifications of relativism seem to use several fashionable and almost predictable arguments as they dutifully snipe away at theories that postulate a noncontingent aesthetic value in the art object. The long and rich tradition that stands under these more universalistic theories does not disturb the progressive modern. Like his positivistic allies in the sciences, he finds that mere age provides the best indication of where next he is to strike. The word has long been out now in naturalistic value theory, and not the most moderate syllable of it can allow for value-realism. Like other values, aesthetic value must never be seen to exist prior to the relationship of object and subject, whether value be said to exist in the subject or in the relationship itself. But objective theorists have convincingly insisted that there is an either/or in the ontology of value: it is either created or it is discovered. Once the complete objectivity of the latter alternative is scorned, no matter what the qualifications, the resulting position, it can be argued, can be shown to reduce itself to subjectivism and thereby to place itself outside the pale of normative considerations.[1]

But here I want rather to consider the charges against the claim for the phenomenal objectivity of value; and we should expect them to be grave indeed, since they call upon us to give up the immense convenience of judging objects as aesthetically good or bad for the refuge of psychological, sociological, or historical *maybe's*. For my present purposes, I shall skirt the epistemological arguments which, of course, lie at the root of the dispute but upon which so many fine minds have expended so much energy, and shall limit myself to the charges of methodological inadequacy which have been levelled at the objectivists. For, in this skeptical age, if objectivism—a position which ultimately demands certain metaphysical assumptions—be denied even the claim of being adequate to our experience, then it probably has little left with which to tempt the incredulous but still uncommitted observer of our philosophic scene.

One of the commonest complaints against objectivism can, in its most basic terms, be put this way: how can value be said to reside in the object prior to my interest when judgments vary so enormously, even judgments of the most universally acclaimed critics? How can it be denied, then, that judgments are largely controlled by the interests of the judge? But, it may be countered, who would deny that subjective interests influence the judgment of the best of us? I am arguing not the uniformity of taste, eighteenth-century fashion, but the objectivity of value. To assert not only that values reside in the object but also that any one of us or any group of us can discover them adequately would be to proclaim a very rare kind of absolutism (or shall I say dogmatism?) indeed. But is it being proclaimed or is it a very convenient and very mythical straw man? The matter would seem to be disposed of efficiently with the claim that evaluation need not be either correct or incorrect; it only need be corrigible with reference to a norm.[2] This, however, involves a distinction between what is and what ought to be, a distinction which no relativist or relationalist can consistently make.

But what must be seen also is the radical circularity which orients this charge against objectivism. Values are assumed, in such an argument, either to reside or not to reside within the object depending on whether or not various gifted observers agree upon them. This in turn assumes, however, that the value of an aesthetic experience is identical with the value of the object, or, to be more precise, that the value of the object is inseparable from and reducible to that of the experience. But this is the very point at issue. For the objectivist is claiming, as it was claimed in my earlier discussion of the aesthetic experience, that the object has a value which is distinct from any experience of it. This position can hardly be refuted by beginning with the assumption that no completely objective value is possible. Yet the initial confusion of the aesthetic experience with the aesthetic object, of universal agreement with objectivism, makes this tautology inescapable for the relativist.

A common variety of this objection, but one that raises some special problems, comes from the historical branch of relativism.[3] The historicist asserts that art may be judged only in terms of the aesthetic values of the era which produced and received it. Thus "the poetry of an age never goes wrong." [4] Obviously, reduced to its presuppositions, this position can scarcely treat value as resident within the object. On the philosophic level, the objectivist would answer the arguments of this school much as he would the others of the relativist group to which it belongs. But even if the objectivist can dismiss the "intentional fallacy" and consider the work as a separate entity, an objective world of values, he still must account for the historically various ways in which these values are embodied artistically. In other words, what place can he give in evaluation to the particular tradition which plays so large a part in fashioning the work? For if aesthetic value is "discoverable" in the object and is therefore noncontingent, how, then, shall he handle the highly variable element of historical convention?

One current attempt to mediate this problem returns us to a modified relativism. In an effort to avoid subjectivism, it has been claimed that an observer's set of expectations with respect to a work of art may legitimately be broadened by other sets of expectations so that he may more completely see what is there before him to be judged.[5] But if this is the relational theory it purports to be, so that value is contingent upon the expectations, then with reference to what norm can these expectations be considered as corrigible? The only consistent answer would be the "vitalistic" one: the wider and more inclusive the sets of expectations, the better. But this would involve our admitting indiscriminately any and all of the possible expectations, a consequence to which few proponents of this position would very happily assent. Yet with value considered a relational matter, there is no basis for exclusion, for the determination of better or worse expectations.

The objectivist must come to terms with this problem differently. First, he would insist that the historical relativist goes much too far, since he uses history not only to explicate the work but also to judge it. For the historicist a work becomes good or bad only in terms of a cultural relativism, and certainly he never dares outlaw an entire period, an entire set of aesthetic values. For they were right for some people. No, for the historicist art "never goes wrong." At the same time, the objectivist would differentiate his position from that of the so-called absolutist with whom, unfortunately, he has invariably been identified. For the absolutist, at the other extreme, would see aesthetic value as so universal an essence that no temporal contingencies can enter into any relations with it. Thus, with the historical relativist on the one hand and the absolutist on the other, we are given the inescapable alternative of all or none with respect to the use of tradition. But to clarify and defend the distinction between absolutism and objectivism, it is necessary to deal immediately with the gravest of the charges of relativism. And the answer to this charge should help solve the other problems which have been bothering us here.

As my discussion of I. A. Richards has shown,[6] the absolutist has often been attacked because he disdains analysis; because, that is, while asserting the independent existence of value, he asserts also that this value, being purely intuited, is therefore unrelated to the objective features of the work. In other words, in some Idealistic fashion he divorces the aesthetic value of the work from its sensuous structure. He must dismiss all technical disputes about artistic success or failure, however objectively grounded these may be, as mere scholastic quibbles. For to analyze structure is to involve "reason" in the investigation of a quality which presents itself nonrationally to our faculty of intuition. This amorphous absolute can have nothing to do with an intellect which, in the case of beauty, must "murder to dissect." But this view of beauty as an objective quality sacrifices all the advantages for criticism with which objectivity presents us. If intuitions cannot be defended with reference to features of the object which are open to inspection (and even the attempt at rationalization is not allowed), then for all practical purposes we are returned to the unmitigated relativism which this theory has challenged. The hard-won distinction between the value of an object in experience and the value of the experience once more collapses. The "thereness" of value, remaining ineffable, serves only to remove aesthetics to the realm of faith.

There is no need, however, for the vulnerability of this position to be assumed by the objectivist. Vivas, for example, is not touched by this most powerful argument against absolutism. For the purposes of criticism he, in Kantian fashion, restricts our concern with objective value to the phenomenal level. As critic he can treat only those values which are "anchored" to the sharable and analyzable structure into which the medium has been manipulated. Clearly this procedure follows consistently from what we have seen to be his conception of the aesthetic experience. While he does not dispute the validity of subjective "unanchored" values, he insists that these, belonging to the subjective experience rather than to the object, can, in view of his discussion of the aesthetic experience, claim no share in our critical judgment of the object as aesthetic. And this because artistic creation takes place in an objective medium which is intrinsically hospitable to a structure that is open to analysis. The artist's success, then, or to put it more critically, the value of his object, is contingent phenomenally only upon the resident capacity of his perceptible structure to house this value. For even if values—unlike secondary qualities to which they must not be reduced—cannot themselves be analyzed, the structure which contains them can be. And if the objectivist cannot prove beauty as he can prove certain describable structural relationships, these relationships may still help him show why he predicates beauty of the object.

Value, then, may ultimately be an intuitive affair for the objectivist also; but rather than the ungrounded and immediate nature of the absolutist's intuitions of value, those of the objectivist, insofar as the intuited value is "anchored," have the mediating properties of the object to permit as well as to justify them. The critic's discourse can lead us toward the value, if not right up to it. If this view reveals the imperfections of critical judgment and thus restricts the critic to a very modest objective, then it tells us no more than we have always known. For the discovery of poetic value rests finally with each of the other fallible members of the poet's audience in his firsthand experience of the poem.

Now the question of history and tradition can be answered, while the untenable extremes of historical relativism and absolutism are equally avoided. If the critic is to reveal the structure which contains the aesthetic worth or poverty of the work, he must use every possible resource in his attempt to discover it. As R. P. Blackmur puts it, "the critic brings to consciousness the means of performance." [7] In order to fulfill this function, the critic is heavily dependent upon all kinds of relevant data. Varying traditions produce different ways of structuring a given medium. And the structure must be disclosed if the work is to be brought to its full "performance" potential. Thus the objective critic can say that while artistic conventions may be historically relative, so that one must be aware of the various methods of molding a structure, yet the structure and the values embedded in it are themselves universally "there," whether or not we have the sensitivity, impartiality, and knowledge to perceive them. For example, what history can tell us about the meanings of words or the function of line and stanza forms in poetry, about the choice of two- or three-dimensional space in painting, all this and much besides must enter into any analysis of the objective qualities in a work. The relativity of artistic means does not prevent the objectivity of judgment; on the contrary, it makes objectivity possible.

I realize that there may be some dissatisfaction with my terminology, especially since objectivism and absolutism have been so commonly confused, both as terms and as concepts. This should not, however, lessen the importance of the distinction between them. The conflict between objectivism and absolutism—and I have wanted to demonstrate that there is one—may be seen on the philosophic level as somewhat akin to that between Realism and Idealism. Perhaps one may prefer these not much less ambiguous terms. But in any case it should be clear that the departure from even the most objective of objective relativisms does not necessitate an escape to untouchable intuitive absolutes. Quite the opposite is true. The relativist, in his anxiety to counter with analysis the critical "dead end" [8] of absolutism, has been forced to analyze many factors (e.g., psychological states of mind and sociological-historical data) besides the work of art and to count heavily upon these factors in rendering his judgment. And even as a measure of objectivity is added to his relativism, the merger becomes a specious one, since the relativist has already cut his normative ground from under him. The objectivist must appeal only, and again and again, to the work and the structure he sees in it. It would be folly to claim that his judgment of any work need be any sounder than that of a relativist, for a philosophic position is hardly a critical cure-all. But objectivism alone can, with logical consistency, at least give its proponent the knowledge that he may be wrong with respect to other judgments and not merely different from them: he is enabled to debate the issue. It can free him from the feeling of incorrigibility and, consequently, from the spiritual pride which underlies absolutism as well as relativism, and can return him to the humility which is both proper and profitable for an imperfect humanity striving to appreciate its noblest accomplishments.

# THE FUNCTION OF POETRY: SCIENCE, POETRY, AND COGNITION

# Some Older Theories about Poetry and Truth

THE particular formulations given to the creative process and to the aesthetic object by the theories I have been tracing are necessitated by the role many new critics insist poetry must play in the human economy. The peculiar function they wish to attribute to poetry is, as it is in most theories, the primary consideration out of which the rest of their theories grow. And yet, in order to serve my interest in the analysis of these theories rather than in their genesis, I can best treat the function of poetry after trying to determine how the poem comes to be created and what, having been thus created, the poem really is. In other words, I have treated first the various factors within the aesthetic process: the creation and the experience of the art object and the kind of object demanded by the creation and the experience. I have now to consider what service this process performs for those who are involved in it.

There are several modes of activity with respect to which we may justly ask about the service poetry performs: we may ask, for example, about poetry's social or political function, about its moral function, about its religious function. Or—and I mean to separate this from the others—we may ask about its cognitive function. It would seem that this problem stands apart from the others and even, perhaps, above them; or at least it would seem to be logically prior to them. For what we think about the social, the moral, or the religious function of poetry depends largely on what we

conceive to be the capacity poetry has to make meaningful statements about these spheres of human activity; and to determine
this capacity we must know whether poetry can make meaningful
statements about anything. In this section, then, my concern will
be restricted to the cognitive claims which poetry can make. If
these claims should be settled, the other functions which may be
attributed to poetry would follow accordingly.

The charge which more than any other has been hurled against
the critics who concern me is that theirs is a formalistic theory of
criticism, one which may be summed up by the familiar phrase, "art
for art's sake." [1] To treat this theory purely as formalistic would
make the handling of this section a very simple matter, since an
"art for art's sake" theory could have nothing to say about the
relation of art to life or about the extra-aesthetic functions of art.
If this were the case, then all that has been urged here about the
organic unity of the poetic context would have been falsely urged.
For what lies at the root of the contextual theory is an insistence
upon the indissolubility of form and content in the analytical or
critical act as well as in the act of perception. It must be claimed,
therefore, that those who launch the charge of formalism are
themselves so trapped by the form-content dichotomy that once
they perceive that a critic does not talk about a separable subject
matter—as our critics certainly do not—they see no alternative but
to label him a pure formalist. To satisfy them a critic would be
required simply to wrench from the poetic context, however dis-
tortedly, meanings which he wishes to relate directly to an extra-
aesthetic interest, regardless of the way these are related organically to the other aesthetic elements which make up the poem.

In terms of my review of them, it may be claimed that the
critics being studied, consciously or otherwise, undertake the more
complex task of approaching the object as aesthetic and yet insisting that, while remaining an aesthetic object, it has the capacity—
and a unique capacity—to influence life. Thus they would have to
maintain that while the aesthetic object does have extra-aesthetic
effects, these effects can be properly produced only when the object
first functions in its aesthetic capacity. Theirs is the firm convic-

tion that poetry is intimately related to life. Indeed they allow poetry to be a greater force in our other activities than could be allowed by a conception of poetry which would treat it as more immediately and directly influential. Thus a distinction must be made between a belief in the autonomy of poetry and a belief in poetry for poetry's sake; the theory toward which this essay means to point would embrace the former and reject the latter. This distinction is crucial, and on it hinges the value for poetics of the theoretical direction I have been investigating. For the autonomy of poetry, I must emphasize, is asserted solely to ensure that, when poetry is asked to serve other interests, it function as only poetry can.

A careful examination is required here to determine just what kind of meaning, in terms of this theory, poetry can be said to have for the complete human being who struggles to appreciate and to use it. It seems profitable first to inspect analytically and exemplify historically the several most common positions critical theorists have had with respect to the relation between poetry and truth. The history of criticism through the nineteenth century seems to feature four general positions, although there are, of course, many variations of each of them.

Before beginning, I should mention that I am not granting a separate position to the imitation theory. For the pure imitationist who takes his imitation seriously, truth simply means lifelikeness. Since the form of the poem is given the artist from the outside, it is his task merely to record this form effectively. Thus if the objects pictured in a work correspond to their counterparts in nature, then for the pure imitationist the work is true, that is, true-to-life. But the imitation theory—except perhaps at times for Plato, and he used it to derogate poetry—has rarely if ever been proposed in these literal terms. Even Aristotle qualifies it by distinguishing art from life when he claims that poetry is more universal than history since history tells us what is and poetry tells us what may be in terms of the laws of probability and necessity.[2] Once the meaning of the term "imitation" begins thus to be stretched, it seems never to spring back to its original limits. Aside from minor perversions of the word which came and went in the history of its use,[3] imitation of nature came commonly to mean with later critics the imitation of general or universal nature. Thus Johnson requires of imitation that it deal with the species rather than the individual.[4] But since in life we are given only particulars, if the poet literally imitates he is not going to come out with general types. In what sense, then, without stretching the word to the point of meaninglessness, can the poet who follows Johnson's prescription be said to be imitating? Some metaphysics may support the claim that there are essences and universals in nature, but they are hardly obvious to the eye. In any case it should be clear that for the later so-called imitationists the truth of a poem would depend on the validity of the general statements it makes or illustrates, since the representative type given us in the poem would have to be a sign pointing to a universal. But this claim that poetry yields general truths characterizes one of the four positions on poetry and truth which I am about to examine. Since it is not a claim that stems from a theory of strict imitation and since almost all so-called imitationists distort the concept of imitation in order to make this claim, it does not seem that the only unique position the imitation theory could hold about poetic truth—that of immediate fidelity to nature—merits consideration here.

The first position to be examined here is that of Plato in his *Republic* and of some Elizabethan Puritans. It maintains that the poet, with respect to universal truths, is a liar.[5] Plato maintains that, as a mere imitator of worldly imitations of ideal truths, the poet is too far removed from the universals. Further he is too concerned with arousing the passions of his audience to restrict himself to the reasonability of any truths he may know. Thus the function of poetry, according to this position, ought to be that of yielding propositional truth. But poetry cannot yield propositional truth and therefore ought to be damned. There are, then, two parts to this position: One states what the function of poetry ought to be and the other states that in fact poetry is incapable of so functioning.

## Some Theories about Poetry and Truth

Each of the remaining three positions stems from one of the two parts of the first position. Each accepts one of the two statements and contradicts the other. Thus the second position would agree that poetry ought to yield propositional truth and that, contrary to Plato, it does in fact do so. The third and fourth positions would agree with Plato's other statement while contradicting the first: Poetry does not in fact yield propositional truth, but ought not to do so since it has another function. These two positions disagree about what this other function ought to be. Let us examine each of these three positions more closely.

Sir Philip Sidney, in *An Apology for Poetry*, is a representative and extremely systematic exponent of the second position, although he does not differ essentially from the majority of Renaissance and later neoclassicists or for that matter, from many critics we have had since.[6] Sidney reverses Plato in order to justify poetry in terms of its Platonic function. Plato, he claims, in denying to poetry the capacity to give propositional truth, is really attacking not all poetry but the abuses of inferior poets. Sidney sees poetry, as does Aristotle, as better than history, but in addition for Sidney, poetry, when properly practiced, is better than philosophy too. History describes particulars only; as descriptive it can never give us universal truth or tell us how to act. Philosophy can do both, but its terms are too general for us to apply the universal truth or general precept to the individual case. Poetry surpasses history in that it tells us how life *ought* to be and surpasses philosophy in that it gives us the particular example. In this way Sidney solves the ever present problem of poetic theory, which asks how poetry can be at once universal and particular. For him poetry is allegory; it is argument by example rather than by the abstract or syllogistic reasoning, which characterized so much of philosophy for so long. Thus poetry becomes a kind of inductive philosophizing; its proper function, which the proper poet can ably make it serve, is propositional truth. In such a poetics, where the only justification of poetry is the truth it exemplifies, it is difficult to see how those qualities that make poetry poetry and not another thing—to use Eliot's phrase—could be viewed as more than what has so frequently been termed the sugar-coating of the pill. It may be a simplification, but hardly an unjust reduction, to claim that this is no more than a decoration-theory which cannot give a unique role to poetry, and to claim also that any theorist who maintains that poetry can and ought to yield propositional truth inescapably joins Sidney in his limited view.

The third position, theoretically considered, is ultimately that of aesthetic hedonism. As I have anticipated, it grants Plato's claim that poetry cannot give us propositional truth. But, it goes on, there is no reason why poetry should be concerned with knowledge. Why not let this concern be saved for those more austere disciplines like science or philosophy which are explicitly governed by it? And if these writers deny to poetry any cognitive function whatsoever, then they usually are forced to claim that the only justification for its existence is the pleasure it can provide. Since poetry can make no meaningful statement about life, then obviously, not being granted the capacity to function cognitively, neither can it have any other function with respect to our other modes of activity. If it cannot minister to our interests as knowers and doers, then it must be said to minister to our emotions. If the second position largely concentrated on the content or teaching aspects of poetry, this position largely concentrates on the formal or pleasing aspects of poetry.

This position has only been less widely held than the second I have examined, although as far as any common acceptance is concerned, it is a relative newcomer to the critical scene. Among the Italian critics of the sixteenth century there were but a very few, notably Castelvetro and Mazzoni, who, in the midst of the flourishing of didactic theories, variously expounded forms of this heresy.[7] Both these men seem to accept Plato's attack on poetry and merely shift the defense to other aspects of poetry by claiming, though in different ways, that, as pleasure-giving, it is its own justification. But this justification comes at a high price. For implicit in Castelvetro and explicit in Mazzoni is the concession that, after all, poetry is not a very important part of man's activities. While it may be needed as an escape from our more serious affairs, it does not bear at all significantly upon our conducting of these affairs. This seems from the first to be the cost of buying for art an autonomy so complete that the separation of art from life once made, there is no possibility of return. This position, only a faint, dissident voice in the Renaissance, was comparatively without adherents until the nineteenth century. But from the time that Gautier enunciated the slogan "l'art pour l'art," the movement grew. It has since dominated the French Symbolist and English Aesthetic movements. And more recently it has dominated the "formalists" in the plastic arts, like Clive Bell and Roger Fry,[8] and as we have already seen in detail, those who may very well form the only equivalent school in current literary criticism, the neo-Aristotelians.

The many forms that this position has taken indicate equally that once older critics have denied literature any cognitive function—and, consequently, any practical function—unless they have been ready to dispense with it altogether, as Plato seems to have been, they have been likely to give it some hedonistic function.* Conversely, critics who have seen art's primary purpose as hedonistic, have refused to allow it to compete with the more ascetic knowledge-giving disciplines. But in taking this position these critics have had to deny literature any real importance in the human economy. Now it is true that many of the art-for-art's-sake theorists have claimed that aesthetic pleasure is the most important part of our lives so long as we can keep the pleasure purely aesthetic. These theorists might not be able to substantiate psychologically the claim that pleasures as subjective phenomena—that is, in abstraction from the objects that arouse them—are different in kind one from another.[9] And if pleasures do not so differ, so that aesthetic pleasure qua pleasure could not be clearly dis-

---

* Occasionally such a critic has disguised his intention by claiming to defend poetry as functioning not for a commonplace pleasure but for its own sake alone. But invariably we find somewhere the appeal to pleasure, even if it be to the pure and rarefied aesthetic pleasure—a concept which, like that of aesthetic emotion, I have already had occasion to question (see note on p. 154 and also notes on pp. 49, 50).

tinguished from other pleasures, then their justification collapses and poetry for them could easily be replaced by another pleasure-giving stimulant. But even if we grant the questionable claim that aesthetic pleasure is a pleasure unique in its kind, we are not much better off. For if we view the matter from the standpoint of society and culture, from the standpoint of men's other and more time-consuming activities, we must recognize—unless we are to make the serious and prideful error of denying significance to all but aesthetic activities—that art considered as pleasure-provoking only (no matter how rare its kind of pleasure) may not seem sufficiently important to justify all the effort men have put into creating it, even when there was little promise of reward, and all the effort societies have put into sustaining it, even when their resources were too taxed to allow them to sustain some more practical activities, to say nothing of more commonly, if more vulgarly, pleasurable activities.

Like the third position, the fourth admits Plato's charge that poetry does not produce what we would term propositional truth but denies that poetry ought to concern itself with this inferior kind of truth. Rather proponents of this position claim that poetry is dedicated only to what it terms intuitive or imaginative truth; and it is this intuitive, rather than propositional, truth that is the highest form of knowledge. Now this opposition between propositional and intuitive or imaginative truth is a rather awkward one. Normally we mean by truth that which is capable of being formulated into demonstrable propositions, although the principle of verification would vary widely as we moved from one science to another, from science to philosophy, and from one philosophic system to another. And it is irrelevant to our purposes to argue here how untranscendental a philosophy must be in order for its statements to be considered propositions capable of verification. At any rate, this would not seem to be a problem capable of solution on a priori grounds, since surely even the vaguest of our thinkers, so long as they choose to present their ideas in philosophic form, do so in an effort to expound what seem to them to be truthful propositions. Thus when we characterize truth as propositional, we are characterizing it in accordance with the form in which it appears.

But claims to intuitive truth also may be and are formulated into propositions. For what would characterize truth as intuitive is not its formulation but the way in which it was apprehended. One comes at truth, for the intuitionist, through the immediacy of an act of imagination and not through the mediating powers of reasoning, whether it be reasoning about abstractions or upon mere observation. It must, however, be granted too that the intuitionist would deny the efficacy of attempts to verify his truths. They are intuited and as intuited are self-evidently known. The defenders of intuitive or imaginative truth have usually opposed their kind of truth to what they have preferred to call "rational" rather than "propositional" truth, allowing this opposition to reflect the opposition in their transcendental psychology between the faculties of imagination and of reason. While this mentalistic terminology would hardly be widely acceptable today, it does enable us to see how an independent position was found which could dedicate poetry to truth without making it, as Sidney did, an auxiliary to philosophy. For the intuitionist scorned that kind of truth which was the product of reason or which depended for its validity on rational or empirical verification.

As I have observed, this romantic and irrationalistic position clearly rests on the postulation of a faculty of imagination which is superior in its vision to the faculty of reason. Since we can arrive at intuitive truth only through poetry or another form of imaginative art, art usually becomes for the intuitionist the most important cognitive activity of man. The first hint we get of this position may very well also come from Plato who in his *Ion* pictures the poet as divinely inspired and even as possessed. He is the man chosen by the gods to intuit the highest truths.* This definition of the poet was developed into the first theories of

---

* The ambivalence in Plato's attitude toward poetry is a reflection of the dual picture we have of him as rationalist and as mystic—the Plato of the dialectic and the Plato of the myths. Some commentators may resolve this inconsistency on the matter of poetry by claiming that in the *Republic* Plato's attitude is conditioned by his objective, the setting up in rational terms of an

imagination by Dion Chrysostom, Philostratus, and finally by the neo-Platonic Plotinus. But it does not attain its most systematic and influential expression until the conception of imagination becomes a central concern of German absolute Idealism and is passed on to segments of British as well as of German romanticism.

This position would seem to demand a special metaphysic. If we look, for example, at the influential theory of Schelling,[10] the theory that provided Coleridge with his concept of imagination, we find that he can grant such cognitive powers to the imagination only because he posits a monistic universe whose divine essence or ground lies immanently within every particular object. If the whole is in every part and never exists except in the part—if the ground, in other words, is only immanent and never transcendent—then only by fully apprehending the part can we intuit the indwelling whole. This activity certainly is not to be entrusted to our abstract reasoning power, which can never fully appreciate the particular. Nor need our intuition be subject, like propositional truth, to a rational check since imagination, beyond reason, can hardly be contained by the inferior disciplines which reason provides. The imagination, then, is the faculty which produces art since it captures the particular completely and sees through it to the underlying essence.

Schelling has taken one reckless step beyond his master, Kant. From Kant he learned that the understanding can never see an object in its particularity. Kant claimed also that the imagination treated the object *as if* it held a telic significance, *as if* it revealed the operation of an objective will which lay behind and structured the phenomena of the universe. But in Kant's scheme the imagination could so conceive the universe and the object only in order to create beauty; it could so conceive them only because it could not know. There is no question of the imagination taking its

ideally successful state. How much less stern his judgment would be in another context is a matter of conjecture. In any case the Plato of the *Ion* laid much of the groundwork of romantic aesthetics just as the Plato of the *Republic* furnished the neoclassicists, thanks to the qualifications of Aristotle, with the theory of imitation and, thanks to the qualifications of Horace, with a moral objective for poetry.

supposition seriously as knowledge.[11] But Schelling, and Coleridge after him in his less dualistic moments, claimed that the act of the imagination—the perception of a particular and seemingly lifeless object, which infuses it, through the power of mind, with the dynamic essence of the universe—is literally an act of cognition, the most crucial act of cognition we can perform. Of course the relation between the universal and particular given us by Schelling is not at all like that of Sidney. Sidney considered poetry, with its use of particulars, as another path to propositional truth— from below, as it were, rather than from above. For Schelling the truth of poetry is the only final truth. Truth comes intuitively or it comes not at all.

We have, then, to consider the merits of three of these positions; the first position need not concern us here since the assumption is that we want to defend rather than to abolish poetry. Indeed if poetry did not have its great staying power, it would have vanished long ago. To summarize briefly, we may say of the positions remaining that the second position claims that poetry through example yields propositional truth, the third that poetry has nothing to do with knowledge but exists for the pleasure it furnishes, and the fourth that poetry yields intuitive truth which is the kind of truth most worth having. A brief survey of the way in which certain developments in the history of ideas affected these theories, coupled with a further examination into their theoretical adequacy, should bring clearly into focus the demands made upon the modern theorist.

We may begin by asking why the pleasure-theory gained so wide a following during the nineteenth century. The historical reasons for the fact that this position did not attain great popularity until then are not far to seek. From the start of the Renaissance, science was making serious inroads into what had previously been thought of as the area of the humanities. Science was constantly refining its procedures and getting more and more spectacular results from them. And these results were increasingly exact, as well as increasingly predictive—more so than the results of any of the fuzzier disciplines could hope to be. Finally the inevitable day came when, inflated with the successes of science, some of its idolaters (they could hardly be called purely scientific themselves) pushed the application of scientific method—which, by their redefining of truth, they made the only path to knowledge—into fields with respect to which they had no evidence to support such application.

Out of this reductionism arose scientific positivism. Knowledge had to allow of proof in the laboratory manner or it was not knowledge. Since even speculative philosophy was driven to cover so that eventually even the word *metaphysics* found itself in bad repute, what claims could possibly be made for the cognitive powers of literature? For philosophy always had disciplines which were directed only to enquiry after truth. If its methods were denied, what could be said for poetry whose disciplines and techniques have always served other gods, even in the days when poets thought they were serving truth as well? What, other than pleasure, then, could now be said to be the function of poetry by those who thought they had to justify, if they were to preserve, its existence?

I have thus far speculated generally about why the denial of truth to poetry came about and I showed earlier why any position that stems from this denial necessarily fails to do justice to the immense importance which poetry, or any other art, for that matter, has always had in all societies. But what are the alternatives of this theory, in view of the advance of science? Now the position that poetry gives us propositional truth has been by far the most popular one in the history of criticism. But if positivism has helped to demolish this claim, it has done aesthetics a real service. For actually, long before this position was challenged by science it was hardly one that could either do justice to poetry or give it a thoroughly unique function. Poetry, it claims, gives us particular illustrations of propositional truths. There are several weaknesses here, as we have seen. If poetry gives us propositional truth through arguing by examples, then poetry exists primarily for its "message" and the content of poetry is irrecoverably separated from the form, which can act only as embellishment. Why, in this case, bother with the poem? Why should we not be given the message straight out instead of being tricked into accepting it by the pleasantries of language? If we are told that the pleasantries help to persuade, we may still observe that the distinction between poetry and rhetoric has been lost. For the truth itself, which poetry is illustrating, can be discovered by other more rational, if less pleasurable, techniques. Indeed, this justification of poetry can hardly be said to justify its existence at all. The importance of poetry's role in the human economy is as much undermined by this position as it is by aesthetic hedonism. If, on the one hand, the hedonist sees poetry as occupying—from the standpoint of moral and cognitive pursuits—a pure but insignificant place, unburdened by life and possibly replaceable by the latest gadget of the Huxleyan nightmare, our brave new world; the allegorist, on the other hand, sees poetry as philosophy's handmaiden who, for all her beauty, may if necessary be forsaken when the queen's throne is threatened.

Paradoxical as it may sound, this feeble defense of poetry could be offered only at a time when no stronger one was needed, when poetry was flourishing, when its role was secure and its existence not seriously threatened. For at that time the only serious complaints about poetry concerned its morality. Its apologists could justify poetry on moral grounds without probing the problem to its roots. Since philosophy itself was still not endangered, poetry had merely to be made into philosophy. Poetry was not, as it recently has seemed to be, with its back to the wall, having to show that it has a unique function or none at all that is really serious.

When this view of poetry as allegory is revealed in its stark clarity, there appears another reason for the rise of the art-for-art's-sake position. For the poet was left with so little to do, the unified context of his poem was so utterly disrupted, the prolonged and difficult struggle of the artist with his medium so neglected—and all for the sake of a "message" that was hardly intrinsic to the poetry at all—that to save his technique, the artist's contact with reality was to be relinquished. If the allegorist, working with a rigid form-content dichotomy, seized upon the content and hoped only that the form would be suitably palatable, the hedonist, accepting the terms of the allegorist, seized worshipfully upon the form in utter disdain of the content. The critical position into which scientism has thrust poetry, is, ironically, a blessing for those who theorize about it. For now poetry must be justified as an irreplaceable discipline or it is simply to be relegated to an insignificant place among our playthings.

The other position, the fourth, in many ways the position of Coleridge at those times when he was closer to Schelling than to Kant, does attempt to give poetry a unique role; it does so, as we have seen, by denying the value of rational truth in order to assert the primacy of intuitive or imaginative truth. Insofar as it seems to give poetry a peculiar and important function, this position would appear to meet the theoretical problem more cogently than do the others. But is the function it attributes to poetry really a unique one after all? I have shown in my earlier sections that this romantic theory has several difficulties. Although it was designed specifically to meet the challenge of science, somehow it fostered a poetry that ended by competing with science. This may not be accidental. It may very well be claimed that it was the failure of this theory to differentiate poetry from science by grounding poetry in a language context that led to the flabby philosophical poetry which it often sponsored. For, after all, we have observed that there is no reason why intuitions cannot be expressed in propositional form. Since a proper distinction can be made between intuitive and rational truth but not between intuitive and propositional truth, the distinction can be seen to be founded on psychology rather than on the work done. In the discourse itself it may tend to disappear. Thus principally, as my examination of Hulme was intended to reveal, the theory is too completely focused on the faculty of mind and too slightly on the objective stuff of the poem. The creative power it postulates is not sufficiently bound to matter; it need not work in a medium. The imagination merely perceives and, perceiving, knows. And the working poet, provided he has the visionary power, need not indulge in the give-and-take struggle with language in order to crystallize his insights. If the seer chooses to write poetry, he is condescending to communicate his prior revelations, so that the poet appears simply to be the mystic who has chosen to share his "vision splendid."

When carefully examined, then, this theory does not give poetry the unique role it may at first seem to give it. For the imagination and the truth it yields are not solely in the service of poetry; rather poetry is but a translation of this irrational approach to knowledge. And once again the poem is seen as the ornament for a pre-existing entity. As Sidney made of poetry the handmaiden of rational philosophy, so the romantics make of it a handmaiden of mysticism. This neglect of language as necessary for the realization of the poet's insights can have regrettable practical consequences, as so much romantic poetry shows us. With so much emphasis on the uninhibited expression of the poet's intuitions and so little emphasis on the controlling disciplines of the linguistic medium, it is inevitable that what we get so often is not poetry at all. But to proceed further would be to indulge in further repetition of what has been discussed frequently and in detail throughout my first section.

Neither can this Idealistic theory be utterly discounted, however. For to retreat to a complete Realism, one which would deny completely the poet's creativity, would be to return to a naive theory of imitation in which we would again be locked in the form-content dichotomy. I intended to show throughout my first section how promising this theory of the creative imagination may be, if united to it is a proper recognition of the role of language: the resultant is an imagination which can do its work only in a medium but which, left to its own resources, can never advance beyond the vague, the unrefined. And the poem created in these terms is the only expression and the only way of expressing what the imagination of its poet has created. Thus it may again seem to be as an extension and radical modification of this romantic theory—and certainly it has been thoroughly wrenched from its philosophical context—that a different approach to the cognitive problem has come to be tentatively explored by recent theorists.

# Chapter 12

# Some Conditions for an Apology

THIS historical examination has not led away from the primary purpose of this section. In revealing the influential alternatives inherited by recent theorists for defining the meaning of poetry, it has revealed also what made each of these alternatives unacceptable to them. Thus it has implied the now restricted directions they could still pursue while they avoided what seemed to their immodest twentieth-century minds to be the errors which constituted the history of critical theory.

Yet in more recent theory there are some remnants of the positions I have examined. This observation should convince us that there is some continuity between twentieth-century critics and their forebears, even though those moderns who concern us here, in recognition of what seemed to be the unique burden forced on them by history, try to take up an entirely new stance. If, since we are, I assume, trying here to defend poetry rather than indict it, we again disregard the first of the positions discussed above—that ascribed to the Plato of the *Republic*, which claims that poetry ought to yield truth but does not—then we would find that of them all only the second position—that poetry is concerned with propositional truth—has been unqualifiedly rejected by our critics.[1] At least this much the progress of scientism has accomplished, and in doing so it has provided a boon to the study of poetics.

To begin once more with I. A. Richards,[2] who seemed to propose a new solution to this old problem of poetic meaning, we see that his claims at first blush appear to bear some relation to the third position, the hedonic approach to the function of poetry. And strangely enough, the concept into which that of Richards was transformed by those who followed him—yet another novel proposal—seems more closely allied to the fourth position, which sees poetry as yielding intuitive truth. That is to say, Richards finds for poetry an other-than-cognitive function, while theorists like Cleanth Brooks see poetry as yielding a knowledge which is distinct from and certainly not inferior to that given by science. If we are initially confused at finding two such positions thus related to each other, our difficulties disappear when we distinguish Richards' position from the hedonic and the position of a Brooks from the intuitional.

Of course Richards himself explicitly renounces any pleasure-theory.[3] However, in denying meaning to poetry and in claiming that poetry operates therapeutically by improving our neurological health, he may still seem dangerously close to such a theory. On the other hand, Richards countered what seemed to be the arid formalism into which this viewpoint often degenerated. He recognized that the role which, according to him, an advancing science left to poetry had to be more vital if poetry was to serve a culture bereft of its religion. The culture had to be so served since our psyches, created with the need for religion and thus now unable to front an emotional void, demanded that poetry arise out of religion's dissolution. Thus poetry, a kind of objectless religion which gave us the satisfaction without demanding the commitment, would have to fill the gap at least until science changed our psyches or learned ways to satisfy them more economically. As a surrogate for a defunct religion, poetry could hardly manage without a content. Yet of course the content could not function as content or else poetry would make the claim to have meaning, to be truth, which is precisely what destroyed its more deluded predecessor, religion. So the content functions only as a component of the total psychological effect the poetic occasion has on its subject. That is, the content operates only within a formal context and makes no claims beyond what is necessary to the aesthetic experience. If Richards, then, denies meaning to poetry, he does it to save the integrity of the poetic experience and the sanctity of poetry's function in our world. He does not, like the hedonist, see poetry as existing to ornament our leisure pleasurably but rather, like his master, Matthew Arnold, relates it to the needs of our nature in its wholeness. Nor does he profess the dilettante's interest in the prettiness or even the perfection of poetic techniques and arrangements, but here is dedicated to relating himself as reader to the nature of the poem in its wholeness.

Unfortunately the referential-emotive dichotomy does not always serve an intention so benignly disposed toward poetry and our humanistic needs as it does in the hands of Richards. The commonly more insidious use of this dichotomy by many contemporary positivists should be evidence enough of the threat it poses to our culture.[4] Indeed once Richards himself has denied meaning to poetry, he at times feels free, as a positivist, to call much of speculative philosophy mere poetry.[5]

Even an anti-positivistic theorist like Eliot, who would seem to be very far from a position that denies meaning to poetry, may, as was observed earlier,[6] be ensnared in it. For, finding Richards' formula about poetry and beliefs much in keeping with his own objective correlative, he adapted it too uncritically. Thus he separates beliefs from poetry, insists that a poet can only borrow beliefs but can never contribute to their formation, and sees the function of poetry to consist in conveying in objective form the emotional equivalents for the beliefs. Thus for him too the poem has nothing to do with knowledge and, with the beliefs thrust aside—as decent beliefs should allow themselves to be thrust—the poetry, self-justified, can carry out its emotive assignment.

But others of Richards' anti-positivistic contemporaries did not accept this much of his orientation, so that their adaptation of his ideas involved far more radical changes. They would not accept salvation for poetry at the sacrifice of all the stuff of poetry, as the emotive theory seemed to demand. Perhaps as poets themselves, many of them felt personally affronted. Nor did they feel that the sanctuary Richards found for poetry within the now unassailable walls of psychic therapy would protect it for long from the hordes of modernism. Instead of a sanctuary, it would prove to be merely a sanitarium: poetry would be safe not because of what it uniquely was but only because of what it could do that for now nothing else could. And its future would be no more assured than was that of the now exploded religion, since once again something less demanding might come along. But more than this, many of these theorists, not having lost their religious commitment, would not grant so much to Richards' Arnoldian view of the historical role of poetry as a substitute for religion.

In turning from the relation of Richards to the older hedonism in order to consider his relation to the apologists who followed, I use Brooks once more as my chief example because of his attempt at a coherent system. We saw earlier,[7] when Brooks' development of the concepts given him by Richards was discussed, that Brooks made two major transformations. First he transformed the psychologizing of Richards into his claims for the objective poetic context, which we saw to be consistent with the definition of aesthetic experience that I have been using. In other words, he further explored, in terms of different assumptions, the relation between the poet and reader, the relation on which Richards concentrated almost exclusively. But besides developing Richards in this way, Brooks transferred Richards' interest in the poem-reader relation (an interest in the aesthetic experience) to an interest in the relation between the poem and reality (an interest in the cognitive function of poetry). In the latter relation, of course, Richards, in view of his initial assumptions, can have no interest since he can make only negative statements about it. While in my second section I was concerned mainly with the first of these transformations, here it must be the second—the one introducing the relation between the poem and reality—that is crucial.

To review briefly, we should recognize that it is strange to find Richards, whose position emphasizes the therapeutic and noncognitive character of poetry, influentially in the background of this positive view of poetic meaning. Richards, of course, meant to do anything but give poetry a claim to truth. Referential discourse, that used in science, can give propositional truth. In order to do so it must employ signs that are as transparent as possible: the relation of the sign to the thing or concept it represents must be as close to one-to-one as possible. But if this thin discourse is lucid, alas it is also—compared to less exact and more distorted discourse—cold and unfeeling. Thus we also need an emotive discourse, although we can never allow it a claim to truth. For it is not referential in character; if it were it would lose its warmth. Instead of statements, then, it contains "pseudo-statements":[8] it is pure myth. And it exists only to affect our total psychology, a function until now and in the foreseeable future beyond the cold powers of laboratory-controlled knowledge. Since this discourse does not literally mean anything, since it points—as knowledge-giving—nowhere but to itself, there is no need for clarity; ambiguity may be allowed, indeed seriously encouraged, since the denser the discourse the more complex the context and thus the more efficiently it performs its neurological task. Taking off from this point, critics like Brooks make something quite different of this theory.

In moving from Richards' discussion of the poetic context to their own discussion of the meaning of poetry, such writers as Brooks, Tate, and Ransom[9] keep the dichotomy established by Richards but refashion it in order to take the emotive more seriously—that is, in order to transform the emotive into the contextual and thereby to consider it more cognitively. The abstractions from the world made by science for its own purposes, they claim, may properly remain in the referential category assigned them by Richards. But, they immediately add, this is hardly all the knowledge there may be since the abstractions of science hardly exhaust all that there is in the world. Indeed science must leave the most significant aspects of the world unaccounted for, the aspects that must slip through the inhumane sieve of formulae which science must use. But these critics are not merely trying to make room for speculative philosophy. Indeed they find in philosophy the same inadequacy with respect to the complete data furnished by the world.

At least Brooks seems to define this inadequacy in the semanticist's terms which he borrows from Richards. The trouble with philosophy as well as with science, indeed with systematic prose discourse in general, is that it *is* referential. Because this discourse is thin and its relationship to things one-to-one, it cannot help but be generic, abstract. The context of the discourse ought to lend no hand to qualify the terms and give them density. Rather the individual term is ideally to exist in complete isolation with its meaning fixed, static.

The terms of science are abstract symbols which do not change under the pressure of the context. They are pure (or aspire to be pure) denotations; they are defined in advance. They are not to be warped into new meanings. But where is the dictionary which contains the terms of a poem? It is a truism that the poet is con-tinually forced to remake language. As Eliot has put it, his task is to "dislocate language into meaning." And, from the standpoint of a scientific vocabulary, this is precisely what he performs: for, rationally considered, the ideal language would contain one term for each meaning, and the relation between term and meaning would be constant.*

How can these static terms hope to do justice to the complex and dynamic world which they are to symbolize? How can they do more than abstract and abstract severely from the fullness of what might be called our world-in-experience? Here the effect of Bergson, ministered through Hulme, certainly displays itself; and, like Brooks, the others are as convincing as their master in deplor-ing the loss to our ineffable, dynamic flow of experience when

* *The Well Wrought Urn*, p. 192. (Used by permission of Harcourt, Brace and Co. and Dennis Dobson.) Crane launches his most effective attack on the new critics in terms of this shockingly extreme and perhaps naive definition of scientific discourse ("Cleanth Brooks," *Modern Philology*, XLV [1948], pp. 239–43). See Tate, "Literature as Knowledge," *Limits*, p. 21, for a view which may seem in some ways similar to Brooks': the scientist "demands an exact one-to-one relevance of language to the objects and the events to which it refers. In this relevance lies the 'meaning' of all terms and propositions in so far as they are used for the purpose of giving us valid knowledge." But Tate shows a far more sophisticated comprehension of modern science. He sees that, unlike classical science, ours does not claim absolute knowledge but "knowledge for action," so that the idea of meaning, no longer "a real problem . . . has been replaced by a concept of 'operational validity.' " Thus Tate is aware that in scientific discourse there is involved more than the mere referential problem conceived in the simplistic way in which Brooks conceives it.

the fixed, unyielding form of stereotyped discourse tries vainly to exhaust it. They insist too that prose discourse admits of not the slightest flexibility in its dealings with whatever resists the category. If discourse is rigid—and the systematic purposes of prose discourse do not allow it to be otherwise—then all that it can transmit to us are those mechanical aspects of the world which lend themselves to this callous treatment. But most of what characterizes the experiential world for us as humans must resist these fixities and, as a result, must be lost to us unless we can pose an alternative which escapes the limitations of prose discourse.

These critics base their theory on the claim that poetry can be made into such an alternative. And the reasoning behind this claim rests, as the second section of this essay has shown, on their definition of the poetic context. This context, we saw, is contained by verbal complexities: endless qualifications, double meanings, even outright contradictions provided they are ironically controlled. It is these complexities which prevent the alert reader from "using" the poem crudely, from treating it as a mere sign. The involved data of human experience must be sifted as little as the poet can aesthetically manage with, so that as much as can be accommodated may come through into his poem. The words themselves and the context which they form and which in turn "informs" them must be many-faceted in order to do justice to the ever changing, ever confusing flow of experience. Here there must be no place for the single-mindedness and the resistance to contextual qualification which ought to characterize referential discourse.

Thus for these critics poetry must meet experience head-on, must see life whole. If this discourse cannot give us the certainty of a proposition or the prescription for action of a moral tract, it can give us in its fullness that experience to which the scientist, because of his quest for systematic certainty, and the moralist, because of his devotion to systematic guidance, have had to be half blind. For these theorists, then, poetry, in one sense less useful because it is literally confounded, can give us a kind of knowledge afforded by no other discipline precisely because it is in this sense less useful.[10] While poetry cannot substitute for either science or philosophy, neither can science or philosophy substitute for poetry. Poetry alone refuses to abstract from experience, nor does it have to since it does not share the precise purposefulness of these other disciplines.

Just as Richards' claims were not simply a new formulation of the hedonistic position, so these theorists are not merely restating the essentially romantic doctrine that poetry reveals imaginative or intuitive truth. Their view differs in a number of important ways, most of which have been anticipated earlier. For one thing, the knowledge that they claim poetry affords is not opposed to that of our reason; indeed, it is not the reflection of any faculty. With their central concern for the object rather than for the process which creates it, this knowledge must be for them a characteristic of the mode of discourse and not of the poet's psychology. It arises from the controlling poetic context and not from a clairvoyance that precedes and transcends the poem. Moreover, it is not to the essential realities of a noumenal world that poetry is, for them, to break through. They see poetry as more closely related to the immediate world of experience than are the abstractions of science, instead of, like the romantic intuitionist, relating poetry to what Hulme disparagingly called some vague infinite in opposition to science's concern with the matter-of-fact. Indeed, this knowledge given by poetry is not, for our theorists, to compete with any other kind of knowledge. It is simply different from propositional knowledge and has to do with a world differently conceived in accordance with the difference of purpose. It is, then, a knowledge which has its own rightful place, a knowledge of experience in its fullness.

It may very well be asked whether the interest of clarity is best served or even the interest of poetry necessarily furthered by the insistence on calling this product of poetry by the honorific name of *knowledge*. After all the work done in the theory of meaning by recent philosophy in order to narrow what this term may legitimately signify, it may seem needlessly cavalier to demand that this very word be applied to an admittedly preconceptual affair simply because the term is so soothing to the self-confidence of the harassed humanist. If we yield up the word *knowledge,* or the word *truth,* we might then see these theorists as meaning something much like what Eliseo Vivas means when he speaks so often of poetry as presenting us with "the organization of the primary subject matter (or the data) of experience." [11]

Once the word *knowledge* is dropped simply as inconvenient and possibly misleading—even while the same ideas are maintained but now expressed through some such phrase as Vivas' or a phrase like "presentational" immediacy [12]—this view may appear similar to several which at first seem to be opposed to it. For example, it is especially ironic to find that, in assigning the function it does to poetry, it touches at a crucial point the utterly antithetical approach of Max Eastman. This is the very writer whose phrase "the Cult of Unintelligibility," used to characterize "obscure" modern poets, earned him the disrespect of this entire school of poet-critics.[13] In addition, in the modern critical scene he played the role of a rather obvious representative of scientism, who sanctioned, with considerably more crudity than Richards, the retreat of the humanities under the impact of science and their relegation to areas which science could well spare or which it had not yet found the time to appropriate. Yet there is a moment of contact between our theorists and him. It occurs in his post-Kantian attack on what seems to him to be Richards' inadequate concept of the "given" and thus his naive philosophy of science.[14] He objects to Richards' handling of the referential-emotive dichotomy, which keeps pure knowledge for science but hands over to poetry, as the manipulator of attitudes, the control over action. Thus, in separating knowledge from action, Richards runs counter to the modern "operational" approach to science in accordance with which scientists "have more and more clearly realized that their theories do not tell us what reality is, but only how we must conceive of it if we wish to perform these miracles." [15] It is poetry, then, that is contemplative, since science springs not from the pure contemplation of things but from the need to operate on them. Poetry alone deals with things for their own sakes and thus gives us what Eastman terms "reality," since science is interested only in constructing from reality whatever conception its practical purpose demands. Poetry, that is to say, gives its reader "the quality of experience." The distinction formulated by John Hospers, who is admittedly in considerable agreement with Eastman, between the poetic "truth-to" life and the propositional "truth-about" life is perhaps a more cogent statement of the same view.[16]

Of course, this claim of similarity must be strongly qualified. For it is clear that, although Eastman invokes a concept of experience similar to that of our critics, he has too primitive a view of poetry to ground this concept in a doctrine of context.* And his Philistine tastes would hardly allow him to entertain the idea of poetic complexity. Probably as disdainful of "obscurity" in poetic theory as he is of it in poetry, Eastman cannot be expected to be interested in attempting an organic theory which would avoid the form-content dichotomy. Indeed, his inversion of Richards seems strangely to lead him to consider poetry as the referential discourse, with the data of experience as its object: "Poetic words . . . point to details in the given experience." [17] Further, his positivistic version of poetry's experiential function seems unlimitedly anarchic in failing to distinguish art from life: "How can such [poetic] words help us to order, consolidate and control our experience? . . . It would be truer to say that their very essence is disorder, disconsolidation and complete loss or abandonment of control." [18] Finally we may note that Eastman's concern for a peculiar language of poetry, a "poetic diction," attests to his pre-twentieth-century aesthetic orientation, which would seem to preclude any more sophisticated approach.

Despite these and other important differences, all would agree to see poetry as functioning to catch for us the nuances of our experience—an experience too recalcitrant for the exact and exact-

---

* It is true also that Hospers, despite the far greater maturity of his work than Eastman's, similarly fails to commit himself to the contextual doctrine which would lend depth to his claim that poetry is "true-to" experience.

ing character of propositional discourse. But since the contextual theorists have most satisfactorily earned this position theoretically, it would probably be most rewarding to return to their version of it in order to seek the solution to several problems it raises. There is, first, an immediate and serious difficulty which undermines the contextualist although the shallower theorizing of Eastman rides blithely clear of it. This difficulty, already examined at length in Section II, may be simply phrased: How can poetry tell us something about our world that we can learn nowhere else when for the contextualist it is not in any obvious sense referential? We have seen how great the cost of making poetry referential would be. If it were referential in the sense in which prose discourse is, then obviously what it would tell us about the world we could learn anywhere else. But if it were not referential, how could it tell us anything? If, like Richards, the contextual theorist assigns the referential to science, how, unlike Richards, can he allow poetry to have meaning?

Of course this problem cannot occur in Eastman's version of this theory since, through his inversion of Richards, it is poetry rather than science which for him "points to" reality. Clearly this is no way out, as Eastman's failure to view the poem as a unified aesthetic object ought to convince us. How, when poetry, unordered and uncontrolled, is obligated only to render bit by bit the individual things-in-experience, can we expect more? But what seems to be Eastman's referential view of poetry ought to alert us to the need for the poem to reach out beyond itself if it is to have the cognitive value for us which our contextual theorists seem to be claiming. If they are to retain at all their concept of the poetic experience, they must insist that poetry, making no referential assumption, assumes that what it is saying somehow refers only to the unique world created by the irreducible poetic context. Only the poem, as its system develops, need not cast a backward glance over its shoulder at the world which spawned it; if it does, it risks violating its own nature by failing to remain true to the laws it creates for itself as it comes into being. Yet the apologist must make sense of the seemingly paradoxical claim that this self-containedness allows poetry to tell us something about the world that we cannot learn from less self-contained discourse.

Eastman's failure, also noted earlier, to provide the poem with any element of control at all, again warns us of a similar weakness in the more sophisticated contextual view, even though Eastman's is once more seen to be but a parody of serious theorizing in this direction. If we look at this conception of the function of poetry from the austere vantage point of Yvor Winters, this weakness is immediately revealed. Without exception Winters would charge all who held this view with being exponents of the essentially romantic "fallacy of imitative or expressive form." [19] Indeed, he would see this view as largely responsible for what he most dislikes about much recent poetry. Because the world about which the poem is to be concerned is confused, these theorists appear to advocate that the poem itself be equally confused. Instead of having the poet impose a form on experience, refracting it through this form until it becomes meaningful, these theorists appear to claim that the poem should chaotically capture, indeed should "imitate," the chaos of experience. We may note Brooks' extreme statement of this imitationist position which, in the following passage, provides not at all for poetry to refine the mass of experience it tries to assimilate:

Yet there are better reasons than that of rhetorical vain-glory that have induced poet after poet to choose ambiguity and paradox rather than plain, discursive simplicity. It is not enough for the poet to analyse his experience as the scientist does, breaking it up into parts, distinguishing part from part, classifying the various parts. His task is finally to unify experience. He must return to us the unity of experience itself as man knows it in his own experience. The poem, if it be a true poem is a simulacrum of reality—in this sense, at least, it is an "imitation"—by *being* an experience rather than any mere statement about experience or any mere abstraction from experience.[20]

Now it must in fairness be admitted that in places Brooks would seem to exempt himself from this charge by suggesting that the poem *is* to order the fullness of experience rather than merely to reproduce it. Here is a strikingly explicit example:

What does Mr. Stauffer's "simplicity" mean? What can it be made to mean? If one means that a poet may be able to write without giving a sense of pomposity—that he can give a sense of casual and simple directness—the point can surely be granted at once. If the statement means that the poet can make his poem one by reducing to order the confusions and disorders and irrelevancies of ordinary experience in terms of one unifying insight, again granted. The poet not only may do this; he must.[21]

Agree as we may with this latter statement, we would be hard put to demonstrate how Brooks has theoretically earned what may seem to be only an *ad hoc* claim that his critical good sense occasions him to make; how he can keep it from clashing with his definition of poetry as "a simulacrum of reality" or his demand for "poetry of inclusion." For what sort of poetic unity would it be which, as Brooks sometimes says, is to order experience and yet, as he usually maintains, is to imitate experience without abridging its fullness? And in accordance with what principles can a reduction to order take place when the reduction is not to distill our experiential complexity?

Winters, then, would seem considerably justified in coming forward with his objection; it is but another and more forceful way of putting my earlier charge that this theory has recklessly removed all the brakes and can provide no check upon runaway complexity. But we must recall that the corrective suggested by Winters was itself not totally acceptable since he can envision no form through which experience is to be refracted by the poet except one that is unswervingly argumentative. And to strain experience through the fixed demands of logical consistency would involve poetry in abstracting as meagerly from experience, in using experience as crudely, as does propositional discourse.

Here, then, is the second problem the apologist must deal with: unless he is to be satisfied with Eastman's romantic view of poetic disorder, he must maintain that some forming of experience has to occur in order for the complexities of our full experience to be made more meaningful to us in poetry than we find them in life. It is the meaning-producing order which, after all, is to lift the poem beyond mere "imitation" and is to constitute the poet's addition to what experience has furnished him. Yet this ordering must not be accomplished in accordance with those principles that systematize other disciplines. For if poetry orders experience by rarefying it until it lends itself to the rigorous restrictions of logical consistency, then poetry too becomes conceptual: it becomes abstract, removed from the primary level of experience, as are other forms of systematic discourse. Thus poetry would find itself back where it was with Sidney, aping philosophy by searching for propositional truth. But what principles other than logical and argumentative ones can form this order? Which is but to ask what could be meant a moment ago by the term "meaning" when applied to something denser and less abstract than the sort of thing we get from prose discourse and yet somehow more refined than the sort of thing we get from unmodified experience. And this is to return to the old aesthetic riddle which asks what it means to place art between the percept and the concept.

But if the apologist thus recognizes that poetry must have some controlling form although there is a need to distinguish between the logical structure of prose discourse and whatever is meant by the formal structure of poetic discourse, he is merely returned to another difficulty which I have considered before in another connection. For if prose has a logical structure, then it too, contrary to Brooks, is contextually controlled. D. G. James and the Chicago neo-Aristotelians showed us earlier in this study, and Eastman has just shown us, that the referential-emotive dichotomy, as formulated by Richards, or its transformed version in the referential-contextual dichotomy of a Brooks, rests on too simple a view of language.[22] Richards and Brooks seem concerned to ask but one question when trying to distinguish among various kinds of discourse: does it point directly or doesn't it? We saw earlier that, for Brooks, the terms of referential discourse should be so utterly fixed in their meanings that ideally each word would reach out individually— that is, without regard for any context—and point to its referent.

In their attack upon the contextual critics, the neo-Aristotelians have already shown us the naiveté of this notion, insisting that in prose too there is a limiting framework which determines to a great extent the meanings of the individual terms.* But we have witnessed a far more extended statement of this view made by D. G. James. To review for a moment, it should be recalled that he saw no difference in kind between the operation of the imagination in poetry and its operation in our other activities. For man is, as Cassirer and Langer have it, a symbolizing animal. As James views language, the terms which man uses, whatever form of discourse he engages in, are determined wholly by the purpose of this discourse and, consequently, by the symbolic view of the world imposed by this purpose. There are as many ways of viewing the world—that is, depending on one's metaphysic, as many ways of abstracting from the world or projecting upon it—as there are purposes in the viewers. Each piece of discourse, then, James would say, whether it be poetry or prose, is a self-contained symbolic structure obliged only to the motives that brought it into existence. In its extremest form with James, this theory would see no purely referential problem since the demand for self-consistency would abolish it. The terms in discourse, thus conceived, would be no more than cross-referential. Within this framework poetry would be conceived as no more symbolic than prose discourse, as not in any essential sense differently symbolic from prose discourse. It is no more constructive of an independent world than is prose discourse. And since no discourse can tell us about the neutral world, there is no talking across any two discourses, no comparing of them in terms of a third entity (the world), which may act as a standard. Each discourse is inviolable: so long as it is logically self-consistent in terms of its purposes we can ask nothing more of it.

Like Eastman, who has in many ways a similar view of the relation of language to reality, James is unable to work out a satisfactory poetic theory from this conception. In addition to its

* It is from their notion that what discourses are about is determined by their differing purposes and assumptions that the neo-Aristotelians derive their admitted "pluralism," in accordance with which there is no arguing across discourses—a strange perversion, perhaps, of the Aristotelian theory of classes. See R. S. Crane, "Introduction," *Critics and Criticism*, pp. 5–12, for one of several

inadequacies on the aesthetic level, so extremely solipsistic a view has obvious inconveniences on the practical level. While refraining from entering upon epistemological issues which are not directly pertinent here, I may surely point to the obvious advantages of a more moderate position; one which would claim that if the scientist or philosopher cannot talk about the whole world, he can yet talk about an aspect of it as objective. To put it another way, the abstractions made by prose discourse may not refer to the world-in-experience, but they do refer to an abstraction of this world made for the special purposes of the writer. It is necessary to his purpose that certain aspects of the world be abstracted into a certain systematic pattern and that his discourse refer to this pattern which, however rarefied, is still a part of a whole and a real world. Of course, this abstraction is not the full world-in-experience, which resists any such violation. Experience as we know it—whether moral, religious, aesthetic, or cognitive—is, it must be conceded to Brooks, infinitely complex; in its wholeness it withstands any attempt, scientific or philosophic, to systematize it within the limits of a consistent purpose.

But James has at least shown us that we err if, like Brooks, we assume that what gives poetry a special dispensation to capture the whole of experience is its contextual character; if, that is to say, we deny to so-called referential discourse a controlling context to which the individual denotations are subservient and by which they may be strongly qualified.* If the context has its role in prose as well as in poetic discourse, it would seem that any distinction must collapse if it is based on the notion that only poetry is contextually determined.

statements by them of this position. For an excellent critique of it, one that attacks the concept itself as well as the inconsistency with which they invoke it, see Wimsatt, "The Chicago Critics: the Fallacy of the Neoclassic Species," *The Verbal Icon*, pp. 41–65; originally printed as "The Chicago Critics," *Comparative Literature*, V (1953), pp. 50–74.

* I am assuming here my modification of James for which, I admit, I have not argued. Otherwise I should have here to make a far stronger statement to the effect that the terms are utterly dependent for their meaning upon the systematic context formed in response to the purpose which ordered the discourse.

But once a completely constructivistic view like that of James has been modified, it becomes possible to point out that there is a great difference between the way context operates in prose and in poetry. After all, I have just claimed that the terms of any piece of prose discourse are only in part determined by their context, that despite its abstracting nature the discourse has a referential intention. In other words, it is not a closed system. Further, the logical procedures in accordance with which its system gains coherence are hardly unique to this particular discourse. They are the logical procedures which are applicable to all prose discourse. On the other hand, taking the contextual view of poetry, the theorist can claim a closed system for the poem. The organicism behind such a view can lead him to assert further that the context which seals off the poem is a unique and thus an unrepeatable one; a form which is created not in response to any principles external to the needs of the growing thing that becomes the poem. Not that there are not more general or conventional forms which can be found in many poems, but any problem which might arise here can be dismissed with the classic formulation of Coleridge that set the pattern for organic theory:

The true ground of the mistake lies in the confounding mechanical regularity with organic form. The form is mechanic, when on any given material we impress a predetermined form, not necessarily arising out of the properties of the material . . . The organic form, on the other hand, is innate; it shapes, as it developes, itself from within, and the fulness of its development is one and the same with the perfection of its outward form. Such as the life is, such is the form.[23]

Poetic form, then, varies with the particular demands of every context. It is a uniqueness, a particular adaptation to the peculiar purpose of the poem, somehow achieved by the poet through distorting, but never utterly destroying, the normal operational procedures of his language and the conventional formal patterns of his poetic tradition. Somehow the distortions occur although, if it is a good poem, they never appear in the poem or perhaps even present themselves to the poet except as already distorted.

More than this the contextualist cannot say, any more than he can say precisely how the transformation (or should I say transubstantiation?) of the elements into the unique and accommodating form occurs.

It might seem, then, that the contextual theorist can still distinguish between poetic discourse and prose by claiming that, although the context operates in both, the way it operates in poetry—as a force unique with every poem and one which supervises a closed system—is different in kind from the way it operates in prose. But each of these characteristics of the poetic context returns us to one of the other two difficulties of the contextual position which I have been examining. For, forced now to insist on the poetic system as utterly closed in order to keep it distinguished from prose, the contextualist has only aggravated his need to allow this system theoretically to open the experiential world for us as it has never been opened before. And forced also to insist on the utter uniqueness of every organic form, the contextualist, even if he could explain what this means—which is doubtful since the very nature of the formulation precludes the possibility of definition—has pretty well cut himself off from any device that could refine the stuff of life for aesthetic purposes. After all, a completely organic form, at the service only of the growing demands of the developing poem, can hardly provide the controls which a self-complicating context may need in order to become successfully poetic.

But these are hardly new problems. By now they may seem to be chasing each other around since, if the theorist entertains even a faint possibility of disentangling one, he can do so only by knotting the others more inextricably than ever. And yet any alternative to the contextual approach is far less satisfactory unless he is willing to forgo the demand that a theory try to be adequate to the data of poetic experience.

It is worth reviewing briefly the burden of this final critique of contextualism, since it assembles the burden which the modern theorist must carry with him in search of an apology. First, he may grant the referential-contextual dichotomy and distinguish poetry as uniquely contextual. But then he is troubled by the difficulty of showing how poetry, thus defined, can manage to present our experiential world to us. Secondly, if he should for a moment waive the seeming paradox, he may grant that poetry can present this world. But then he is troubled by the difficulty of showing how, in this case, poetry can manage, as art, to order experience without using the same agent of order as would prose discourse. Further, this second view reverses the first's conception of the referential-contextual dichotomy. For while, according to the first view, poetry has a context which renders it independent of the outside world of meanings, the second view, by conceding to prose discourse logical procedures which order it and set it off from experience and by denying such an ordering agent to poetry, considers poetry as directly and uninhibitedly involved with experience, and prose, with its logically ordered context, as somewhat shut off from it. Finally, the theorist may grant the obvious need to recognize contextual qualification in both poetry and prose. Although he can still claim a distinction between the kinds of context, with the unique form of the poem operating analogously to but differently from the logical coherence of prose, this view has serious repercussions on the partial truths contained in the other two. In addition, it is in urgent need of an explication which the very concept, with its emphasis on uniqueness, seems to prohibit.

Such, then, is the maze of incompatible assumptions, formulations, and theoretical problems, each with a partially just claim that on its treatment a satisfactory apology depends. The apologist must ask far more than he can answer since there is little enough that he can be certain he knows. He may know that unless he is to fall into the chaos of experience through the trap of imitative form—a trap which Brooksian complexity cannot theoretically escape—he cannot hope for poetry to be as complex as life. The forms of poetry cannot be so unlimitedly flexible as to accommodate all the nuances of experience. Only life itself can afford such infinite variety; and life is hardly poetry, which is probably a blessing for both. He may know that the various forms of what has been called prose discourse abstract painfully from life to give us the particular meaning which their various purposes allow to their words. But if poetry is to give any meaning to the peculiar segment of experience with which it deals, it too must sacrifice to some extent the unabridged fullness of that experience, even if the precise agent of that sacrifice escapes him. He might like to know not merely that poetry, still somehow uniquely revelatory of life, is several degrees closer to experience than is prose discourse, but that it holds with respect to experience a relation which is different in kind from that of prose. He might, then, like to say that poetry does not abstract; rather it forms. For he may feel that there is a universe of discourse between the two activities—even if he needs a discourse other than he knows to say what it is he means by this.

The little that he does know must be supplemented by an enormous amount that he is perhaps not likely to know before the apologist dare relax in the knowledge that he can answer those who would do less than justice to the object of his devotion. Perhaps his foreknowledge that his answer, had he one to give, would hardly be either understood or sympathetically received by them—perhaps two ways of saying the same thing—can comfort him in the long meanwhile of his ignorance. But, despite the insecurities of the self-conscious theorist, perhaps poetry after all asks not to be apologized for but only to be read. So if this bitter comfort is little assurance, fortunately there is and will be the thing itself—poetry—and the assurance of the rightness of his convictions that poetry bestows.

*NOTES AND INDEX*

# Notes

I HAVE put at the foot of pages in the text only those notes that seem to me to contain urgently supplementary material. Other supplementary materials—perhaps as interesting, perhaps as urgent—together, of course, with references, I have put below as numbered notes.

## Introductory

[1] For many points in my treatment of the poem I am indebted to the analysis by Cleanth Brooks in *The Well Wrought Urn* (New York: Reynal and Hitchcock, 1947), pp. 10–17. I hope that I have managed to make these my own in terms of the peculiar purposes of this chapter. See also Leonard Unger, *Donne's Poetry and Modern Criticism* (Chicago, 1950), pp. 26–30.

[2] Douglas N. Morgan, "Creativity Today: a Constructive Analytic Review of Certain Philosophical and Psychological Work," *Journal of Aesthetics and Art Criticism*, XII (1953), 12. The tone of the subtitle is indicative of the austere, if barren, brand of philosophical modernism which characterizes the essay.

[3] Eliseo Vivas, "A Definition of the Esthetic Experience," *Creation and Discovery* (New York: The Noonday Press, 1955), pp. 95–96; this essay is reprinted from *Journal of Philosophy*, XXXIV (1937), 628–34.

[4] *Loc. cit.*

[5] I. A. Richards, *Science and Poetry* (New York: W. W. Norton and Co., Inc., 1926), pp. 66–79.

[6] Morris Weitz, *Philosophy of the Arts* (Cambridge, Mass., 1950), pp. 134–47.

[7] These will all be discussed more fully in my last chapter.

## Chapter 1. T. E. Hulme

[1] For one of many such examples, see Brooks, *The Well Wrought Urn*, especially pp. 17, 230–31.

[2] See, for example, Coleridge's psychological treatment of Shakespeare as poet in *Coleridge's Essays and Lectures on Shakespeare and Some Other Old Poets and Dramatists* (London: J. M. Dent and Co., 1907), pp. 38–42; a

somewhat similar faculty-analysis of Wordsworth appears in *Biographia Literaria*, ed. J. Shawcross (Oxford: Clarendon Press, 1907), I, 124–49.

³ *Speculations* (London: Routledge and Kegan Paul, Ltd., 1936), pp. 116–18. This collection is the source of all quotations from Hulme and all summaries of his position.

⁴ For Hulme's source see especially Henri Bergson, *Laughter: an Essay on the Meaning of the Comic*, trans. C. Bereton and F. Rothwell (New York, 1911).

⁵ *Biographia Literaria*, II, 6.

⁶ *Modern Painters*, Part III, Chapter III.

⁷ *Biographia Literaria*, I, 15, 62.

⁸ This is the term used by Hulme. See *Speculations*, pp. 24–30.

⁹ Hulme's attempt to unite these positions is similar, often in detail as well as in principle, to Eliot's in his famous "Tradition and the Individual Talent."

## Chapter 2. T. S. Eliot

¹ *Selected Essays*, new ed. (New York: Harcourt, Brace, and Co., 1950), p. 247.

² *Ibid.*, p. 243.

³ One may claim that these are equally the grounds on which Allen Tate defends a concept of imagination which seems to be Coleridgean in spite of his criticisms of Coleridge. See *On the Limits of Poetry* (New York: The Swallow Press and William Morrow and Co., 1948) for his use of imagination (pp. 91–114) and for his objection to the subjective and psychological basis of Coleridge's distinction between fancy and imagination (pp. 35–41). It may be that Tate, even with his disclaimers, could be used in this discussion as profitably as can Brooks.

⁴ Coleridge, *Biographia Literaria*, ed. J. Shawcross (Oxford: Clarendon Press, 1907), II, 12; and quoted in Brooks, *The Well Wrought Urn* (New York: Reynal and Hitchcock, 1947), pp. 17, 230n.

⁵ *Coleridge's Essays and Lectures on Shakespeare* (London: J. M. Dent and Co., 1907), p. 40. See I. A. Richards, *Coleridge on Imagination* (London: Routledge and Kegan Paul, Ltd., 1934), pp. 82–83.

⁶ *Coleridge's Essays and Lectures*, p. 39; and quoted by Richards, *Coleridge on Imagination*, p. 77.

⁷ *Coleridge's Essays and Lectures*, p. 39.

⁸ Coleridge, *Specimens of the Table Talk* (London, 1836), p. 306. The italics are mine.

⁹ Eliot, *The Use of Poetry and the Use of Criticism* (Cambridge, Mass.: Harvard University Press, 1933), pp. 67–71.

¹⁰ *Selected Essays*, p. 248.

¹¹ It is most fully discussed in "Tradition and the Individual Talent" and "Hamlet and His Problems." But, assumed rather than discussed, it furnishes the basis for important conceptions of the function of poetry in "The Social Function of Poetry," in *Critiques and Essays in Criticism*, ed. R. W. Stallman (New York: The Ronald Press Company, 1949), pp. 105–16; reprinted from *Adelphi*, XXI (1945), 152–61.

¹² It is this aspect of Eliot's theorizing which Eliseo Vivas criticizes so effectively. See "The Objective Correlative of T. S. Eliot," *Creation and Discovery* (New York: The Noonday Press, 1955), pp. 175–89; reprinted from *American Bookman*, I (1944), 7–18.

[13] *Selected Essays*, pp. 124–25.

[14] *Ibid.*, p. 125.

[15] Vivas, in his essay on Eliot (see note 12, above), distinguishes carefully among these various emotions while pointing out Eliot's failure to do so.

[16] *Selected Essays*, p. 10.

[17] "The Social Function of Poetry," in *Critiques and Essays in Criticism.*

[18] W. K. Wimsatt, Jr. and M. C. Beardsley, "The Intentional Fallacy," *The Verbal Icon* (Lexington, Ky., 1954), pp. 3–18; reprinted from *Sewanee Review*, LIV (1946), 468–88. The poem may be read as reflecting the emotional life of its author, it would seem from parts of Eliot. And Eliot's practical criticism frequently harks back, via the poem, to the qualities of the poet—this from one of the founders of the new criticism.

[19] *Selected Essays*, p. 9.

[20] *Loc. cit.*

[21] *The Use of Poetry and the Use of Criticism*, pp. 21–22.

[22] From *The Three Voices of Poetry* by T. S. Eliot (Copyright 1953 by Cambridge University Press. Used by permission of the author), pp. 17–18.

## Chapter 3. I. A. Richards

[1] For a brilliant exposure of Richards' primitive behaviorism, see R. S. Crane, "I. A. Richards on the Art of Interpretation," in *Critics and Criticism, Ancient and Modern*, ed. R. S. Crane (Chicago: University of Chicago Press, 1952), pp. 27–44; reprinted from *Ethics*, LIX (1949), 112–26. Crane's perhaps overly rhetorical exploitation of the analogy Richards draws between the reader of literature and Pavlov's dog does succeed in reducing Richards' theory—insofar as it is a theory of literary criticism—to absurdity. My treatment here and later (see also Chapters 7 and 12) is not intended to be a complete summary of Richards' theory. Rather I mean to present, in terms of its primary assumptions, as much of the theory of the early and the most influential Richards as appears to be essential in view of the needs and interests of this essay. Richards' own retractions of his early concepts do not make them any less crucial to the student of modern poetics.

[2] *Principles of Literary Criticism* (London: Routledge and Kegan Paul, Ltd., 1925), pp. 44–62.

[3] *Ibid.*, pp. 107–33.

[4] *Ibid.*, pp. 11–18.

[5] *Ibid.*, pp. 25–33, 180–85, 190–98.

[6] *Ibid.*, pp. 147–74.

[7] *Ibid.*, e.g., pp. 64–65, 72–73, 229–31.

[8] For the following discussion, *ibid.*, pp. 23–24, 199–206.

[9] One may find for this too a passage in Eliot which is roughly similar, except that Eliot candidly admits his form-content dichotomy while Richards only denounces any use of it. But the fact remains that both these influential writers display this mechanical distinction even though the movement which they began—jointly, if inadvertently—is more united in its assertion of an insoluble organic unity than it is, perhaps, in any other single concept. An example of Eliot's form-content distinction occurs in "The Social Function of Poetry," in *Critiques and Essays in Criticism*, ed. R. W. Stallman (New York: The Ronald Press, 1949), p. 109 (used by permission of T. S. Eliot and his publishers):

"I find that, in reading the work of a good poet, I am apt to be struck by a certain ambiguity. At moments I feel that his language is merely the perfect instrument for what he has to say; at other moments I feel that he is simply making use of, even exploiting, his beliefs for the sake of the verbal beauty in which he can express them. He appears to be both inside and outside of his beliefs and interests. Where this doubt about the attitude of the poet cannot arise, one is tempted to suspect the poetry. If we can enjoy the form while indifferent to the content, that poetry is for us mere virtuosity; if we can attend to the ideas and be indifferent to the words in which they are expressed, what we are reading is for us merely bad prose."

[10] E. Legouis and L. Cazamian, *A History of English Literature* (New York, 1929), p. 293, as cited in René Wellek and Austin Warren, *Theory of Literature* (New York, 1949), p. 134.

[11] London: Routledge and Kegan Paul, Ltd., 1934, p. 19.

[12] *Coleridge on Imagination*, p. 18.

[13] *Ibid.*, p. 61.

[14] *Ibid.*, pp. 67–71. This distinction, first made in *Principles of Literary Criticism*, pp. 8–10, underlies his entire theory. The reader is again referred to Crane (see note 1 to this chapter).

## Chapter 4. Requirements of an Organic Theory

[1] The source of much of what I say about the first of these problems may be found in Benedetto Croce, *Aesthetic*, trans. D. Ainslie (London, 1922), pp. 1–38; R. G. Collingwood, *The Principles of Art* (Oxford, 1938); and the passages already cited in Coleridge. The source of much of what I say about the second of these problems may be found in Samuel Alexander, *Beauty and Other Forms of Value* (London, 1933), pp. 53–74, and John Dewey, *Art as Experience* (New York, 1934), pp. 58–81. See also the important distinction between "subject" and "susbtance" in A. C. Bradley, "Poetry for Poetry's Sake," *Oxford Lectures on Poetry* (London, 1909), pp. 5–27. What I mean to do in this chapter is to apply these theories, which have already been developed in aesthetics, to the peculiar literary problems raised by my treatment of Hulme, Eliot, and Richards.

[2] Eliot, *Selected Essays*, new ed. (New York: Harcourt, Brace & Co., 1950), pp. 3–7.

[3] *Beauty and Other Forms of Value*, pp. 53–74. Alexander's terms, "material passion" and "formal passion," may be seen as analogous to my distinction between the vague impulse or idea and the formal demands. I have avoided his terminology because of the ambiguity which surrounds the unusual (for him) use of "material" as subject matter (or A. C. Bradley's "subject") rather than as the physical medium, to which his term "formal" seems to refer.

[4] To the point here is Dewey's valuable distinction between mere "discharge" and "expression": *Art as Experience*, pp. 60–64.

## Chapter 5. The Organic Theory

[1] Eliot, for example, says in "The Social Function of Poetry"—in *Critiques and Essays on Criticism*, ed. R. W. Stallman (New York: The Ronald Press Company, 1949), p. 110—"For any other answer would immediately take us into speculations about aesthetics, for which I have neither the competence

nor the interest." And Allen Tate states in *On the Limits of Poetry* (New York: The Swallow Press and William Morrow and Co., 1948), p. x: "Criticism, unless it is backed by formal aesthetics, is at best opinion; and aesthetics frequently does well enough for its own purposes, without attending too closely to works of literature as they are commonly known. I have tried to remember, from the time I began to write essays, that I was writing, in the end, opinion, and neither aesthetics nor poetry in prose."

[2] It must in fairness be added that Cleanth Brooks and René Wellek and Austin Warren indicate in some passages here and there that their conception of the creative act would be much like that given above. See *The Well Wrought Urn* (New York: Reynal and Hitchcock, 1947), pp. 182–83, where Brooks approvingly quotes W. M. Urban's similar position in *Language and Reality* (London, 1939); and René Wellek and Austin Warren, *Theory of Literature* (New York, 1949), pp. 80, 128.

[3] I refer the reader again to the moving and enlightening description of the creation of "meditative" poetry in Eliot's *The Three Voices of Poetry* (London: Cambridge University Press, 1953), pp. 17–18, quoted on page 55 above, and call attention to the similarities between it and my description in Chapter 4.

[4] Yvor Winters, *In Defense of Reason* (New York: The Swallow Press and William Morrow and Co., 1947), pp. 134–42.

[5] The reader is urged to see Wimsatt's incisive and important discussion of Winters' use and misuse of the logical terms "denotation" and "connotation" as well as Tate's of "extension" and "intension" (to be treated later in this chapter) in "The Substantive Level," *The Verbal Icon* (Lexington, Ky., 1954), pp. 145–49; reprinted from *Sewanee Review*, LIX (1951), 626–31.

[6] *In Defense of Reason*, p. 11.

[7] *Ibid.*, pp. 18–19.

[8] *Ibid.*, pp. 549–51.

[9] See, for example, Winters' criticism of Eliot's *The Waste Land*, *ibid.*, pp. 497–501, and his approval of Allen Tate's *The Subway*, pp. 19–21.

[10] *Ibid.*, p. 497.

[11] For this entire discussion of Ransom's, see especially *The New Criticism* (Norfolk, Conn.: New Directions, 1941), pp. 294–336. As with some other critics treated here, especially Richards, the view under examination is the writer's most influential rather than his current view. Ransom not only has modified his earlier notions, but recently has gone a long way toward retracting them. See his "The Concrete Universal: Observations on the Understanding of Poetry," *Kenyon Review*, XVI (1954), 558–60.

[12] *Theory of Literature*, pp. 139–58; reprinted in a somewhat altered form from "The Mode of Existence of a Literary Work of Art," *Southern Review*, VII (1942), 735–54.

[13] See, for example, "Poetry: I. The Formal Analysis," *Kenyon Review*, IX (1947), 436–56; "The Literary Criticism of Aristotle," *Kenyon Review*, X (1948), 382–402.

[14] This view may best be seen in "Poetry: a Note in Ontology," *The World's Body* (New York, 1938), pp. 111–142, and "Criticism as Pure Speculation," in *The Intent of the Critic*, ed. Donald A. Stauffer (Princeton, 1941), pp. 91–124. It is instructive to note the similar consequence of a similar anti-Platonism in Allen Tate's earlier "Three Types of Poetry," *On*

*the Limits of Poetry* (New York: The Swallow Press and William Morrow and Co., 1948), pp. 91–114.

[15] *Biographia Literaria*, ed. J. Shawcross (Oxford: Clarendon Press, 1907), II, 11.

[16] *The New Criticism*, pp. 314–16.

[17] *Ibid.*, p. 316. For the definition of "icon," see C. W. Morris, "Aesthetics and the Theory of Signs," *Journal of Unified Science*, VIII (1939), 131–50; "Science, Art and Technology," *Kenyon Review*, I (1939), 409–23.

[18] See his "Poetry: a Note in Ontology."

[19] *On the Limits of Poetry*, pp. 75–90.

[20] *In Defense of Reason*, pp. 40–57.

[21] *On the Limits of Poetry*, p. 83. What seems to be a similar and a more profoundly metaphysical statement occurs, in a very different context, as the conclusion to Tate's "The Symbolic Imagination: the Mirrors of Dante," *The Forlorn Demon* (Chicago: Henry Regnery Co., 1953), p. 55; reprinted from *Kenyon Review*, XIV (1952), 277:

". . . [the symbolic imagination] does not reject, it includes; it sees not only with but through the natural world, to what may lie beyond it. Its humility is witnessed by its modesty. It never begins at the top; it carries the bottom along with it, however high it may climb."

[22] *In Defense of Reason*, p. 551.

## Chapter 6. The Uniqueness of the Poetic Imagination

[1] Sigmund Freud, "The Relation of the Poet to Day-Dreaming," *Collected Papers* (London, 1925), IV, 173–83.

[2] For an excellent and incisively detailed discussion, from the point of view of modern criticism, of the relation of psychology to literature, see René Wellek and Austin Warren, *Theory of Literature* (New York, 1949), pp. 75–88.

[3] R. S. Crane, "Cleanth Brooks; or, the Bankruptcy of Critical Monism," *Modern Philology*, XLV (1948), 226–45. Similar attacks, launched from much the same position may be found in Elder Olson's review—*Modern Philology*, XLV (1948), 275–79—of Robert Penn Warren's essay on *The Rime of the Ancient Mariner*, and his "William Empson, Contemporary Criticism and Poetic Diction," *Modern Philology*, XLVII (1950), 222–52. These essays are all reprinted, with other allied work, in the monolithic *Critics and Criticism, Ancient and Modern*, ed. R. S. Crane (Chicago: University of Chicago Press, 1952).

[4] For Coleridge's distinction between "poem" and "poetry" see *Biographia Literaria*, ed. J. Shawcross (Oxford: Clarendon Press, 1907), II, 8–13. For Crane's discussion of this distinction and its relation to the new critics, see "Cleanth Brooks . . .," *Modern Philology*, XLV (1948), 228–33. As one example of the refusal to countenance this distinction, see Allen Tate's attack on what he considers Coleridge's confusion in this matter (*On the Limits of Poetry*, pp. 35–41), an attack based on a misunderstanding of what Coleridge means by "poem" and "poetry." A more blatant and more misdirected attack on Coleridge's distinction occurs in Richards' *Coleridge on Imagination*, pp. 100–21.

[5] Richards, *Coleridge on Imagination* (London: Routledge and Kegan Paul, Ltd., 1934), pp. 72–99.

<sup>6</sup> R. S. Crane, N. F. Maclean, and Elder Olson, "Two Essays in Practical Criticism," *University Review*, VIII (1942), 199–219; R. S. Crane, "The Plot of *Tom Jones*," *Journal of General Education*, IV (1950), 112–30. The latter is reprinted in *Critics and Criticism*, pp. 616–47.

<sup>7</sup> Elder Olson, "An Outline of Poetic Theory," in *Critiques and Essays in Criticism*, ed. Robert Wooster Stallman (Copyright 1949, The Ronald Press Company), p. 281n.

<sup>8</sup> Cleanth Brooks, "Forward" in *Critiques and Essays in Criticism*, ed. Robert Wooster Stallman (Copyright 1949, The Ronald Press Company), pp. xix–xx.

<sup>9</sup> *The Well Wrought Urn*, p. 8.

<sup>10</sup> *Theory of Literature*, p. 152. It is interesting to note that the organization of the succeeding portion of the book is largely controlled by this concept of the ever-expanding power of words: Chapter XIII on "Euphony, Rhythm and Meter"; Chapter XIV on "Style and Stylistics"; Chapter XV on "Image, Metaphor, Symbol, Myth."

<sup>11</sup> Although the book never aroused much fanfare, we find that strangely divergent writers have mentioned it favorably, sometimes as a uniquely provoking and influential work. See, for example, Susanne K. Langer, *Philosophy in a New Key* (Cambridge, Mass., 1942), p. 89n; John Hospers, *Meaning and Truth in the Arts* (Chapel Hill, 1946), pp. 129, 196–203; Frederick A. Pottle, "The Eye and the Object in the Poetry of Wordsworth," *Wordsworth Centenary Studies Presented at Cornell and Princeton Universities*, ed. G. T. Dunklin (Princeton, 1951), p. 37n. Thus, in addition to its bearing on my discussion of the imagination, I think it important, in view of what appears to me to be its glaring weaknesses, to give the book a more critical treatment than I have seen it receive.

<sup>12</sup> Some attempt in this direction is made in Herbert J. Muller, *Science and Criticism* (New Haven, 1943), but there is little here of use to critical theory. And such key works as Susanne K. Langer, *Philosophy in a New Key* and Ernst Cassirer, *An Essay on Man* (New Haven, 1944) are not obviously applicable to problems of poetics. In my final chapter I shall discuss Max Eastman's use of a similar concept of the "given" in *The Literary Mind* (New York, 1931).

<sup>13</sup> For the following discussion see *Scepticism and Poetry* (London: George Allen and Unwin, Ltd., 1937), pp. 15–43.

<sup>14</sup> *Biographia Literaria*, ed. J. Shawcross (Oxford: Clarendon Press, 1907), I, 102–5.

<sup>15</sup> *Scepticism and Poetry*, p. 29.

<sup>16</sup> Ibid., p. 25.

<sup>17</sup> *Kant's Kritik of Judgment*, trans. J. H. Bernard (London, 1892), pp. 67–90.

<sup>18</sup> *Biographia Literaria*, I, 202.

<sup>19</sup> Ibid., II, 6.

<sup>20</sup> For the following discussion see *Scepticism and Poetry*, pp. 75–137.

<sup>21</sup> Ibid., pp. 68–69 (for a comparison of "Tintern Abbey" with *King Lear*) and pp. 115–17 (for a comparison of Shelley's "Lines Written in Dejection" with *King Lear* and *Othello*).

<sup>22</sup> Ibid., pp. 47–49.

<sup>23</sup> *On the Limits of Poetry* (New York: The Swallow Press and William Morrow and Co., 1948), p. 94.

<sup>24</sup> *Scepticism and Poetry*, p. 69n.

<sup>25</sup> Ibid., pp. 83–87.

[20] *Ibid.*, pp. 85, 96.

[21] *Ibid.*, p. 261.

[28] *Ibid.*, p. 265. Also see p. 207 for a similar passage on the imaginative failure of Shakespeare.

[29] *Ibid.*, p. 81. Here we see that the reader, since he is to create his own art object, is to be made a poet. Apparently the only task of the original poet is to provide him with this possibility for construction.

[30] *Ibid.*, p. 58.

[31] *Ibid.*, p. 78.

[32] *Ibid.*, pp. 242–74.

## Chapter 7. I. A. Richards and Organic Criticism

[1] Of course, not all our critics need fall into this trap. We have seen that Hulme, at least in his more Bergsonian moments, is a notable exception—perhaps because he has a greater philosophic awareness. And we have seen also that in Wellek and Warren, who have tried not unsuccessfully to theorize for the group, there are indications of the theory of poetic creativity advanced here. And again this may be the result of a greater consciousness of philosophic requirements. Again reference is made to *Theory of Literature* (New York, 1949), pp. 80, 128.

[2] *Principles of Literary Criticism* (London: Routledge and Kegan Paul, Ltd., 1925), pp. 225–27.

[3] See *Principles of Literary Criticism*, pp. 98–102, 114–33. For an excellent exposition and criticism of this concept, the reader is again referred to R. S. Crane, "I. A. Richards on the Art of Interpretation," in *Critics and Criticism, Ancient and Modern,* ed. R. S. Crane (Chicago: University of Chicago Press, 1952), pp. 27–44.

[4] See the discussion of Richards' development of Coleridge's distinction between fancy and imagination, Chapter 3 above.

[5] It is because of this associational theory that Richards dismisses such primitively behavioristic laboratory experiments as those of Fechner, since they are non-contextual (*Principles of Literary Criticism*, pp. 8–10).

[6] By way of contrast see *Theory of Literature*, pp. 151–58.

[7] *Principles of Literary Criticism*, pp. 11–22, 38–43.

[8] Eliseo Vivas, "The Objective Basis of Criticism," *Creation and Discovery* (New York: The Noonday Press, 1955), pp. 191–206; reprinted from *Western Review*, XII (1948), 197–210.

[9] *Theory of Literature*, pp. 151–58.

[10] Vivas, "The Objective Basis of Criticism," *Creation and Discovery*, p. 195.

[11] A fuller discussion of these problems occurs in Chapter 10 below.

[12] For the following discussion see *Principles of Literary Criticism*, pp. 261–87.

[13] *Ibid.*, pp. 107–13, 243–52.

[14] *Ibid.*, p. 250.

[15] *Ibid.*, p. 248.

## Chapter 8. The Transformation of Richards

[1] For excellent treatments of these reductions, see the following articles: for the reduction of the poem to the psychology of the poet, Wimsatt and Beards-

ley, "The Intentional Fallacy," *The Verbal Icon* (Lexington, Ky., 1954), pp. 3–18; and for the reduction of the poem to the psychology of the audience, their "The Affective Fallacy," *The Verbal Icon*, pp. 21–39. The latter is reprinted from *Sewanee Review*, LVII (1949), 31–55.

[2] *Principles of Literary Criticism* (London: Routledge and Kegan Paul, Ltd., 1925), p. 248.

[3] This is of course previous to his more recent retraction of his condemnation of Milton in his "Milton," *Sewanee Review*, LVI (1948), 185–209.

[4] This fusion lies behind his entire approach in *Modern Poetry and the Tradition* (Chapel Hill, 1939). See also Brooks' *The Well Wrought Urn* (New York, 1947), pp. 3–20, 176–225.

[5] London, 1930. The marked influence of Freud upon him as well as his relativistic tendencies make Empson a far less satisfactory example, for my purposes, than Brooks.

[6] An obvious example of what might be thought of as reckless eclecticism may be seen in Brooks' attempt to unite such antipathetic views as those of Urban and Langer even as he keeps so many of Richards' concepts. See *The Well Wrought Urn*, pp. 182, 186, 189, 232–38.

[7] *Ibid.*, pp. 176–96, 226–38.

[8] This metaphor serves as the title of one of Ransom's more important works: *The World's Body* (New York, 1938).

[9] *Biographia Literaria*, ed. J. Shawcross (Oxford: Clarendon Press, 1907), II, 12; and quoted by Brooks in *The Well Wrought Urn*, pp. 17, 230n.

[10] E. M. W. Tillyard, *Poetry Direct and Oblique* (London, 1934).

[11] Brooks, *The Well Wrought Urn*, pp. 176–96, 226–38; Tate, *On the Limits of Poetry*, pp. 16–48, 91–114, 115–28; R. P. Warren, "Pure and Impure Poetry," in *Critiques and Essays in Criticism*, ed. R. W. Stallman (New York: The Ronald Press Company, 1949), pp. 85–104; reprinted from *Kenyon Review*, V (1943), 228–54.

[12] Tate, *On the Limits of Poetry*, pp. 21–35. Ransom joins this group in his discussion of Morris; see *The New Criticism*, pp. 281–94.

[13] Charles W. Morris, "Science, Art and Technology," *Kenyon Review*, I (1939), 411n:

"The number of the primary forms of discourse corresponds to the three dimensions of sign functioning: scientific discourse brings into prominence the relation of signs to objects denoted (the semantical dimension), aesthetic discourse accents in a distinctive way the sign structure itself (the syntactical dimension), technological discourse emphasizes the efficacy of the signs in the practice of the users (the pragmatical dimension)."

[14] See note on p. 72 above.

[15] "A Definition of the Esthetic Experience," *Creation and Discovery* (New York: The Noonday Press, 1955), pp. 93–99. See also his "A Natural History of the Aesthetic Transaction," in *Naturalism and the Human Spirit*, ed. Y. H. Krikorian (New York, 1944), pp. 96–120.

[16] *The Well Wrought Urn*, p. 229.

[17] "Animadversions on Naturalistic Ethics," *Ethics*, LVI (1946), 160–61.

[18] For the following discussion, see Eliot, *Selected Essays*, new ed. (New York: Harcourt, Brace, and Co., 1950), pp. 218–31; *The Use of Poetry and the Use of Criticism* (Cambridge, Mass.: Harvard University Press, 1933),

pp. 79–91; and "The Social Function of Poetry," in *Critiques and Essays in Criticism*, pp. 105–16.

[19] Eliot himself, with less embarrassment than we might hope for, admits the closeness of his claims about poetry and beliefs to those of Richards. See *Selected Essays*, new ed., pp. 229–31, and *The Use of Poetry*, pp. 86–87, 90–91.

[20] *The Well Wrought Urn*, pp. 227–29; *On the Limits of Poetry*, p. 112.

[21] Ransom here is very close to the other critics I have been discussing. His "Poetry: a Note in Ontology" (*The World's Body*, pp. 111–42) is similar in its statements about Platonic or allegorical poetry to Tate's "Three Types of Poetry" (*On the Limits of Poetry*, pp. 91–114), written just slightly earlier.

[22] *The Well Wrought Urn*, pp. 176–96.

[23] For a concise statement of Croce's general position, see his "The Breviary of Aesthetic," *Rice Institute Pamphlets*, II (1915), 223–310; reprinted as *The Essence of Aesthetic* (London, 1921). It is true that in some areas Croce's position has been far from constant, as is made clear, for example, in René Wellek's rich and ample farewell tribute, "Benedetto Croce: Literary Critic and Historian," *Comparative Literature*, V (1953), 75–82. I do not intend here, however, to follow his views on their divergent and frequently baffling paths. Rather I shall assume his to be a unitary position, one capable of systematic extension. It represents primarily the early Croce who was a major influence upon English and American aesthetics; the Croce who insists on the integrity and untranslatability of the artistic intuition and who defends this intuition against any violation by what he refers to as intellectualist errors. See his *Aesthetic*, trans. Douglas Ainslie, 2nd ed. (London, 1922), pp. 32–38.

[24] *Aesthetic*, pp. 118–21.

[25] I cannot resist quoting in full Robert Penn Warren's brilliant parable on critical modesty from "Pure and Impure Poetry," with which William Van O'Connor tastefully concludes *An Age of Criticism 1900–1950* (Chicago, 1952), p. 175:

"Critics are rarely faithful to their labels and their special strategies. Usually the critic will confess that no one strategy—the psychological, the moralistic, the formalistic, the historical—or combination of strategies, will quite work the defeat of the poem. For the poem is like the monstrous Orillo in Boiardo's *Orlando Innamorato*. When the sword lops off any member of the monster, that member is immediately rejoined to the body, and the monster is as formidable as ever. But the poem is even more formidable than the monster, for Orillo's adversary finally gained a victory by an astonishing feat of dexterity: he slashed off both the monster's arms and quick as a wink seized them and flung them into the river. The critic who vaingloriously trusts his method to account for the poem, to exhaust the poem, is trying to emulate this dexterity: he thinks that he, too, can win by throwing the lopped-off arms into the river. But he is doomed to failure. Neither fire nor water will suffice to prevent the rejoining of the mutilated members to the monstrous torso. There is only one way to conquer the monster: you must eat it, bones, blood, skin, pelt, and gristle. And even then the monster is not dead, for it lives in you, is assimilated into you, and you are different, and somewhat monstrous yourself, for having eaten it.

So the monster will always win, and the critic knows this. He does not want to win. He knows that he must always play stooge to the monster. All he wants to do is to give the monster a chance to exhibit again its miraculous power."

²⁰ René Wellek and Austin Warren may also seem to believe in complexity for its own sake, in view of what they say about inclusive art or "difficult beauty" in their chapter on "Evaluation" in *Theory of Literature* (New York, 1949), pp. 253–55.

## Chapter 9. The Contextual Theory

¹ Shelley's *A Defense of Poetry* is perhaps the best repository of the conceptions discussed here. Allen Tate's commentary on this romantic tendency is also to the point: "The history of this fallacy [the fallacy of communication], which is as old as poetry but which towards the end of the eighteenth century began to dominate not only poetry, but other arts as well—its history would probably show that the poets gave up the language of denotation to the scientists, and kept for themselves a continually thinning flux of peripheral connotations." (*On the Limits of Poetry*, p. 82.)

² This is what Winters, after Kenneth Burke, calls "qualitative progression" as opposed to "rational progression." See Winters' *In Defense of Reason*, pp. 57–64, and Kenneth Burke, "Lexicon Rhetoricae," *Counter-Statement* (New York, 1931), pp. 157–59.

³ Warren, "Pure and Impure Poetry," in *Critiques and Essays in Criticism*, ed. R. W. Stallman (New York: The Ronald Press Company, 1949), p. 102.

⁴ For Brooks on Ransom, see *The Well Wrought Urn* (New York: Reynal and Hitchcock, 1947), pp. 190–94, 219–22; for Ransom on Brooks, see "Poetry: I. The Formal Analysis," *Kenyon Review*, IX (1947), 436–56. See also the second note on p. 83 above.

⁵ For Brooks on Winters, see *The Well Wrought Urn*, pp. 183–84, 215–19.

⁶ Ransom has devoted one of the major sections of *The New Criticism* (Norfolk, Conn.: New Directions, 1941) to his critique of Winters (pp. 211–75). For Winters' extended retaliation, see *In Defense of Reason* (New York: The Swallow Press and William Morrow and Co., 1947), pp. 502–55.

⁷ See p. 84 above.

⁸ For a critique of the use and misuse of terms like "connotation" and "intension" in this entire paragraph, the reader is again referred to Wimsatt's "The Substantive Level," *The Verbal Icon* (Lexington, Ky., 1954), pp. 145–49.

⁹ The reader is referred to my initial discussion of the neo-Aristotelians in Section I (pp. 93–98). And it must be remembered that there we saw them opposed to any attempt to define poetry in terms of language; that is, to any consideration of poetry as a mode of discourse.

¹⁰ See R. S. Crane, "Cleanth Brooks: or, the Bankruptcy of Critical Monism," *Modern Philology*, XLV (1948), 226–45; Elder Olson, "William Empson, Contemporary Criticism and Poetic Diction," *Modern Philology*, XLVII (1950), 222–52; and Olson's "An Outline of Poetic Theory," in *Critiques and Essays in Criticism*, ed. R. W. Stallman (New York: The Ronald Press Company, 1949), pp. 264–83.

¹¹ Crane, "Cleanth Brooks . . .," *Modern Philology*, 243.

¹² Olson, "An Outline of Poetic Theory," in *Critiques and Essays in Criti-*

cism, pp. 268–70. See also Hoyt Trowbridge, "Aristotle and the 'New Criticism'," *Sewanee Review,* LII (1944), 537–55.

[13] Crane, Olson, and N. F. Maclean, "Two Essays in Practical Criticism," *University Review,* VIII (1942), 199–219; Trowbridge, *op. cit.*

[14] For the discussion which follows, see especially Olson, "An Outline of Poetic Theory."

[15] Olson, for example, commenting on Robert Penn Warren's essay on *The Rime of the Ancient Mariner,* says (*Critics and Criticism, Ancient and Modern,* p. 139n.):

"We may indeed worry about whether, on the contrary, it is not an absurdity to conceive of a poem—i.e., any imitative poem—as having a theme or meaning. The words have a meaning; they mean the poem; but why should the poem itself have any further meaning? . . . Such interpretation springs from the use of a very arid grammatical apparatus and wholly blinks the question of how powerfully we are affected by the spectacle of human fortunes . . ."

Besides noticing the perhaps more "arid" formalism implied by this statement, we may indeed wonder how a poem can be "imitative" and yet mean only itself.

[16] Again I refer the reader to Crane's "The Plot of Tom Jones," *Journal of General Education,* IV (1950), 112–30. See also my first note on p. 96.

[17] Ransom, "The Bases of Criticism," *Sewanee Review,* LII (1944), 556-71.

[18] It should be mentioned that Kenneth Burke has very different assumptions from which to attempt the definition of poetry. Although he is popularly referred to as a new critic and his is an unusual attempt, one which has not been without its influence, he is not being treated in this essay by very reason of his different assumptions. Burke's science-poetry dichotomy cannot be maintained theoretically since he is justifying poetry by the use of tools borrowed from the sciences or would-be sciences of psychology, sociology, and semantics. As a result the poem, for him, must be defined as a response to the needs of the spectator (see "Psychology and Form" and "Lexicon Rhetoricae," *Counter-Statement* [New York, 1931], pp. 38–56 and 156–232) and as a response to the neurosis of the author (see "Lexicon Rhetoricae," *Counter-Statement,* and "The Philosophy of Literary Form," *The Philosophy of Literary Form* [Baton Rouge, 1941]). In the work which is to satisfy the psychology of the poet and the psychology of the audience, there is insufficient provision made for the dislocations of stereotyped expression; rather "experience has worn a path" and the language of poetry is allowed to fall into this groove, into this "prior form"—prior, that is, to art ("Lexicon Rhetoricae"). This framework leads to Burke's "dramatistic" theory, which ends by denying any barrier between art and life. For all of life, like all of art, is conceived in dramatistic terms: every action is a "strategy" called forth by a "situation"; and the literary work, as "symbolic action," has the same function for the same reason. Although it would be profitable to argue the merits and defects of this position, it hardly falls within the scope of this essay. While Richards differs from most of our critics in a similar way, his theories lent themselves to adaptation and transformation by those critics who are my central concern. Burke, on the other hand, simply represents an extremely divergent approach, one that hardly bears on the apology for poetry I am here trying to trace. I must leave him for such "scientifically" minded historians of criticism as Stanley Edgar Hyman.

## Chapter 10. A Note on the Objectivity of Value

[1] Again I am anxious to make it clear that I am trying to avoid getting into any detailed discussion of pure theory of value. Here I am rather interested in the advantages to practical criticism (as well as the practical need for the theoretical direction I have been pursuing) of an objective theory of value. For the arguments of objective value-theorists who attempt to reduce the most objective of objective relativists to pure subjectivism, the reader is referred to C. E. M. Joad, *Matter, Life and Value* (Oxford, 1929), pp. 266–83; and to Eliseo Vivas, "The Nature of Aesthetics," in *The Return to Reason*, ed. John Wild (Chicago, 1953), pp. 203–7, or, for a more lengthy treatment, to his *The Moral Life and the Ethical Life* (Chicago, 1950), Part I, especially pp. 61–79.

[2] Vivas, "The Objective Basis of Criticism," *Creation and Discovery* (New York: The Noonday Press, 1955), pp. 191–206. My other references to Vivas in the discussion which follows are also based on this essay.

[3] A good statement of this position is found in Frederick A. Pottle, *The Idiom of Poetry* (Ithaca, 1946). A refutation of this position appears in Brooks, "Criticism, History, and Critical Relativism," *The Well Wrought Urn*, pp. 197–225, and is implied in Wimsatt and Beardsley, "The Intentional Fallacy."

[4] Pottle, *Idiom of Poetry*, p. 22.

[5] For a very fine statement of this position, see Helmut Hungerland, "Consistency as a Criterion in Art Criticism," *Journal of Aesthetics and Art Criticism*, VII (1948), 93–112.

[6] See pp. 116–18 above.

[7] R. P. Blackmur, "A Burden for Critics," *Hudson Review*, I (1948), 171.

[8] The phrase is taken from Richards (*Principles of Literary Criticism*, p. 41), who, as we have seen, furnishes an excellent example of the extra-artistic analytical interests of relativism.

## Chapter 11. Some Theories about Poetry and Truth

[1] Just one of the more recent versions of this charge may be found in Peter Viereck, "Pure Poetry, Impure Politics, and Ezra Pound," *Commentary* (April 1951), pp. 340–46.

[2] *Poetics*, 9.

[3] In contrast to his literal use of the term elsewhere, in his *Republic*, Books II and III, Plato uses imitation to mean what we would call the dramatic "point-of-view": the mimicking of somebody's speech. In *The Art of Poetry* (1527) Vida gives us a common Renaissance distortion of the term: the writer is to "imitate," that is, almost literally to plagiarize from the works of the ancients. In his *Poetics* (1570) Castelvetro transforms *imitation* into *verisimilitude* and thereby calls for the three unities. The play is to "imitate," and therefore to be restricted by, the physical limits (of time and space) of the stage on which it is to be performed.

[4] See Johnson's *Preface to Shakespeare* (1765).

[5] *Republic*, Book X, and Stephen Gosson, *The School of Abuse* (1579).

[6] His treatment of poetry primarily as allegory, in large part inherited by Renaissance theory from medieval tradition as well as, perhaps, from the Horatian tradition, is not basically unlike what we find in Dante, Boccaccio, and Savonarola; and it is very close to most of the sixteenth-century Italian

critics. Or, to look forward, we find similarities of course in the English neo-classicists—Dryden, Pope, Addison, Johnson, and a host of others. For this, we have seen, is the position into which most so-called imitation theories fall. Nor indeed is the primary interest in content, within the terms of a form-content dichotomy, markedly different in Victorian critics like Arnold or in the later neo-Humanists. Even today, in the theory of a self-styled analytical philosopher like Morris Weitz (*Philosophy of the Arts* [Cambridge, Mass., 1950], pp. 134–47), although the terms are more technical, we find the same insistence that art yields propositions, true or false. Finally, depending upon which selections one uses, whether Winters can be included in this position or not could be argued either way.

[7] Castelvetro, "Poetics," and Mazzoni, "Defense of the *Divine Comedy*," in *Literary Criticism: Plato to Dryden*, ed. Allan H. Gilbert (New York, 1940), pp. 305–57 and 359–403, respectively. While this may seem an odd heresy to be credited to Castelvetro (who, we are never allowed to forget, was the first to insist on the three unities), it is nonetheless true. In his commentary on the *Poetics* Castelvetro again and again insists (and insists—as would the modern Aristotelian school—that Aristotle insists) that the sole end of poetry is delight. It is not concerned with truth (except in so far as verisimilitude is required to delight the audience); nor is it concerned with morality. Castelvetro was one of the first to see an opposition between poetry and science, indeed an opposition between poetry and any discipline which has truth or morality as its end. Thus neither Lucretius nor the historians are poets for him. Morality, he claims (and rightly, it would seem, from an examination of *Poetics* 15), is made a quality of character by Aristotle rather than a quality of the all-controlling plot or action. Thus we cannot demand that the effect of a work be moral.

While Mazzoni often attacks Castelvetro by name in his "Defense of the *Divine Comedy*," there is some similarity between them. He goes even farther than Castelvetro in considering art for its own sake alone. For him the end of poetry is the imitation or representation itself. This is a self-justifying activity for both artist and spectator. And this too sounds like much of Aristotle. But he incorporates Plato too. While representation is the end of poetry considered in isolation, one may, for nonaesthetic purposes, think of poetry in terms of recreation or in terms of civic good. In terms of recreation its end is conceived as play and delight; in terms of society its end is conceived as moral. But neither of these considerations mars the true end of poetry considered in its own terms. Thus Mazzoni admits too that the concern of poetry is not with truth (also intimating a dichotomy between poetry and science) and that poetry can be conceived as moral only as this objective is, for practical reasons, imposed from the outside.

[8] See Bell, *Art* (London, 1914) and Fry, *Vision and Design* (London, 1920).

[9] The reader is again referred to my note on p. 154.

[10] The ideas which run through much of Schelling's *Transcendental Idealism* (1800) are perhaps more concisely seen in his *Concerning the Relation of the Plastic Arts to Nature* (1807). An English translation of the latter by Michael Bullock is appended to Sir Herbert Read's *The True Voice of Feeling* (New York, 1953), pp. 321–64.

[11] *Kant's Kritik of Judgment*, trans. J. H. Bernard (London, 1892), pp. 188–206.

## Chapter 12. Some Conditions for an Apology

¹ But it is much less than entirely neglected by twentieth-century theorists outside the group we are considering. See, as just a single example but one especially surprising in view of his philosophical affiliations and his claimed allegiance to organicism, Morris Weitz, as cited in note 6 to Chapter 11.

² It should by now be needless to add that here, as elsewhere, I mean the early Richards only: the Richards of *Principles of Literary Criticism* (1924), *Science and Poetry* (1926), and, with qualifications, *Coleridge on Imagination* (1934). So often we use a man's name as if the name and a single position were synonymous when actually he has held several positions during his career. Richards has later held other positions. But if these are less extreme, they were less influential and less likely, therefore, to be the ones most frequently associated with his name.

³ *Principles of Literary Criticism* (London: Routledge and Kegan Paul, 1925), pp. 92–97.

⁴ See, for one of many such examples, A. J. Ayer, *Language, Truth and Logic* (London, 1936), pp. 44–45.

⁵ This claim may be seen in *Principles of Literary Criticism*, pp. 272–87, and, in a somewhat modified form, in *Coleridge on Imagination* (London: Routledge and Kegan Paul, 1934), pp. 172–80, 220–30.

⁶ See Chapter 8 above, pp. 132–33 and note 19 to that chapter.

⁷ Once again in Chapter 8 above, pp. 125–27.

⁸ Richards, *Science and Poetry* (New York, 1926), pp. 66–79.

⁹ See especially Brooks, "The Problem of Belief and the Problem of Cognition," *The Well Wrought Urn* (New York: Reynal and Hitchcock, 1947), pp. 226–38; Tate, "Literature as Knowledge," *On the Limits of Poetry* (New York: The Swallow Press and William Morrow and Co., 1948), pp. 41–48; Ransom, "Wanted: an Ontological Critic," *The New Criticism* (Norfolk, Conn.: New Directions, 1941), pp. 279–336.

¹⁰ Allen Tate comments approvingly upon Richards' surprisingly strong claim in *Coleridge on Imagination* (p. 163) that "Poetry is the completest mode of utterance."

"It is neither the world of verifiable science nor a projection of ourselves; yet it is *complete*. And because it is complete knowledge we may, I think, claim for it a unique kind of responsibility, and see in it at times an irresponsibility equally distinct. The order of completeness that it achieves in the great works of the imagination is not the order of experimental completeness aimed at by the positive sciences, whose responsibility is directed towards the verification of limited techniques. The completeness of science is an abstraction covering an ideal of co-operation among specialized methods. No one can have an experience of science, or of a single science. For the completeness of *Hamlet* is not of the experimental order but of the experienced order . . ."

And a bit later:

"We must return to, we must never leave, the poem itself. Its 'interest' value is a cognitive one; it is sufficient that here, in the poem, we get knowledge of a whole object. . . . I have been concerned in this commentary with the compulsive, almost obsessed, application of an all-engrossing principle of pragmatic reduction to a formed realm of our experience, the distinction of which is its complete knowledge, the full body of the experience that it offers us."

(These quotations are reprinted from pp. 47 and 48 of *On the Limits of Poetry* by permission of Alan Swallow, publisher. Copyright 1948 by Allen Tate.)

[11] For one of many such passages in the work of Vivas, see "Literature and Knowledge," *Creation and Discovery* (New York: The Noonday Press, 1955), pp. 117–23; reprinted from *Sewanee Review*, LX (1952), 580–87. His emphasis on organization and order, however, may exempt him from the charges of imitationism which follow.

[12] One attempt to work toward what he calls a "presentational" aesthetic, although it is concerned mainly with the plastic arts, may be found in Arnold Isenberg, "Perception, Meaning, and the Subject-Matter of Art," in *The Problems of Aesthetics*, ed. E. Vivas and M. Krieger (New York, 1953), pp. 211–25; reprinted from *Journal of Philosophy*, XLI (1944), 561–75.

[13] Eastman, *The Literary Mind* (New York: Charles Scribner's Sons, 1931), pp. 57–122. For one of the more rewarding reactions by a member of the school he attacks, see Tate, "Understanding Modern Poetry," *On the Limits of Poetry*, pp. 115–19.

[14] For his explicit discussion of Richards, see *The Literary Mind*, pp. 297–317.

[15] *The Literary Mind*, p. 220. It is instructive to note the similarity of Eastman's statements here to the views of D. G. James which were discussed at length in Chapter 6.

[16] Hospers, *Meaning and Truth in the Arts* (Chapel Hill, 1946), pp. 141–207. And, as one would expect from the philosopher of experience, John Dewey expresses a similar view. See *Art as Experience* (New York, 1934), pp. 83–86.

[17] *The Literary Mind*, p. 304.

[18] *Loc. cit.*

[19] For this discussion the reader is referred to my earlier consideration of Winters in Chapter 5 above.

[20] *The Well Wrought Urn* (New York: Reynal and Hitchcock, 1947; quoted by permission of Harcourt, Brace and Co. and Dennis Dobson), p. 194.

[21] *Ibid.*, p. 203.

[22] See note on p. 187 above, for an important difference between Brooks and Tate on this issue.

[23] *Coleridge's Essays and Lectures on Shakespeare* (London: J. M. Dent and Co., 1907), pp. 46–47.

# Index

# Index

# Index